The Sutton-Taylor Feud

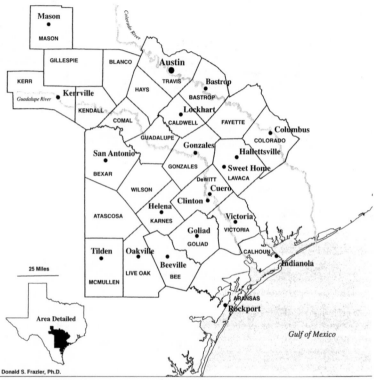

The area of Texas where the Sutton-Taylor Feud was hottest. *Map courtesy Donald S. Frazier.*

THE SUTTON-TAYLOR FEUD:
The Deadliest Blood Feud in Texas

by Chuck Parsons

Number 7 in the A.C. Greene Series

University of North Texas Press
Denton, Texas

Printed in the United States of America.

10 9 8 7 6 5 4 3 2

Permissions:
University of North Texas Press
1155 Union Circle #311336
Denton, TX 76203-5017

The paper used in this book meets the minimum requirements
of the American National Standard for Permanence of Paper
for Printed Library Materials, z39.48.1984. Binding materials
have been chosen for durability.

*Cover and interior page design and layout
by Stephen Tiano, Book Designer, Page Compositor & Layout Artist
www.tianodesign.com • steve@tianodesign.com • twitter.com/stephentiano*

Library of Congress Cataloging-in-Publication Data

Parsons, Chuck.
   The Sutton-Taylor feud : the deadliest blood feud in Texas / by Chuck
Parsons.
      p. cm. -- (A.C. Greene series ; no. 7)
   Includes bibliographical references and index.
   ISBN 978-1-57441-257-4 (cloth : alk. paper)
   ISBN 978-1-57441-534-6 (paper : alk. paper)
   ISBN 978-1-57441-367-0 (ebook)
   1. Sutton family. 2. Taylor family. 3. Pioneers—Texas—Biography.
4. Frontier and pioneer life--Texas. 5. Vendetta—Texas—History—19th
century. 6. Violence—Texas—History—19th century. 7. Peace treaties—
History—19th century. 8. Texas—History—1846-1950. I. Title.

F391.P264 2009
976.4'0610922—dc22

                              2008038369

The Sutton-Taylor Feud: The Deadliest Blood Feud in Texas is Number 7
in the A. C. Greene Series

The electronic edition of this book was made possible by the support of
the Vick Family Foundation.

And if you wrong us shall we not revenge?
—SHYLOCK TO SALERIO, 3:1, 61–62
from *The Merchant of Venice*

William Shakespeare: The Complete Works
General Eds. Stanley Wells and Gary Taylor
Clarendon Press, Oxford, 1988 Compact Edition

*Dedicated to Pat, for her continued assistance,
love and support.*

Contents

List of Illustrations

Acknowledgments

Bruce Allardice;

James Back, Cuero, for grateful assistance in helping locate the lost McCrabb Cemetery;

T. Lindsay Baker, W. K. Gordon Endowed Chair, Tarleton State University;

Sheron Barnes, Special Collections Librarian Victoria College/ University of Houston-Victoria, Texas for her assistance with the Barry A. Crouch Collection;

Donaly E. Brice, Research Specialist at the Texas State Library and Archives, Austin, who has assisted greatly whenever asked;

Amy N. Cockerham, Alkek Library Special Collection, Texas State University, San Marcos;

Tracie Evans, Texas Ranger Hall of Fame and Museum, Waco;

Frank S. Faulkner Jr., Texana/Genealogy Department, San Antonio Public Library;

Patsy Hand, Victoria;

Jane Hoerster, so knowledgeable about the events of Mason and Mason County;

Dave Johnson, Zionsville, Indiana, a long time friend who provided considerable assistance with the shaping of the manuscript;

Bena Taylor Kirkscey, Rosebud, who for years has edited the *Taylor Family News,* preserving a wealth of family information;

Dennis McCown, Austin; his knowledge of the violence of Texas and New Mexico in the 1870s and 1880s is nearly all encompassing, and for his continued advice and support;

Robert G. McCubbin, Santa Fe, whose collection of original photographs is accessible and incomparable in quality;

Rick Miller, long time friend, historian and authority on a number of Texas historical figures, Harker Heights;

Pat Mosher, Records and Archives Assistant, Gonzales County Court House Annex;

Jim Mundie, Kenner, Louisiana;

Elva Petersen, DeWitt County Clerk, Cuero;

Cynthia Salm, great-great-granddaughter of William E. and Laura E. Sutton;

Steve Schiwetz, great-grandson of Frank O. Skidmore, Corpus Christi;

Robert W. Shook, long time friend and authority on Victoria and Victoria County history, Victoria;

M. G. "Jerry" Spencer, second cousin of Randolph and William A. Spencer, once removed, Grapevine;

Charles and Pat Spurlin, Victoria;

E. J. Thormaehlen, great-great-grandson of Pitkin B. Taylor, New Braunfels;

Oralia Vela, Wilson County, Texas County Clerk's office, for going beyond the minimum effort of county clerks;

Lisa Struthers, San Jacinto Museum, La Porte;

And to my wife Pat who has patiently read and re-read more chapters and drafts of the manuscript than she probably wished, and for her constant love, support and encouragement.

INTRODUCTION

The Sutton-Taylor Feud

Bill Sutton stepped down from the hack first, and then helped his pregnant wife Laura, holding her arm gently. She was now in her early months, strong, smiling, and confident, but to loving husband Bill she was delicate and fragile, and he was more than ordinarily concerned about her. Good friend Gabe Slaughter, fellow cattleman and friend John N. Keeran, and Ed McDonough also descended from the conveyance, glad to have their feet back on the ground. Then the group walked together up the gangplank. Before them in Lavaca Bay, the steamer *Clinton* gently rocked in the waters.

Bill Sutton had grown weary of always watching his back trail; he was tired of being a target for the Taylors and their friends. Too many men had been shot down or strung up to dangle on a tree limb until death stopped their struggles. Brother Jim Sutton had already left the country, maybe even had already forgotten about the violence of the feud with the Taylors. Bill now wondered why he had not left as well.

With Laura four months pregnant, he now had no real reason not to leave. A trip from Indianola to New Orleans, up the river and then another leg across Missouri to Kansas City would be what he needed to get his mind off the feud. As a cattleman, he had already hired good men to drive his herds up the trail overland. He would meet them in Kansas, settle accounts, and possibly consider remaining there away from

1

the Texas troubles. Life was good. Laura was radiant, and their first child was less than five months away. Would it be a girl or a boy?

But in spite of his careful planning for Laura, his friends, and his herds, there were others who intended to destroy the idyllic dream. Jim Taylor and his friends wanted Bill Sutton dead, and on this day, the eleventh of March 1874, at Indianola, Texas, their dream was about to come true. Jim Taylor, with cousin Bill Taylor, now stalked up the same *Clinton* gangplank and approached the Sutton group. Their pistols were already in their hands, cocked, and ready to fire.

Moments later, the smoke had wafted away and the echoes of the gunshots were no longer heard. But Laura Sutton's screams still rang loudly over the rippling waters of Lavaca Bay.

The double killing of William E. Sutton and Gabriel Webster Slaughter on the deck of the steamer *Clinton* on March 11, 1874, in front of numerous witnesses including Mrs. Sutton, was the apex of the Sutton-Taylor blood feud. The years of bloodshed beginning in the late 1860s reached what now could be the terminating factor: the death of William E. Sutton. He had been the target of several assassination attempts, and with his body growing cold the Taylors believed themselves the victors. Jim Taylor had achieved his goal of slaying the man he held responsible for the death of his father and other kinfolk, and no doubt he felt that blood had answered blood. After all, the family motto of "Who sheds a Taylor's blood, by a Taylor's hand must fall" was now satisfied. After Sutton's killing of Charley Taylor in Bastrop back in 1868, and then his killing of Buck Taylor in Clinton that Christmas, avenging their deaths became an imperative to Jim Taylor. In another time and place, attorneys might have settled matters in a court room, but in the tumultuous days of Reconstruction in Texas, the more common means of settling disputes was with a gun.

The early Taylor killings led to two groups of people, both having sided with the Confederacy, now taking arms against each other, swearing death to the other. Of the multitudinous conflicts in Texas history, the violence acted out between the followers of William E. Sutton and the Taylor faction became the epitome of the blood feud.

The troubles began during the tragic period known as Reconstruction. Many small conflicts between neighbors and groups of people, united by ethnic background or race or family ties, began during that nine-year period of civil tumult. In the decades prior to the war the greatest threat had been from the displaced Native Americans who were forced to move farther west, fighting against the white invaders every step of the way. Now after the war between North and South was over, Central and East Texas were safe. Men no longer feared Comanche or Kiowa raiding parties, but nevertheless continued to keep their weapons close, and loaded. The legal system could not catch up with the societal changes wrought by the Civil War. Many men who had lost much or everything in the war, now with only themselves to deal with their problems, found recourse in violence. Now the residents of DeWitt, Gonzales, Karnes, and Bastrop counties—the heartland of the feud—could only focus partially on establishing homes in the land, tending their cattle herds to drive to northern markets, or merely raising their families. But Reconstruction spread its own problems and for many the period of blood feuds began.

The Taylors were descendants of Virginia-born Josiah and Hephzibeth Taylor. Sons William Riley, Creed, Josiah Jr., Rufus P., Pitkin, their sons and nephews and other in-laws and friends, became the Taylor party, or faction.

The initial problems began when Creed Taylor's sons Hays and Doboy killed two Union soldiers in Mason County. Then William E. Sutton, believing Charley Taylor and a friend were guilty of theft, pursued them into Bastrop County with a posse.

Taylor was killed first, shot down on a street in Bastrop. Then his friend was taken, then shot down on a road in neighboring Caldwell County, vigilante style. Before many months passed Sutton was responsible for the killing of two more Taylors, William P. "Buck" and his cousin Richard Chisholm. One must consider these events as the beginnings of what has become the Sutton-Taylor Blood Feud which lasted into the next decade. The conflict was long and bloody. It cost more lives than any other Texas feud.

Some of the Sutton faction, those associated with William E. Sutton although no others of that name were involved, were members of the State Police and several became deputy sheriffs, thus giving them legal sanction. Although not criminals, the Taylors did not choose to become deputies or policemen, which may have been a costly misjudgment on their part.

A period of vigilantism became common during the late '60s and '70s, and many men associated with the Taylors, or related to them, were accused of theft and then murdered, the excuse being "killed while attempting to escape." The decade of the 1870s witnessed the double murder of the Kelly brothers, sons-in-law of Pitkin Taylor; the murder of Martin Taylor and father-in-law Dave Morris, the double murder of John Choate and his cousin Crockett Choate, and many others, all connected to the Taylor faction by blood or marriage or friendship.

The Taylors did not sit idly by and allow their ranks to be thinned without retaliation. One-time DeWitt County Sheriff Jack Helm was gunned down by Jim Taylor and John Wesley Hardin. Then Jim Cox and Jake Christman fell before Taylor guns in a well-planned ambush. The Taylors several times laid ambushes to get Bill Sutton, but he managed to escape. Pitkin Taylor himself was lured from his home during the night and shot to death. Finally Jim Taylor's plans to kill Sutton and possibly end the feud were realized on the deck of the *Clinton*.

Even after Sutton's death, his followers chose to carry on the violence. After the Sutton killing, cousins Bill Taylor and Jim Taylor became fugitives. Jim joined forces with John Wesley Hardin and the pair left the area, gathering their cattle for a drive to Kansas markets. Cousin Bill Taylor remained in DeWitt County. He should have left with Jim and Wes, but he did not. He was arrested and jailed, but eventually escaped and did leave the area, but only after killing Reuben H. Brown, the new leader of the Sutton faction. Meanwhile a Brown County deputy sheriff attempted to arrest, or kill, Wes Hardin, but he himself was gunned down. In the aftermath, Hardin's brother and two cousins were arrested. Mobs formed and deemed their vigilante justice was supreme: brother Joe Hardin and the two Dixon brothers were taken out and lynched; two other cousins of Hardin were shot to death. Other associates of Hardin were captured, turned over to a DeWitt County mob and lynched. The "crimes" of these eight men were nothing more than being associates of Jim Taylor and John Wesley Hardin.

The bloody year of 1874, with the death of Sutton and Slaughter and the increased vigilante activity above mentioned, resulted in Captain McNelly and his Texas Rangers being sent to DeWitt County. His constant patrolling throughout the "battlefield" of DeWitt County caused the feudists to reduce their vigilante work, but violence resumed when he was sent to the Rio Grande frontier. Certainly the feudists could control their passions, but apparently only when McNelly and his squads kept a close damper on their activities.

In December of 1875 the Sutton group surrounded Jim Taylor and two friends and shot them down on the streets of Clinton. This battle ought to have ended the feud, as William E. Sutton and the leaders of the Taylor faction now were either dead or out of the country. But the subsequent killings belied this assumption. The most noted killing was the double murder of

Doctor Brassell and his son George, taken from their home in the middle of the night and shot to death. The Texas Rangers were called in again under Lieutenant Hall. Hall arrested the suspected murderers and with the court system finally taking charge the shooting phase of the feud ended. Trials of those charged with the Brassell murders were costly in time and money, but eventually only one man was convicted of murder. He was quickly pardoned. From the initial killings until the pardon of Dave Augustine, some three decades elapsed. The blood feud had cost the lives of some eighty individuals.

Among those four score men shot or lynched during the feud, the best known is one-time State Police Captain Jack Helm, shot to death in 1873 by Jim Taylor and John Wesley Hardin. Hatred for Helm was deeply ingrained in the Taylor men as he was, or so it was believed, responsible for the deaths of many innocent men, among them numerous Taylor friends or relatives. Hardin, in his self-serving autobiography written years later, still felt remorse over the vigilante action that cost the lives of his brother, cousins, and friends. The year of 1874 was perhaps the bloodiest year with more mob activity than any previous year in Texas history. Hardin believed that mobs had become the law in Texas that year, although he himself did not realize the irony of the situation with his organizing successful ambushes resulting in the deaths of various Sutton followers.

The men who participated in the Sutton-Taylor Feud were neither soldiers carrying on a lost cause nor a group of outlaws acting against legitimate authority, but men who believed that they had been wronged and that the legal system was inadequate to provide justice. Thus they had to take its place with the gun and the rope. They believed their extra-legal means of righting the wrongs was totally acceptable. Captain McNelly expressed it best when he wrote his superior in Austin that the leaders of the Suttons and the Taylors, meaning the leaders of both factions, were "long accustomed to doing as they pleased" and had "never experienced restraint upon their movements. ..." The Sutton-Taylor conflict that originated in DeWitt County was not a crime wave led by the Taylors, but an authentic blood feud with two families each swearing to eradicate the other.

Although only one man named Sutton was involved, his friends and followers were collectively called the Sutton Party. This terminology, identifying the collective shootings and lynchings as the Sutton-Taylor Feud, or vice versa, the Taylor-Sutton Feud, was recognized and accepted during the 1870s by Texas Rangers as well as by newspaper reporters and participants who themselves realized completely that the actions they took to eradicate their enemies were for revenge. Their actions were not to enrich themselves, although there may have been cattle theft at times during the feud. Their actions were not for sociopathic pleasure, although there may have been murderous sociopaths on each side. The troubles, the difficulties, the killings of DeWitt County that poured over into numerous other counties of Texas, became the archetype of what a blood feud was, a model for other groups to follow. Texas men who carried on a feud did not have to have a model to follow; carrying on a blood feud came naturally to those who believed revenge was obligatory.

It was natural in DeWitt County and natural for the men of Mason County several years after Hays and Doboy Taylor killed the Union soldiers. There, the animosity that led to what is commonly called the "Hoo Doo" War of 1875 tended to pit Anglos against men of Germanic extraction. A corrupt sheriff, the accusation of cattle theft and revenge killings made the violence of Mason County almost a mirror image of the vendetta in DeWitt County, although more lives were taken in the latter feud. The men of Mason County, like those of DeWitt, had no need for training in feud activity.

In frontier Lampasas County, northwest of DeWitt County and close to Mason County, Pink Higgins took the law into his own hands. He certainly was aware of the DeWitt County troubles, and shooting a man he *believed* was a cow thief certainly was a natural reaction when he found the legal system had failed. He shot to death Merritt Horrell, the *alleged* cow thief. This started the Horrell-Higgins feud, which cost several lives and ended only when Texas Rangers convinced the leaders of both sides that the continued killing was senseless. The leaders signed an agreement to cease and desist their animosity, which effectively ended the feud, although there followed a vigilante action of shooting to death two Horrell brothers in a jail cell in Bosque County.

When the feudists in Lampasas County signed a treaty of peace, they kept it. In contrast the Suttons and the Taylors signed treaties, and then for a real or imagined infraction resumed their feuding. It was as if not quite enough blood had yet been spilled. The Horrell men of Lampasas County would have felt at home either in Mason or DeWitt counties, as they too were among rough men who believed in handling their own problems in their fashion. Pink Higgins' shooting a suspected thief was hardly different from William Sutton believing Charley Taylor had stolen his stock, and shooting him and a companion to death, nearly a decade before.

There were no treaties of peace in the Mason County troubles, however. The treaties between the Suttons and the Taylors amounted to nothing more than a waste of pen and ink. Feuding blood ran hotter in their veins.

William E. "Bill" Sutton and wife Laura Eudora McDonald Sutton, possibly their wedding photograph. *Courtesy Robert W. Shook.*

CHAPTER ONE

The Taylors and the Suttons—
Texas Pioneers

"Mrs. Susan Taylor. . . . and her husband, the late Pitkin
Taylor, were among the earliest settlers of the county, and
were exposed to many dangers from the frequent incursions
of Indians in those early days."
—*Cuero Star,* OCTOBER 30, 1885

Duٛring the tumultuous days following the Civil War, Reconstruction and its aftermath, and into the decade of the 1870s, some considered the Taylors as outlaws, but although several were fugitives from the law, the Taylors in truth were Texas pioneers. Grassroots historian C. L. "Doc" Sonnichsen depicted them accurately as "a large tribe" living in DeWitt County. He described the sons and grandsons of patriarch Josiah Taylor Sr. as "American pioneers," men who "had small opportunity to acquire refinement and culture, but they were much respected by Indian war parties who had occasion to test their shooting ability." The Taylors "did not have the reputation of being interested in other people's cattle when such distinction was rare." They were without a doubt "clannish and quick to resent a wrong to any member of the tribe." Further, Sonnichsen says, the Taylors "were Southern to the core and too high-spirited to stay out of trouble with the Yankee army of occupation after the surrender."[1] What Doc Sonnichsen wrote was not only true for the Taylors, but numerous others in that area of the state as well.

Today there are numerous state historical markers recording the family's accomplishments, providing a solid record that they contributed significantly to the settlement of Texas. After enduring the transition from the dangerous wilderness of pre-Republic to settled statehood, the offspring of Josiah and Hephzibeth Luker Taylor became involved in what has become known as the Sutton-Taylor Feud, a conflict that drew family members against family members, as well as numerous outsiders.

Josiah Taylor and Hephzibeth Luker were married on October 6, 1807, in the Mars Hill Baptist Church at Clarke County, Georgia, by itinerant Minister of the Gospel Isaac Settles. Josiah was described as an "educated man of quiet and gentle disposition with light hair and beard, fair complexion and blue grey eyes." His wife Hephzibeth was "a woman of resolute will and independence ... of a very charitable nature. She was [of] very dark complexion, black hair and eyes, and boasted of being 1/8 Cherokee Indian blood."[2] Josiah and Hephzibeth Taylor gave six sons and three daughters to the world. Their sons and grandsons and extended family members were most affected by the turmoil following the Civil War; they lived, and some died, fighting for their lives and livelihood. The Taylor children, in order of their birth, were William Riley, born February 16, 1811; daughter Hardinia,[3] born 1814; Johanna, born 1817; Creed, born April 10, 1820; Josiah Jr., born circa 1821; Pitkin B., born 1822; Rufus P., born November 10, 1824; James, born 1825; and Mary Jane, born July 31, 1826. William, Hardinia, and Johanna were Georgia-born, but typical of pioneers the family moved often. Josiah Jr. was born in Tennessee, while sons Creed, Pitkin, and Rufus were born in Alabama. Son James and daughter Mary Jane were both born in Texas.[4]

Years later, Creed recalled that he and his father left Alabama in 1824 when he was four years old. He perhaps meant that he and the entire family moved, traveling together and settling below Liberty on the Trinity River (present-day Liberty County). Another move placed them at Taylor's Bayou, then another placed them in DeWitt County. Green DeWitt was successful and acquired a land grant from the Mexican government in April 1825, which allowed him to bring in four hundred Anglo-Americans on the Guadalupe River to settle, in the area now including and surrounding DeWitt County. The opportunity was there and Josiah Taylor took advantage of it. He immediately attended to the legal requirements to assure that the land would remain his, and that would be his last move. On February 1, 1829, Josiah registered his brand and the marks of Hephzibeth as well as marks and brands of Johanna, Creed, and Josiah Taylor Jr., who were minors. Green DeWitt himself witnessed the registration. The family settled on the banks of the Guadalupe River, near where the present Taylor-Bennett Cemetery is located, just south of Cuero.[5]

Patriarch Josiah Taylor was a soldier. In 1811–1812 he was in Texas; in 1812 he became involved in the Gutiérrez-Magee Expedition, an abortive attempt by various Americans to free Mexico from Spanish rule. Made a captain, Taylor and his company were on more than one occasion in the brunt of the fighting during this expedition. He engaged the enemy at the battles of La Bahía, Alazán, Rosales, and Medina which cost the filibusters dearly. Captain Taylor was one of about three hundred who survived out of the original force of nearly fourteen hundred. He was wounded seven times during this period.[6]

Josiah Taylor died in 1830; his widow survived him until about 1841. The family placed their remains in what is now the Taylor-Bennett Cemetery. In 1973 the DeWitt County Historical Commission erected historical markers at Josiah Taylor's grave. The commission honored Hephzibeth Taylor as well, but with a separate marker that identifies her nine children by Josiah and the one son by her second husband, Patrick Dowlearn, whom she married by bond on July 20, 1830.[7]

Of the children of Josiah and Hephzibeth Taylor none had such an adventurous career nor lived as long as did Creed. When father Josiah died, widow Hephzibeth sent Creed to Gonzales to receive an education. He boarded at the home of Almaron Dickinson who was later to die in the Alamo. In 1835, Creed and other Gonzales citizens fought Mexican dragoons to maintain possession of a cannon used to defend themselves against raiding parties. Their defiance is considered the first act of the Texas Revolution. "Come and take it" became their battle cry, and Creed was one of the colonists defending it. Later, as a soldier under the command of Captain John J. Tumlinson Jr., Taylor participated in the battle of Concepción, then took part in the "Grass Fight" and the siege of Bexar. Creed then returned to Gonzales, thus being absent from the Alamo. He was with his mother and other families, ready to depart Gonzales if necessary. Creed participated in the "Runaway Scrape," that retreat from the burning of Gonzales when the settlers feared they would be overtaken and massacred as the defenders of the Alamo had been. Creed then returned to action and, although not attached to any particular company of General Sam Houston's army, participated in the Battle of San Jacinto on April 21, 1836.[8]

Taylor again became a fighter in 1840. Comanches had descended from the Hill Country and attacked the coastal cities of Linnville and Victoria. As they retreated back to the Hill Country with their plunder, settlers attacked them near Plum Creek in present-day Caldwell County. Taylor was in the company of Captain Daniel B. Friar in this engagement and "killed several Indians in personal combat" according to early historian A. J. Sowell. Later, he joined the company of Captain John Coffee "Jack" Hays and fought Indians again at the Battle of

Bandera Pass in 1843, and perhaps here Creed Taylor learned the effectiveness of the Colt revolver at close range, as it was that weapon that assured victory against the Comanches. Creed survived all his battles and many wounds and left the DeWitt County area strong enough to eventually establish a ranch near present-day Junction in Kimble County.[9]

Creed married Nancy Goodbread on March 30, 1840, and they had two sons: John Hays, born in 1842 and named after Captain Jack Hays and Phillip Goodbread, born in 1843. They also had one daughter, Caroline Hephzibeth. The boys were usually known by their middle or nicknames, Hays and Doboy (a play on his middle name, suggesting "Doughboy"). Creed's first wife, Nancy, died on June 15, 1857.[10] Creed married Lavinia Spencer on February 18, 1873, and they had five children. Years later Taylor dictated his memoirs to James T. DeShields and they were published in 1935 under the title *Tall Men with Long Rifles*. Creed died on December 27, 1906, and is buried in the Noxville Cemetery, near Junction.[11] In 1936 the State Historical Commission dedicated a marker in his memory.[12] That same year the Commission erected a marker in Cuero, which mentions him twice, both as a soldier in the Texas army in 1836 and as a soldier at the Battle of Salado in 1842.[13] Another historical marker, erected near Junction in 1967, marks the site of his original native stone ranch home, built in 1869–1871.[14]

Creed Taylor's sister Johanna, born in Clarke County, Georgia, in 1817, married Joseph Tumlinson on April 2, 1834. Joseph's sister Elizabeth had married William Riley Taylor in Gonzales County on March 14, 1830.[15] Thus the Tumlinson and Taylor families became related by double marriages. One may be tempted to make of this double marriage a scenario where the children of two feuding families were torn as "star-crossed lovers," in the fashion of Romeo and Juliet, but such is not the case. The actual animosities between the Tumlinson and

Taylor families and William E. Sutton would not blossom for several decades.

Joe Tumlinson first married Johanna Taylor, sister of Creed and Pitkin, but later chose to fight on the opposing side during the feud. He had fought Indians prior to his involvement in the feud where he fought against the Taylors. Tumlinson's marker, shown here, is in the small family cemetery, now nearly lost and difficult to access on private property. *Author's photo.*

Johanna's husband, Joseph Tumlinson, experienced adventures as a young man as well, although his did not rival those of Creed Taylor. Born in Tennessee on February 16, 1811, the son of John Jackson and Elizabeth Plemmons Tumlinson, he arrived in Texas in 1829 and received title to ¼ *sitio* of land (about 1,100 acres) in 1831. Joseph and older brother John Jackson Jr., with other settlers, pursued the Indians who killed their father, but they never recovered his body. Joseph Tumlinson and Johanna Taylor signed their marriage bond on April 2, 1834, stating in part that the couple was "held and firmly bound ... in the penal sum" of $10,000 lawful money of the Mexican United States. Each claimed residence of the Mexican State of Coahuila of Texas and DeWitt's Colony. With no church or legally established ecclesiastical authority in the colony by means of which a couple could be legally united, both parties agreed to be lawfully married, until such time as they could appear before a minister of the gospel.[16] One of the sureties was Richard H. Chisholm, who married Creed Taylor's older sister Hardinia, thus linking together another family who would become involved in the lengthy blood feud of the future.

Johanna Taylor Tumlinson died in the late 1830s, hardly out of her teens. "Captain Joe" as he was frequently called, then married Elizabeth Newman in 1840. Captain Joe passed away from natural causes in late 1874; widow Elizabeth survived him many years, dying in 1906. There were no children from the first marriage but several from Joseph's union with Elizabeth Newman.[17]

William Riley Taylor, Creed's older brother and the first born of Josiah and Hephzibeth Taylor, was born in Clarke County, Georgia. He arrived in DeWitt's Colony in 1828 and on March 14, 1830, married by bond in Gonzales County Elizabeth Tumlinson, sister of Joseph Tumlinson.[18] In October 1848, settlers commanded by Captain John York fought back against a raiding party of Lipan Apaches. The group consisted of William Riley Taylor and his brother Rufus, Richard H. Chisholm, John and Joseph Tumlinson, Henderson McBride Pridgen and Newton Porter, and others, thirty-two men in all. Captain John York, his son-in-law James Bell, and James Sykes were killed in this engagement; Joseph Tumlinson, James York, son of Captain York, and Hugh R. Young were wounded. It was the last Indian raid in the area, fought on the Escondida, west of the San Antonio River and near the mouth of the Cibolo.[19]

William Riley Taylor died January 12, 1850, in DeWitt County, but he left widow Elizabeth financially comfortable; she continued as head of household and never remarried. Widowed at the age of thirty-six, she lived another thirty-six years. When the feud began she "was moved to Junction to distance her from its cruelties." There she lived out her remaining days on the edge of Junction in Kimble County near the North Llano River.[20]

Josiah Jr. was born October 1, 1821, and also fought in wars. He enrolled on May 8, 1836, in the Texas Army and served until December 25, 1838. He later served as a captain in the 36th Cavalry, Company G, Texas Troops, CSA. Josiah Taylor Jr. died March 23, 1864 and is buried in a small family cemetery near Yorktown, DeWitt County.[21]

Pitkin Barnes Taylor was born in Alabama in 1822 and experienced violence at an early age. As a thirteen-year-old he participated in the Texas Revolution, playing his part in the battle of Salado Creek and the Grass Fight. He married Susan Cochrum on December 13, 1846, their marriage being the first in the newly created DeWitt County.[22] He served as a county commissioner, proving the citizens had confidence in his leadership abilities. He and Susan were parents of two children who would experience tragedy in their lives due to the feud: daughter Amanda Jane, born August 1, 1848; and son James Creed, "Jim," born January 15, 1851. Amanda married Henry Kelly, who became an early victim in the feud; her brother Jim married Mary Elizabeth "Mollie" Kelly, sister of Henry Kelly.

Rufus Taylor was born in Alabama on November 10, 1824, and was also in Texas early. On July 1, 1842, he appeared before Gonzales County Clerk Ezekiel Williams and applied for a marriage license. On the Fourth of July of the same year he and Miss Elizabeth Lowe were united in matrimony in Gonzales County.[23] As a Texas Ranger he served under Captain Jack Hays from March 1, 1844, to June 1, 1844. Rufus Taylor Sr. died October 31, 1854, and is buried in the Taylor-Bennett Cemetery. The feud claimed two of his sons: Rufus Jr., known as "Scrap," and Martin Luther.[24]

James, the youngest son of Josiah Sr., was born in Texas about 1825. Little is known of his life, but one newspaper reporter described him as "a young man of prepossessing personal appearance [who] followed gambling for a living." He joined the rush for California gold and in Stockton, on Sunday, September 5, 1852, was killed in what is known simply—at least in Texas—as a "difficulty" with a man named William Turner.[25]

The sons of Josiah and Hephzibeth Taylor were men who were not afraid to fight for what they believed in. As Texas Rangers, farmers, ranchers, Indian fighters, they embodied the pioneer spirit of heads of households who traveled west to locate better opportunities for themselves and their families. When called to fight they were always ready, whether the enemy was an Indian, Mexican, or an Anglo. The "warrior tradition" would continue throughout the decades of the sixties and seventies.

Opposing the Taylors, at least in the informal nomenclature of feuding terminology, was a member of the Sutton family. William E. Sutton had no uncles or brothers involved in the feud; his one brother, James, married young and removed himself and his wife from the difficulties of the feud and lived a long life elsewhere. James Sutton proved it was possible to avoid the conflict, but only by leaving the immediate area and living out his years in Wilson County, not far from the center of the feud. James T. Johnson, a fellow cattleman, recalled that in the early seventies he "experienced quite a lot of difficulty trying to play neutral in the Taylor, Sutton and Tumlinson feuds," as his "sole desire was to work for wages and not get mixed up with either side."[26] That the troubles amounted to a genuine family feud was accepted by all who lived in the area.

William E. Sutton, whose surname will be forever linked with that of Taylor, was the second-born son of John S. "Jack" and Cynthia Shults Sutton. Jack Sutton, the eldest of twelve children, was born in Spotsylvania, Virginia. Jack gathered up his wife, Elizabeth Turner Sutton, and the children and moved to Tennessee, but in 1840 the Suttons were in Texas. In 1842 widower Jack Sutton married Cynthia Shults in Fayette County. The couple had two sons: James, born October 10, 1844, and William E., born October 20, 1846. No one today knows what the middle initial "E." stood for, but when asked, William jokingly explained that his initials represented "watermelon, eggs and sugar."[27] By 1850, the Sutton boys had lost their father; then the widow Sutton and her sons Jim and Bill moved in with her parents, C. W. and Mary Shults, along with her brothers Martin and Joseph. In 1856 Mrs. Sutton married William J. McDonald of DeWitt County. McDonald was a well-to-do stock raiser with real estate valued at $1000 and personal estate valued at $9500 in 1860. William J. McDonald had two daughters of his own: Lucy Charlotte and Sarah J. McDonald.[28]

When the Civil War erupted, both Sutton boys marched off to fight for the Confederacy. Jim enrolled in Captain James B. P. January's Company A of Waller's Battalion, 13th Texas Cavalry on May 15, 1862, at Victoria, Victoria County. Waller's Bat-

James and William Sutton, as young men before the Civil War. James took no part in the difficulties. *Courtesy Robert W. Shook.*

talion became part of Bagby's Brigade under General Thomas Green's famed Cavalry Division. On September 7, 1862, James Sutton lost his $175 horse and $35 worth of equipment in a skirmish at Bonnet Carre, Louisiana. Yellow fever incapacitated young Jim, forcing him to leave the service before war's end. His service record further reveals that he was admitted to the General Hospital in Houston on April 22, 1863, suffering from what was diagnosed as "Debilitas"—probably simply exhausted from his military duties—and was placed on furlough for thirty days. Apparently he did not return to the battle fields of the South. Captain January also returned to Victoria to assist with yellow fever patients; in his absence the command was placed under Lieutenant R. N. Weisiger. The close family ties between the Suttons and the Weisigers began during these years of war. Young Bill Sutton was drafted into the army on August 18, 1863, for a six-month term of service under Captain Harrison Gregg, Company C, 24th Militia Brigade, Texas State Troops. He was seventeen. His official record exhibits no outstanding traits or acts of heroism; Bill Sutton was simply a good soldier.[29]

Both Suttons survived the war, apparently healthy except for Jim's bout with yellow fever. On returning home, Jim courted a young lady named Martha Ann Dees; they were married on January 15, 1868, at Helena, then the county seat of Karnes County. Later they moved to Wilson County and made their home near Stockdale where they lived out their lives. Jim lived in peace with all his neighbors; no evidence has been uncovered indicating that he took part in any of the troubles in DeWitt County or the surrounding area where his brother fought and died.[30]

Not long after the end of the Civil War, young Bill Sutton chose the woman who became his wife, Laura Eudora McDonald, the daughter of John William and Leah Kirsch McDonald. They had known each since before the war, and in part had grown up together. After Jim and Bill's father died in 1850, their mother remained a widow until 1856 when she married William John McDonald. His brother, John William, was married to Leah Kirsch. John W. and Leah K. McDonald had a daughter, Laura Eudora, born June 22, 1853. Uncle William J. and Aunt Cynthia now took the five-year-old girl to live with them when her

James Sutton, brother of Bill, who chose to leave the feud behind him. *Courtesy Robert. W. Shook.*

parents died in 1858. Thus Laura McDonald and Bill Sutton, along with siblings Jim Sutton and Lucy and Sarah McDonald, lived together in the same household prior to the boys going off to war. Sutton family lore records Bill and Laura finding love early in their lives, a love which lasted through the war and the turmoil that followed in Reconstruction, until their own deaths. Bill and Laura married on October 20, 1869, at the home of the bride's aunt, Mrs. William J. McDonald. He was twenty-three; the bride was sixteen.[31]

Even though Bill Sutton was pleased with his courting success and happy with his young bride, dangerous events roiled around him. Lawlessness and violence were increasing. The policies of the Reconstruction government could not be implemented. Southern society was demoralized in its defeat; much of the state existed in frontier conditions. In many portions of the Lone Star State there was not even a semblance of peace. Mexicans, Indians, freedmen, and defeated white men found reasons to continue their animosities toward each other. In many cases the military simply threw out men who had been elected to their official positions prior to the war, replacing them with their own choice of "loyal" officials. Vigilante groups determined in many cases who was guilty and how the guilty would be punished. The old Southern social organization was now gone; the economic future of most Texans was bleak.[32] It was within this tumultuous social situation that the conflict now known as the Sutton-Taylor Feud began in deadly earnest.

"Capt. Creed Taylor" as he appeared in 1901. From the original photograph by Nicholas Ankenman and M. L. Butler, Mason, Texas. *Courtesy the Robert G. McCubbin Collection.*

CHAPTER TWO

Homicides and Private Quarrels

*"... many of these homicides have resulted from private
quarrels. There is much bad blood in the land."*
— Report of Special Committee on Lawlessness and
Violence in Texas, JUNE 30, 1868

Hays and Doboy Taylor, the sons of Creed, were the
first of the Taylors to be involved in difficulties with
the occupying Federal forces. Anyone associated with
them naturally became part of the "Taylor gang," although the
Taylors certainly never considered themselves a gang. We cannot know today who all comprised the Taylor party, those men
Union officials identified as outlaws, but certainly their cousin
Buck Taylor would have been a welcome member, if indeed
such a notorious band of outlaws did exist. Hays, Doboy, and
Buck became the first to draw the full attention of the military.
Its efforts merged with the attempts of various civilian officers,
the initial troubles ultimately bringing on the feud.

Hays Taylor's first recorded act of violence occurred on
April 15, 1867, when he and William North argued about the
winnings at a horse race in DeWitt County. The twenty-five-
year-old Taylor shot North through the thigh, and at the time it
was believed he could not recover.[1] The rumor mill also recorded
that Hays and Doboy had seriously wounded Captain Nolan

of the 18th New York Cavalry in Clinton in 1865, certainly the same Captain Nolan later reported shot in La Vernia. Additional rumors maintained that two soldiers were killed by the Taylors.[2] Unfounded rumors undoubtedly plagued the Taylors, rumors that resulted in the military expending great energy to capture or kill them. The violent incident that colored the name of every Taylor as a desperado took place in the town of Mason, in Mason County, on the fourteenth of November, 1867.

Taylor brothers Hays and Doboy, along with kinsman Randolph W. Spencer,[3] moved to Mason County, then on the edge of the frontier. A relatively small number of soldiers were stationed at Fort Mason situated a little over a mile from the town of Mason itself. They were there mainly to give the settlers a semblance of protection against Indian raiding parties. Ohio-born John A. Thompson, Company F 4th Cavalry, commanded the fifty or so soldiers stationed at the fort. Appointed 2nd Lieutenant in the 1st Dragoons on June 25, 1855, he was transferred to the 1st Cavalry later that same year. After joining the 4th Cavalry on August 3, 1861, Thompson served throughout the Civil War, and was then named post commander of Fort Mason on August 25, 1867, with the rank of major.[4] On November 14 he was waiting for an officer to relieve him so that he could proceed to a new command in Kansas with the 7th Regiment of U.S. Cavalry. Major Thompson was considered by his contemporaries "a man of noble qualities and a genial nature [and was] universally beloved by his fellow officers and men under his command. ..."[5]

On that day, Spencer, with Hays and Doboy, brothers quite different in personality—Hays quiet and good-humored and polite while Doboy boastful and quarrelsome—returned from a cow hunt and stopped in front of James W. Ranck's general store located on the northwest corner of the town square. Some soldiers, in various stages of intoxication, insulted Hays for no apparent reason. Doboy advised the soldiers to leave his brother alone, but before further action was taken by either side Major Thompson rode up in his buggy, accompanied by his wife. Seeing the disturbance, Thompson ordered Sergeant John McDougall to arrest the civilians. He stated he would discipline the soldiers if he determined they were at fault. But there was no time to determine where guilt lay or to consider discipline, because the Taylors and Spencer resisted with gunfire when the blue-coated sergeant attempted the arrest. Both Major Thompson and Sergeant McDougall were shot and killed. No matter whose bullet entered Major Thompson's right cheek, or whose bullet entered the sergeant's body, both men were fatally shot and all three shooters would be considered guilty. Dr. John J. Hulse was at the side of the dying Thompson within minutes, but could do nothing to save his life, nor could he do anything for McDougall. Dr. Hulse had to report what happened, explaining that it was with "the deepest regret, it becomes my painful duty to inform you of the death of Major John A. Thompson." The death-causing ball had "struck the right cheek emerging below the left ear, cutting the internal Carotid artery with fatal Hemorrhage in about twenty minutes."[6]

Now in flight, the two Taylors and Spencer certainly believed they had acted in self-defense. Two men familiar with the Taylors left accounts of what happened, providing additional details, although not in total agreement with official reports. Mason resident Thomas W. Gamel knew the Taylors and in some way learned their version of what had happened, that when Major Thompson jumped out of his buggy he held something in his hand that they believed was a pistol. This, while hearing the insults of the drunken soldiers, caused them to resist with deadly force.[7] The other account comes from Joseph B. Polley, who knew the Taylors well. Polley wrote that several soldiers insulted Hays simply because he was known to be a former Rebel. Doboy warned them to leave his brother alone, which warning seemed to only encourage more insults. When one of them pulled Hays's hat down

Site of the death of Major John Thompson, killed by Hays and Doboy Taylor in Mason, Texas. *Courtesy the Robert G. McCubbin Collection.*

over his face, Hays jumped up, "drew his pistol and shot the impudent private through the heart." Polley's memory in this case is not reliable as no private was shot, although one may have been involved in the fracas. It was at this point, according to Polley, that Major Thompson drove up, observed what was happening, and ordered the arrest of the three civilians. The

Taylors, and no doubt Spencer as well, answered with gunfire. The three then reached their horses quickly and left Mason. They now became hunted fugitives, eluding Union patrols. At least part of the time they were in hiding, out of the state, hunting horses in Louisiana.[8] The only fact that all accounts agree on was that Thompson and McDougall, perhaps the "private" of Polley's account, were killed.

Philip Goodbread "Doboy" Taylor, son of Creed and Nancy Goodbread Taylor. He was killed in Kerrville in 1871. *Courtesy the Robert G. McCubbin Collection.*

The death of Major Thompson resulted in considerable notoriety for the trio. The U.S. government quickly offered a reward of one thousand dollars for their arrest.[9] While the fugitives were heading back to more familiar ground in Karnes County, Texas Governor Elisha M. Pease reacted to the news. He ultimately increased the amount to $1500, five hundred dollars for each, to be paid whether brought in alive, or dead.[10] More than one Texan now thought the state's population was made up of three classes: the Yankees, the ex-Confederates, and the Taylors.[11]

Naturally the home of Creed Taylor was watched, not only by the military but by various bounty hunters, interested only in the reward for his sons. One group, described sarcastically as "expeditionary forces" (a term which officially described Creed Taylor's company of volunteers mustered into service for the Confederacy in 1864[12]) raided the Taylor home but found only the wives of Creed and Doboy present. In their frustration they insulted the women, stating that "the old man had been hung and the boys soon would be and that they had an idea of burning the house down, which, however, they did not do." They did, however, gratify themselves with taking a good race horse belonging to Creed Taylor, as well as the horses of several neighbors. Many people experienced mixed feelings towards the entire affair, condemning the killing of Thompson and McDougall, but also condemning the unreasonable treatment given Creed Taylor. Alfred Horatio Belo, highly respected editor of the *Galveston Daily News*, expressed his feelings in an editorial: "When the murderers of Major Thompson are caught we shall be in favor of their trial by military commission. ... But to prey upon the property of their father and his family ... is something we think highly censurable."[13] No doubt editor Belo was aware of Creed Taylor's contribution to making Texas a safer land for early settlers during his younger years, and found this tactic reprehensible.

Just as the sons of Creed Taylor found themselves wanted by the military during the Reconstruction years, so did their cousin,

"Buck" Taylor, son of William Riley and Elizabeth Tumlinson Taylor. William Riley was as much a pioneer as any other man, always ready to fight Indians or anyone else who impinged upon him. He was certainly brave and perhaps reckless. A good example is what he did in the fall of 1838, when he and brother-in-law John Tumlinson attempted to rescue Matilda Lockhart and the four Putnam children, who had been kidnapped by a band of Comanches. They failed in their efforts to recover the children, but at least they had made a valiant effort.

Although events would unfold revealing the Tumlinsons and the Taylors as enemies, there was certainly no animosity when William Riley Taylor married Elizabeth Tumlinson, sister of "Captain Joe" Tumlinson. The couple gave nine children to the world, one of whom was William P., always known as "Buck," born in 1837. Buck grew up much like every other child did in that time and place; he was an avid hunter, but perhaps with an urge to use firearms as a first resort. Buck married Mary Anderson, daughter of Walter A. "Watt" and Lou Bailey Anderson, on February 22, 1866.[14] No one knows what his parents dreamed for him, but certainly they had not wished him to have by the late 1860s a reputation as a rough and notorious character. In 1867 Buck's father-in-law, Watt Anderson, was accused of a murder, stood trial and was acquitted. Details of this incident have been lost, but in spite of his acquittal there remained in the mind of the Reconstruction government and its military arm the belief that he was guilty. Occupational troops considered Watt Anderson and his associates, including son-in-law Buck Taylor, outlaws.[15]

Buck Taylor did develop a reputation for lawlessness, but this was more rumor and innuendo than hard fact. The Freedmen's Bureau office in Victoria received reports of disturbed conditions in South Texas. Capt. Edward Miller, a sub-assistant commissioner for the 5th Military District, investigated, and found that the "only danger apprehended in this neighborhood," at least by freedmen and Unionists, was from the "pillaging expeditions" of men led by the "notorious Buck Taylor of Yorktown." Taylor, according to Miller's findings, not only endangered the lives of local residents but also made it "very unsafe for a simple traveler" to pass through that portion of the country. Captain Miller cited no specific charges against Taylor, suggesting his conclusions were based on hearsay, but did recommend that a detachment of cavalry and a good scout "could terminate the Career of these rascals effectually."[16]

In the mind of Captain Miller, there was no question that Buck Taylor was the leader of an outlaw band, but to others he was a much better man than the soldiers who pursued him. Whether he was as bad as the military portrayed him, or simply an unreconstructed Rebel, his reputation became widespread. An exchange that originally appeared in an out-of-state newspaper, then picked up by the widely read *Galveston Daily News*, reflects both his notoriety and the unfair treatment given him. The traveling correspondent stopped at an unidentified grog shop after visiting Yorktown, and "Not knowing at the moment the character of the place, ... entered into conversation with the proprietor" and inquired if Buck Taylor's party "was still upon the rampage," that he had heard "bad reports at Yorktown" concerning the safety of the road he was to travel.

"Buck Taylor's party—hell!" replied the proprietor. "Buck Taylor will trouble nobody who don't trouble him." The man continued with his defense of Taylor, relating how a "party of soldiers came down here ... surrounded a house on a ranche about ten miles from here, and thinking it was occupied by some of Taylor's men, fired into it and killed two men in bed. Some resistance was offered by others of the party and the soldiers retreated, leaving a horse behind them." The editor, perhaps Confederate veteran Alfred Horatio Belo himself, bravely wrote that the amount of lawlessness in Texas was greatly exaggerated. "All the noise and confusion at the North and everywhere else about lawlessness ... is absurd; there is no more lawlessness here than ... anywhere else in the world; in our opinion ... not so much."[17]

Contributing to the notoriety of Buck Taylor was the accusation that he had killed Capt. Henry J. Nolan of the 18th Infantry near La Vernia in Wilson County, just east of San Antonio. Authorities believed Charley Taylor and James Wright were involved as well. It is impossible today to learn specific details of the killing of Captain Nolan, even exactly when and where he met his death.[18] Nevertheless, the military believed Buck Taylor and the others were involved and the military now listed three Taylors as wanted men: Hays and Doboy, sons of Creed, and Buck, their cousin.[19]

Captain George W. Smith of the 35th Infantry left San Antonio, filled with confidence that he would accomplish great things: the arrests of Buck Taylor, his cousin Martin Taylor, and perhaps Hays and Doboy as well. Smith was leader of a fifty-man detachment: 2nd Lt. Charles A. Vernou with seven men of the 4th Cavalry; 2nd Lt. William V. Wolfe, with forty men of the 30th Infantry, all from the post at San Antonio. Smith also had extra horses and five army wagons for supplies. Captain Smith mounted up at 2:30 p.m. on November 16, heading east toward Seguin in neighboring Guadalupe County to obtain maps and a guide, arriving there at 2:00 a.m. the following day. After an hour's rest the group moved on, arriving at Creed Taylor's ranch the afternoon of the seventeenth, after a forced march of sixty miles in less than twenty-four hours. Neither Hays nor Doboy were there, only a hired man named Burch and two women.[20] Instead of admitting defeat, Captain Smith satisfied himself with taking three muskets, one shotgun, and four horses, all items which any rural home would have at that time.

Then on the eighteenth of November, Smith headed out on the Yorktown-San Antonio road, now adding one more name to his list of wanted fugitives: T. C. West,[21] "who was engaged in Killing the negro at Lavernia [*sic*] with the Taylors," or at least that was the belief. No arrest was made. Now the elements acted against Smith, as darkness fell when he was within six miles from Taylor's house. "The night being dark" Smith explained, "our guide missed the direction, when, after wandering about till late, we laid down to rest." When daylight came "dense fog passed over us." By eight o'clock the fog had lifted and the party proceeded, but now with a different guide, one who presumably would know where Taylor lived, but who also may have intentionally betrayed the presence of the hunters. This guide led the group to a hilltop, which allowed Smith to clearly see Taylor's house, but also permitted any inhabitants of the dwelling to see him. Being in full view, Smith decided all that could be done at that point "was to charge the house." Indeed they had been seen, since Buck and his wife had been in the house only moments before. They had left hurriedly, as Smith discovered they had abandoned "a hot breakfast on the table." Buck had seen the man hunters on the hill, and realizing their mission, fled; his wife was found at a neighbor's house where she was interrogated. She informed Captain Smith that her husband had left the house so quickly he did not take the time to even saddle and bridle his horse. She further informed the captain that "had we caught him there, he would have Killed two or three of us, that he had previously shot Capt. Nolan of the 18th N.Y. and two or three other soldiers and made his escape." She also informed Smith that Buck would never surrender. Rather than admitting total defeat he confiscated Taylor's saddle, a bridle, and a shotgun, then proceeded to Yorktown where they had left their wagons. Captain Smith had by now ruined his chances of capturing any of the Taylors, and it is apparent his failure was due to his choice of poor guides, his use of poor judgment, and his gullibility. He had little to show for all his efforts, having confiscated only some weapons, a saddle and bridle, and several horses from the Taylors, but he had not captured Buck Taylor, Hays nor Doboy, nor Martin Taylor, nor T. C. West.

Still determined to accomplish something, Captain Smith traveled to Watt Anderson's place in Yorktown. They searched the house but found no one they wanted, but satisfied themselves by taking a shotgun. How long Smith and his patrol remained in the Yorktown area is unknown, but they did discuss Buck Taylor and his so-called gang with various citizens. Smith learned from them that neither the county sheriff nor any one else would attempt to arrest Buck Taylor or his friends. He was told again that Captain Nolan and several freedmen killed at La Vernia were victims of Buck Taylor, and that Charley Taylor and James Wright were "directly concerned" in the affray. In addition, Smith learned a man identified as Pease, but certainly either Christopher or Madison "Matt" Peace, was another of Taylor's associates, as well as Edward Glover. Glover, or so Smith was told, was also supposedly involved in the multiple killings in La Vernia. Glover lived in Gonzales County, nearly a day's ride from Yorktown. Captain Smith apparently believed whatever he was told, if it reflected negatively upon the Taylors. Someone further informed him that Glover had threatened to kill him, but was provided no reason as to why. Smith now sent some men to arrest Glover, but they failed to find him, only confiscating a six-shooter, a rifle, and a shotgun from his house. Smith then sent a squad to Atascosa County, southwest of DeWitt County, in search of Charley Taylor, and another to search for Martin Taylor. These squads failed to capture any of the wanted men, and Smith had to abandon the search entirely when the horses played out, having accomplished little but confiscating a few weapons and wearing out horses. In spite of his failure, Smith could not resist complimenting the quality of the men who failed with him. "I cannot speak too highly of the conduct of the officers and men of the mounted detachment. In rushing upon the dens of these desperadoes, each striving to be the first in the house with the full knowledge that no attempt to capture them has ever been made without the loss of life." Smith at least saw some good from his endeavors: with the knowledge gained about the country, with twenty men "well armed and mounted upon good serviceable horses," he believed he could break up "this gang of desperadoes, by capturing, killing, or driving them out of the country," and with such confidence Smith requested permission to lead another scout.[22]

He was acting under the orders of Maj. Gen. Charles Griffin, orders to resort to "extreme measures if necessary," and if the men were not found, he was to "seize their property if they have any and sell it as a fine." Smith felt totally justified in confiscating weapons and horses from those he could not capture. Further, General Griffin had assured him that he would "be sustained in any cause you may take to accomplish the desired object."[23]

Living in the same general area as the Taylors was young William E. "Bill" Sutton. Nothing indicates that Bill Sutton as yet had concerned himself with anything other than his own ranching interests, but in March 1868 he was central to an important initial event in the feud. His experience in the late war had sharpened his leadership ability. DeWitt County Sheriff James Francis Blair[24] learned some livestock had been stolen and gathered a posse to pursue the thieves. Sutton, who may have already worked as an occasional deputy, joined the group. He must have known that the stolen stock included a fine horse with a silver-mounted saddle, because before leaving Clinton, Sutton vowed to recover the horse with the fancy saddle.[25] The stolen cattle belonged to a certain Widow Thomas.[26]

When the thieves split up, the posse divided as well, Sutton taking command of one part, Sheriff Blair the other. Sutton's group, consisting of Alfred P. Taylor, Robert Thomas, Alexander H. Samples, Thomas Pulliam, and several others never identi-

fied, caught up with their prey in Bastrop.[27] Surprisingly, two
of the alleged thieves, Charley Taylor and James Sharp, had
been in Bastrop for several days, apparently ignored by local
authorities. Sutton with his men, identified as "a posse of citizens, eight in number, from Clinton, DeWitt county" observed
the pair on Main Street and demanded their surrender. Both
ignored the order and started running in different directions,
Sharp going into and through the store of Cunningham &
Co., while Taylor headed for Crow & Jones's establishment.
Before he reached the door, however, "he was fired on, and
expired immediately on entering the store." By now Sharp had
managed to exit Cunningham's store, ran through several lots,
and found his way into a house where he "concealed himself
under the kitchen floor." Half an hour later the posse discovered his hiding place and took him into custody.[28] Bastrop
citizens realized that the posse intended to kill Sharp, but somehow prevented them.[29] How Sutton or the other members of
the posse recognized Charley Taylor as the presumed thief is
uncertain, but perhaps they simply recognized the fancy silver-mounted saddle on the horse and presumed the worst.[30]
Sharp had seen what happened to Charley Taylor and surrendered.[31] Two other men on the street, a father and young
son named Longee, were accidentally wounded in the melee.
Mrs. Longee had given birth only a few days previously and
Longee had come to Bastrop to get the physician. The wounds
of the senior Longee proved mortal and he died the night of
April 3 after considerable suffering.[32] The posse claimed to have
shouted an order to Taylor and Sharp to surrender, but several
Bastrop spectators to the affair denied that claim.[33] Nevertheless, Sutton, now in charge of the posse, started the return trek
to Clinton, a three-day ride. Jim Sharp was in their custody, as
well as the horse with the fancy silver-mounted saddle; Charley
Taylor was dead, and two men were wounded back in Bastrop.
The disposition of the widow Thomas's stolen stock is unknown.

From Bastrop the group headed west to Caldwell County. Just outside of county seat Lockhart, the "squad of eight citizens under command of Mr. Sutton ... riddled their prisoner with bullets, a short distance from that place and left the body on the roadside." Being "riddled" with bullets suggests not only Sutton but every other man in the group participated in the killing of the prisoner. Whether the posse was in haste to leave the scene, or simply did not care about the bloody corpse, they left the remains of Jim Sharp on the roadside for someone else to bury.[34] Whether Sharp and Charley Taylor were kin to each other or merely friends is also unknown, just as the relationship of Charley Taylor to the sons of Josiah Taylor Sr. remains a mystery. Creed Taylor, who certainly was in a position to know, claimed Charley was a distant relative.

William E. "Bill" Sutton, by following the thieves and rendering "justice" to them, as well as recovering stolen property, proved that he was not only an efficient man hunter but also a gallant young man whose actions certainly impressed the good people of DeWitt County. The fact that the posse did not bring back a single prisoner, but had killed two men, one in their custody and presumably in some form of restraint, and a third man accidentally, apparently did not pose a problem for anyone. Although Bastrop County officials brought charges of murder against Sutton and the others, ultimately nothing came of them and the posse members were dismissed.[35] It was just another example of vigilante justice, approved by the Bastrop County citizenry.

The majority of the population may not have perceived that type of justice as a problem, but the question of excessive lawlessness was a serious concern for the delegates to the Constitutional Convention, then meeting in Austin. Gathered to write a new constitution, the convention devoted much time and effort to studying the question of lawlessness and violence in the state. The special committee on the subject of lawlessness and violence in Texas signed its final report on June 30, 1868. It had had access to the records of the state department, which included reports from only about forty counties; the records of the Freedmen's Bureau, likewise imperfect as they had material only from sixty counties; and sworn statements from competent and reliable witnesses in various portions of the state, which statements were also incomplete as they were made from memory.[36] The committee reluctantly turned in its depressing report, admitting that the actual picture presented by incomplete records and reluctant witnesses, fearful of assassination, showed "a very imperfect view of the actual violence and disorder in the State."[37]

The report presented Texas as a very violent place indeed. The committee had directed its investigation into the homicides committed between the close of the War of the Rebellion to the first of June 1868, a full three-year period. It had not attempted to detail the attempts to kill, the rapes and robberies, the whipping of freedmen, or other outrages. During the time period under study, and the numbers were incomplete, there were 939 homicides. Of these 939, 470 were of whites, and 429 were of freedmen. Race had not been reported for the other forty homicides. During the year of 1868 alone, from January 1 through May 31, 304 homicides had been reported, allowing anyone to realize that violence definitely was on the increase. The committee could not diminish the significance of these figures, and stated forthrightly that the report presented "a frightful story of blood. ... We cannot shut our eyes upon these appalling scenes of bloodshed; and, instead of attempting to conceal them, it becomes us to face them honestly, and address ourselves to the duty of discovering the cause and locating the responsibility of this slaughter of our fellow-citizens." In an attempt to explain why there was such a frightening number of homicides, the committee stated that many of the roadways of Texas were overrun with bandits who would take a human life "for a horse, or a pistol, or a purse." The committee identified the "desperadoes" as former "confederate officers or soldiers, or bushwhackers, during the late war" but also recognized that many of the homicides "resulted from private quarrels" and that "there is much bad blood in the land."[38]

Indeed, there were "private quarrels" and there was "much bad blood in the land," and much of the blood already spilled and blood that would be spilled within a few years in DeWitt and the surrounding counties of Gonzales, Karnes, and Goliad ran through the veins of the Taylors and their followers and sympathizers.

Certainly the so-called desperadoes or bushwhackers were also aware of the fact that many counties had inadequate facilities to hold them if captured. By the end of 1868 only eighty-two counties possessed a jail, and nearly half of those jails were built of wood. In all, only two dozen jails were considered secure.[39] Because of the condition of many jails during the sixties and seventies, mobs found it easy to take prisoners away from jailers and lynch them, or raid the jail and free the prisoners. In Clinton, a suspected horse thief, a man identified as M. Clannahan, was chained in the lower story of the jail, only accessible through a trap door. One night in June of 1868, while the committee in Austin was finalizing its report on violence, unknown parties opened the trap door, threw in a "fire ball (it being in the night) so as to see their victim," and shot him to death.[40] The murder of a prisoner by a mob was not difficult. In the subsequent decade, the Taylors and their allies would suffer greatly from this fact of life.

The report of the committee on lawlessness and violence had a good number of examples from the south-central portion of the state. Violence was considered rampant and in many cases senseless as well. In April 1867, in DeWitt County, Thomas Dodd killed a freedman named Hintz, for no apparent reason.[41] In neighboring Goliad County similar incidents occurred: on

March 1 of that year William Miller murdered a Mexican named Carlos in a dispute over the ownership of a horse; George Blackburn assaulted Mitchell Walton but failed to kill him, and twelve days later Blackburn and William Brooken attempted to kill a Mexican.[42] In August 1867 August Westfall assaulted an old black woman because she had "rebuked him for using vulgar language in her presence." Mrs. C. Sloan, a white woman, attempted to kill Mary Oglesby, a black woman. Mrs. Sloan shot at her four times, but apparently Oglesby survived.[43] In Victoria County, south of DeWitt, Wiley Pridgen, on September 20, 1867, shot and killed Neill Brown following an argument over a horse. Pridgen was found guilty of this murder and sentenced to five years in prison, but escaped after a few months in the Victoria jail.[44] Wiley Washington Pridgen was a brother of Senator Bolivar Jackson Pridgen, a "pioneer Republican [who] was deeply involved in a multitude of complexities facing Texas after the Civil War."[45] The Pridgens later became involved in the feud between the Taylor faction and the Sutton party. All these incidents clearly demonstrate that lawlessness was perceived by many as being out of control in the area.

The killers of Major Thompson and Sergeant McDougall were still on the loose, but the offer of the sizeable reward of $500 for each, dead or alive, attracted numerous bounty hunters, including Capt. John Littleton. He was an experienced soldier with an impressive record. A native of Tennessee, born about 1825, he joined as a private in Capt. William G. Tobin's company of Mounted Volunteers in 1859 to fight in the Cortina War of South Texas. Littleton rose to the rank of lieutenant and later captain of Mounted Volunteers. While fighting Mexican raiders, at least twice he crossed the Rio Grande in pursuit of raiding parties. After serving with famed John S. "Rip" Ford's battalion he was elected as a delegate to the Secession Convention and served from January 28, 1860, to February 4, 1861, representing Karnes County. Like the Sutton brothers and numerous men of the Taylor clan, he had fought on the losing side in the late war. Commissioned a captain, Littleton served on the frontier against Indian depredations until the end of 1863 when he joined Ford against Federal forces on the lower Rio Grande, an action which culminated in the battle of Palmito Ranch in 1865, the last land action of the Civil War. In February of 1864 he had inspected the men of Capt. Creed Taylor's company, a small group who had volunteered to serve in the Confederate "Provisional Army." Taylor's twenty-five man troop was mustered in at Helena, Karnes County.[46]

Littleton had involved himself in the troubles with the Taylors as early as March 1866 when he gave shelter to a man named Polk who had been shot and severely wounded by Charley Taylor, the same Charley Taylor who was killed in Bastrop County.[47] In spite of Littleton's efforts, Polk did not survive his wounds.[48]

Littleton had been impoverished by the war, and earning the reward for the capture of the Taylors and Spencer would have been of great benefit. He may have laid the best of plans, but he failed to keep them secret, unknowingly revealing his intentions to a relative of the Taylors. When advised that capturing the Taylors was too big and dangerous a task, he responded, "Yes, it is a big load, and it may be mighty hard to carry. But my shoulders are broad and strong, and I'll do it or die." Although known to be "brave, resolute and persistent, cunning and resourceful," Littleton was doomed, as the Taylors quickly "got wind" of Littleton's plans.[49] He had been attempting to arrest the Taylors for some time, and was recognized as "the acknowledged leader of a different faction." This statement was expressed by Maj. John S. Mason who later described Littleton as having "the reputation of being a desperate and unscrupulous man." The idea of factions warring against each other was clearly expressed by Mason.[50]

"Creed Taylor Spring near his residence" is how this photograph is identified but it appears the foreground figure is Creed Taylor. This is not the site of the Littleton and Stannard ambush, but clearly shows the physical geography in which the feudists lived, and how easily an ambush could be arranged. *Courtesy the Robert G. McCubbin Collection.*

In early December 1868, Littleton went to San Antonio for business reasons, traveling in a buggy with friend William Stannard to keep him company. The trip to San Antonio was without incident. Returning by night to avoid the excessive heat of the day, the pair felt confident they could begin their work of capturing the Taylors immediately.

As Littleton and Stannard approached Black Jack Spring, a "wet-weather spring" a few miles west from the little community of Nockenut[51] in northern Wilson County, they suddenly heard the sound of horses, and then saw guns in the hands of the very men they intended to capture. Realizing they had fallen into an ambush, Stannard dropped the reins and both men reached for their weapons. Although "armed" in the sense they had weapons, neither succeeded in grasping their holstered pistols placed beneath the buggy seat. Both received multiple shots in their bodies, the force of the blows knocking Stannard out of the buggy. Littleton cried out "Murder!" twice before his death wound. The frightened horses now galloped on, Littleton's body remaining in the buggy. They did not stop until some three miles later. Littleton was marked for death because he had vowed to capture or kill the Taylors. Stannard happened to be with Littleton when his enemies found him, and paid the supreme price for friendship. Both Littleton and Stannard were buried in what is now known as the Old Masonic Cemetery near Helena, their graves unmarked. Little publicity was given this double killing. The *Goliad Guard* printed a brief item, from details learned from "a gentleman" named Hunter of Gonzales and C. A. Russell, Esq., of Helena, that "Capt. J. Littleton and a man by the name of Stanard [*sic*], were waylaid and shot near Leesburg, from which they both died, on Friday the 3d inst."[52]

Authorities suspected the Taylors of the double killing immediately. A witness later provided a deposition in which the six gunmen were not only fully identified but explained how the ambush was successfully carried out. The witness, William A. G. Lewis, a fifteen-year-old boy out hunting a horse, had met up with the group. He identified the ambush party as Hays and Doboy Taylor, Randolph Spencer, Buck Rowland, Jeff Clark[53] and Fred Pell. Lewis "fell in" with the group and, as they were also hunting horses, asked him "to go along with them" and, apparently with no hesitation, Lewis joined them and the group all camped together. The next morning they asked Lewis to go to Leesville, in neighboring Gonzales County, but about six miles away, "and get something to eat for them, and also asked me to find out if Capt. Littleton was about home, or where he was." At a store in Leesville young Lewis "bought a can of oysters, a box of sardines, some ham and crackers," and also inquired of the "man behind the counter where Capt. Littleton was; he told me [he had] gone to San Antonio." On returning to the Taylor party, presumably after eating, the entire group headed for the head of the Ecleto, which took about a day and a half, where camp was made, some three hundred yards off the road. Now Lewis was again sent off to get food, but not finding any place to acquire food or supplies he started to return when he heard firing. Lewis "went up to the camp, ... and saw the whole party hurriedly loading their guns." They informed Lewis they had killed Stannard and Littleton. With their guns re-loaded, "they mounted their horses, and we all rode pretty fast down the road after the buggy, in which Littleton and Standard [sic] were riding when shot." It was Hays Taylor who caught up with the buggy first and stopped the horses. They saw that Littleton was dead, "shot with a pistol bullet in the right side of his head, above the ear; he was shot in the right breast with buck shot, and also in his right leg with buckshot." The buggy had no top on it and he could observe Littleton, lying back, "with his head hanging on the seat, bleeding from the wound in his head, and one leg hanging out at the side of the buggy." Someone told Lewis that Littleton had cried out "Murder!" twice, but Stannard had made no sound, falling out of the buggy on the ground upon being shot.

Lewis's description of the ambush is as close to the actual truth as we are likely to ever determine. The men apparently were proud of their accomplishment, bragging to Lewis about what each had done. Randolph Spencer initiated the ambush, aiming his shotgun at Stannard's chest, "and put both barrels of his shot gun into him." Doboy Taylor shot Littleton in the head with a pistol while brother Hays shot him in the leg with his shotgun. Jeff Clark claimed it was his shotgun blast that knocked Stannard out of the buggy onto the road. Buck Rowland fired his six-shooter twice but made no claim as to accuracy. Doboy apparently believed Stannard had survived the shotgun blasts as he administered a *coup de grâce* to his head. It was the third of December, 1868.[54]

The Lewis deposition is of great value as it provides details on an early killing of the feud like no others. Ambushing an enemy was as old as human conflict itself, and there would be numerous ambushes between the parties engaged in the Sutton-Taylor Feud in the years ahead. Obviously the ambush party feared nothing. Although Lewis knew what they had done, they "cautioned me not to say any thing to any person about what I had seen and heard." Nevertheless, the deposition was not made until September 9, 1869, nearly ten months after the deed he had witnessed. Lewis told his father, and later both father and son visited military headquarters in Helena, where young William Lewis told his story, "under assurances that he should be protected in so doing."

The Taylors as well as the others realized their actions would result in the military's renewed efforts to capture and kill them. Their names were on the list of wanted fugitives, and would remain there. If cornered they would have to fight. If captured they could expect to be shot to death or lynched from a nearby tree, rather than taken to an inadequate jail from which escape might be easily accomplished. They certainly were aware of what had happened to Charley Taylor and James Sharp earlier that year. The killings of Thompson, McDougall, Littleton, and Stannard by Taylors, and the killing of Taylor and Sharp by a Sutton-led posse, provided the fuel for what became the Sutton-Taylor Feud. Their deaths were the genesis of the war.

Grave marker of William P. "Buck" Taylor, killed with Richard Chisholm in Clinton on Christmas Eve, 1868. *Courtesy Robert W. Shook.*

CHAPTER THREE

A Killing in Clinton

"I have been, an[d] am now activated solely by a desire to discharge my duty as an officer, and to see justice done."
—Jack Helm to Brig. Gen. James Oakes, JULY 15, 1867

Richard H. Chisholm was the first permanent settler in the area that became DeWitt County, establishing a home there in January 1829. Soon other settlers moved in and a settlement grew on the west bank of the Guadalupe River, five miles southeast of the present site of Cuero, today the county seat. It was wild country then and tragedies were numerous.

Chisholm proved to be an entrepreneur: in 1839 he began operating a ferry across the Guadalupe. When DeWitt County was organized in 1846 he worked to have the county seat established on his land. James Norman Smith, pioneer teacher, religious leader, and county surveyor, surveyed the town site and named it Clinton in honor of the daughter of Empresario Green DeWitt. But in spite of Chisholm's efforts, the site of the court house was established on land belonging to John J. Tumlinson and named Cameron. As Clinton grew, its citizens protested the site and during the next few years the actual site of the county seat alternated several times between Clinton and Cameron. An 1850 election settled the question for good between the two settlements, but it was not until 1852 when the first court house

51

was built, a log structure followed by a frame building in 1855. Three years later the county could boast of a two-story court house. Several churches remained active for some time. The first church, Live Oak Presbyterian, established in 1849, was followed by a Methodist church in 1850. The two denominations used the log court house until each finally had its own building. A Masonic Lodge was established in 1852. About 1855 a school was established by the Rev. and Mrs. James M. Connelly, who were teachers. Two attorneys at the time were Henry Clay Pleasants and John W. Stayton.

During the Civil War, when Union troops threatened Victoria, the Victoria Female Academy moved to Clinton. During Reconstruction, Federal troops occupied the town, as well as others in the area. Difficulties between those still sympathetic to the "Lost Cause" and occupational troops were frequent, even though the war was over. When the Gulf, Western Texas & Pacific Railroad bypassed Clinton in favor of Cuero, most of the businesses followed the tracks, leaving Clinton to die gradually over the years. All that remains of Clinton today is the still active cemetery, although portions of it have been abandoned and weeds and brush obliterate numerous graves.[1] A Texas State Historical marker dedicated in 1967 indicates where the town used to be.[2]

The Chisholm brothers came from Scotland, then to Virginia and then to Green DeWitt's colony in Texas in late 1828. One brother never married, and the family lost track of him. Richard H. Chisholm married Hardinia Taylor, the daughter of Josiah and Hephzibeth Taylor. Richard H. and Hardinia Taylor Chisholm produced four children: three sons, Glenn Thornton, Bradford A., and Richard T., and daughter Mary Ann. Richard H. Chisholm died April 8, 1855.[3]

On Christmas Eve, 1868, Richard T. Chisholm and his cousin William P. "Buck" Taylor, were in Clinton. Bill Sutton, Joseph P. "Doc" White, Horace French, and Clayton Sumners were also

in Clinton that night. As it was Christmas Eve, no doubt everyone was in a holiday mood. In addition to those named, others
who were there and witnessed the tragedy that followed, or
learned of it from actual eye-witnesses, included Lewis Delony,
Tobe Kelly, Jack Hays Day, and Mary Elizabeth Humphries.

Most young men in those days went armed. Whether a pistol was worn openly or concealed was a matter of personal
preference. A rifle or shotgun, too heavy to carry around in town,
was left on the horse tied up to the hitching rails. Buck Taylor
and Bill Sutton exchanged harsh words in one of Clinton's
saloons, but what words were actually spoken and led to gunplay are now lost. There may have been a remark about the
deaths of Charley Taylor and Jim Sharp that offended Bill Sutton.
The argument included not only harsh words, according to one
witness, but Buck Taylor's temper flared and he slapped Bill
Sutton's face. Naturally, Bill Sutton could not ignore that slap
in the face, whether it came from a Taylor or anyone else. He
could only take it to the next level, which was gunplay. Gunfire erupted in that Clinton saloon, but no one could determine
who fired first, or how many shots were fired. The battle erupted
out into the street where more shots were fired. Certainly Buck
Taylor was armed, and perhaps Dick Chisholm as well, but the
pair inflicted no wounds on their adversaries. Instead, when the
shooting ended Buck Taylor and Dick Chisholm were both dead
or dying.

This is the only point all agree upon: that Dick Chisholm
and Buck Taylor were killed. Why they were killed, and who
exactly did the killing, remains open to debate. This is a very
important consideration because even if there had not been a
feud-like situation prior to the killings, this tragedy for the
Taylor and Chisholm families demanded that their kin avenge
their deaths. Some consider the killing of Taylor and Chisholm
as the actual cause of the feud. Did the killing of Charley Taylor
and James Sharp in Bastrop provide the genesis for the feud which

lasted for years, or was it the killing of Buck Taylor and Dick Chisholm in Clinton? That is the question impossible to answer definitively today.

Lewis S. Delony was a mere boy at the time but was on the streets of Clinton that Christmas Eve. He and a companion, Tobe Kelly,[4] hurried to the court house after finishing their chores, as the Christmas celebration was to be held there. Distracted by loud talking in one of the saloons, the boys stopped to observe what was happening. The loud talk came from several armed men. Delony, recalling what he saw that night many years later, ran from the immediate area to watch and saw a man run out of the saloon, turn and shoot at someone inside. It was Dick Chisholm who had left the saloon, who then fell within ten feet of the boys. They were close enough to hear him yell, "My God I am killed." When the smoke of the battle cleared, the boys continued to the court house where someone asked who had been shot. Lewis answered "Dick Chisholm is killed" and heard Mrs. Chisholm scream and "fall in a faint." According to Delony this "feud was known as the Sutton and Taylor feud, and lasted for several years."[5]

A descendant, Daniel Fore Chisholm, left a more detailed account of what happened. When Buck Taylor and Dick Chisholm came to town, Taylor stopped at a saloon to have a drink, while companion Chisholm continued to the house of Jim Chisholm. There Dick's mother indicated she would need more candles, and Dick volunteered to go back to town to get some, and also bring Buck back "for the Sutton crowd were all in town, and he was afraid that Buck and them might have trouble." Dick found Buck at Stepp's Store where he was arguing with Sutton, "Doc" White, and Horace French.[6] The words led to gunplay and "Clayton Summers" [*sic:* Sumners], hiding behind some logs, shot Taylor in the back. Chisholm, seeing his cousin fall, started to run to his aid but was then shot in the back by Sutton, but not mortally. Seeing he was attempting to fire his pistol

Sumners then finished off the wounded man with a load of buck-shot. Sutton then took Dick Chisholm's pistol.

Daniel F. Chisholm's memoirs may be based in part on what he actually remembered, but when Dick Chisholm and Buck Taylor were killed, D. F. Chisholm was a mere child, born in 1865. He could only have based his "memoirs" on family tradition or stories. There are a number of errors in his account. The "Clayton Summers" was in reality Joseph Clayton *Sumners*, then an eighteen-year-old friend of Sutton.[7] Most glaring is that at the time the sheriff was not William Weisiger but James Francis Blair, who had been elected on June 25, 1866, and who served until February 15, 1869.[8] It is not surprising that Chisholm "remembered" Weisiger was sheriff, as he did serve some eight years while Chisholm was growing up.[9]

Mary Elizabeth Humphreys Ainsworth, a long-time DeWitt County resident who recorded her memoirs years later, also believed that Buck Taylor had been shot in the back, as was Chisholm. She recalled that Chisholm and Taylor had "an altercation" with "a young Sutton," name not provided but obviously Bill. "When ... Taylor started to draw his gun, one of Sutton's relatives standing to the rear shot Taylor in the back, killing him instantly. Of course bad blood was ingendered [*sic*] and it kept on from there."[10] She does not say she was on the scene when it happened, but she may have been close by as she was old enough to be there, fourteen years of age. It was her belief that this "fracas" was what started the feud between the Suttons and the Taylors.

Jack Hays Day, a member of the Taylor clan, provided another memoir, more accurate than Chisholm's, but quite biased in favor of the Taylors. Born October 28, 1856, he was a young teenager when the Taylor-Chisholm killings took place. Day called the tragedy a "cold blooded killing of my cousin, Buck Taylor," and recalled his cousin as "an industrious, quiet-mannered man, born and reared in the saddle." He also claims that the authorities did nothing, writing that "[w]hen we had fully investigated these murders, efforts were made to bring Sutton and his henchmen to trial, but ended in failure. It was apparent that Sutton was the ring leader of a rowdy clique willing to take human life at the slightest provocation; that he was capable of intense hatreds and fed on trouble." Although Jack Hays Day was in the early years of adulthood when these events transpired, his memoir reveals little objectivity.[11]

Buck Taylor's granddaughter, Alexa Taylor Green, learned of the affair and determined that the argument began when Taylor accused Sutton of sending stolen cattle up the trail with his herd. He accused Sutton of being a thief and then slapped him across the face with his glove, an unmistakable challenge to fight.[12]

Curiously, historian Victor M. Rose gives very little attention to this important incident, merely recording that "in the town of Clinton, a dispute arose between Buck Taylor and William Sutton, ... which resulted in the killing of Taylor and a friend."[13]

No action was taken against Bill Sutton or the others for the killing of Buck Taylor and Dick Chisholm. Daniel F. Chisholm perhaps expressed it best, stating that the authorities did nothing, not even "a token-investigation," which proved to the Taylors that "the Sutton gang controlled the District Court, as well as the Prosecuting Attorney and Sheriff's Office,—and to make bad matters worse, Sheriff Bill Wiesiger [*sic:* Weisiger] appointed Dick Hudson and a couple more of the Sutton faction, as Deputy Sheriffs."[14]

Thus, by the end of 1868 two Taylors had been killed; whether they were closely related or only bore the same surname was unimportant. Kinsman Dick Chisholm had also been killed, and William E. Sutton was involved in the killing of all three men; whether his bullets were the fatal ones or not was immaterial. The Taylor family name was now echoed again in the aftermath of these deaths: "Who sheds a Taylor's blood by a Taylor's hand must fall."[15]

Regardless of what initiated the argument and subsequent killing of Buck Taylor and Dick Chisholm, no one was charged with murder. Word reached San Antonio's *Daily Express,* which reported their deaths, but with considerable editorial comment, much based on rumor. The first report, appearing in the Sunday edition of December 27, 1868, three days after the incident, is considerably at variance with other accounts. The *Express* reported that "a row" occurred in Clinton, "on the occasion of Taylor and his friends going there to settle a difficulty between him and some of the citizens. It is represented to us that the difficulty was supposed to have been settled, but after night, he and one Chisholm, (that is supposed to be his name) were killed." A man identified as White was Taylor's "principal opponent," but no other particulars were given other than that Taylor was dead "in a couple of hours after being shot."

Elsewhere in the same issue appeared Moore's commentary. It is obvious that the objectivity of the initial reporting had now been colored by someone, perhaps by a member of the military entourage. This report, in the same issue, was headlined, "Murder of Buck Taylor," and announced the deceased as a "notorious outlaw and desperado" who had finally "come to his untimely end." All the shootists involved were now classed as *members of the same gang,* the explanation given that Taylor and Chisholm both were killed by their companions. Texas was thus rid of "two desperadoes and blood-thirsty men. It is to be hoped that this entire gang will soon be broken up and delivered to the proper authorities to try them for their acts of inhuman treatment to those who were unfortunate to fall in their clutches."[16]

Some questioned this report, as over a week later a confirmation item appeared. The *Express* now reported that the earlier report of Taylor's death had been confirmed. Not able to resist further comment, the writer continued, describing the two dead men as part of "the Taylor gang of desperadoes [which] got into a fight among them selves on the Division of spoils, the result was the death of Buck Taylor and Dick Chisholm." Identifying the popular revolver of the day, the editor wrote that the difficulty was "a regular pitch[ed] battle with 'army sixes.'"[17] The *Express* never altered its report that those who killed Taylor and Chisholm were members of their own group.

If the average Texan was unaware of the hostilities in DeWitt County before this event, he soon would not be as the incident resulted in considerable publicity, much of it based on hearsay or rumor. Questions were then raised as to what actually did happen. A citizen of Victoria sent a private letter to the *Houston Telegraph* that was then reprinted in the *Galveston Daily News*, declaring that a "young man named White killed Taylor, and it seems to be uncertain whether Chisholm was killed by White or by Will Sutton." Further, this report indicated, there "were several persons in the fight on both sides." The "collision grew out of old difficulties."[18] The *Houston Union* expressed strong feelings against the Taylors, reporting in the "Texas Affairs" column that Taylor and Chisholm were killed "in a general fight." The editor revealed his own prejudices by adding, "We record the death of such scoundrels with pleasure, and hope that the whole race will be speedily exterminated."[19] Did he mean the entire "race" of Taylors?

Some considered the Clinton killings as simple justice administered to lawbreakers; others saw the killers, Sutton and others, as merely lawless men taking the law into their own hands. Victor M. Rose states that at this point the Taylors "meditated revenge" and that General Joseph J. Reynolds now "included all the Taylors, from the Rio Grande to the tall pines on the Sabine, in the edict of excommunication, and forthwith set about letting slip the dogs of war." Because of General Reynolds, the Taylors now became a "doomed family" and their friends had to "dissemble their real sentiments, for to befriend a Taylor was to incur the powerful displeasure of the myrmidons of the satrap."[20]

Two of the "myrmidons of the satrap," or unscrupulous henchmen, who became more involved in the Sutton-Taylor Feud than any other lawmen were Capt. Charles S. Bell and John Jackson Marshall "Jack" Helm. Bell remains an elusive figure in the history of Reconstruction. He claimed to have served under General J. J. Reynolds during the war. As a spy he infiltrated behind enemy lines at least once, was captured but managed to escape. On November 2, 1868, Bell corresponded with Reynolds, inquiring if he needed "the services of a detective, *now*." Bell emphasized the amount of crime that "stalks abroad in Texas," blaming it on "the apathy of the civil authorities, and the hatred of the people to all that love law, order, or the Union." In his letter Bell claimed to have lived in Texas from 1865 until the end of 1868, boasted of being familiar with the northern, eastern and western portions of the state, and was thus "consequently familiar with its geography." He also claimed to have "an extensive acquaintance with the people" and could "pass as a *strong Southern man*." Bell admitted to Reynolds that if he were hired as a detective or scout he would "either arrest or *extirpate*" as many outlaws as he could. He would work in secret. Bell composed this letter from Newcastle, Delaware, perhaps his home. It brought positive results, as Reynolds responded by asking Bell to appear in Austin.[21] The interview resulted in C. S. Bell now being placed in a position to wage war against the Taylors, backed by the military.

Jack Helm had an equally interesting background, although little is known of his early years. He was the son of George W. Helm, who had migrated from Virginia to Missouri where Jack was born before the family journeyed to Texas in 1838. The Helms settled in Lamar County in an area that later became

part of Hopkins County. When the war came, Jack Helm served
in Captain L. D. King's Company, 9th Texas Cavalry. In February 1862, Helm and his father were part of a group of vigilantes who "tried" five men for sympathizing with the Union.
The quintet was found guilty and hanged. Helm and his father
were both arrested for having served on the "jury" and stood
trial themselves, but they were both found not guilty.[22] Willis
Fawcett, who as census taker visited the Helm homestead in
DeWitt County in 1870, recorded incorrectly that Helm was
then thirty years of age, was sheriff by occupation but also
farmed, and was Texas born. He was then married. His wife
Margaret Virginia was from Tennessee and a year younger.
Helm claimed no real estate then but did claim personal estate
of the value of $420.00. The couple had no children.[23]

Prior to relocating in DeWitt County, Helm had had his
own personal problem. During the Civil War, when Helm's
company was converted to infantry he deserted and returned
home. Once home he may have determined his wife, the former
Minerva McCown, had committed adultery during his absence
and then killed her.[24] Shortly after these troubles Jack Helm
appeared in South Texas where he worked for cattleman Abel
Head "Shanghai" Pierce in Matagorda County.[25] Helm worked
as a deputy in neighboring Lavaca County, and then was elected
sheriff of DeWitt County on December 3, 1869. Then Reconstruction's "myrmidon" General Reynolds appointed Helm the
county sheriff on March 23, 1870, by his Special Order # 65.[26]
Unfortunately Helm left no official record of what he had accomplished to earn the confidence of the Lavaca or DeWitt County
citizens, but by the turn of the decade Jack Helm was the law
in DeWitt County, home county of the Taylors.

In spite of his wartime activities before he went to South
Texas, by 1867 he had ingratiated himself enough with men of
the two counties to be considered capable of bringing calm to
the region. An undated document, prepared probably in mid-

1867, petitioned General Charles Griffin, Military Commander of Texas, for help, describing "organized bands of thieves & desperadoes" existing "in our midst and in various other sections of the State" and "who set the Laws at defiance & endanger the lives of our citizens." The petitioners declared the civil authorities were "wholly unable to give Legal protection ... to our people." Because of this dangerous situation, they requested that Jack Helm, then deputy sheriff of Lavaca County, be authorized and empowered to arrest lawbreakers and asked that Griffin provide him with whatever power he needed to accomplish the task. The document was signed by wealthy stock raiser M. G. Jacobs and seven other citizens of DeWitt and Lavaca counties.[27]

Jack Helm went to work, now reporting to General James Oakes, with what could justifiably be termed his posse with authority to arrest malefactors anywhere in the state. Whether the military officially endorsed Helm's actions or not is unknown, but he began a chase after men whom he termed "horse thieves" from Lavaca County "through the interior of this State" many miles north, even as far as the Red River, at least a ten-day ride on horseback. While in his pursuit, "in the discharge of my official duty" he explained, he determined there was "a well organized band of robbers and desperadoes extending throughout the interior of the State." Without naming any individuals he claimed there were eleven armed men in the upper part of Bell County, fourteen on the Brazos River in McLennan County, and "22 or 23" in Johnson County, making a total of nearly fifty men. These men, Helm wrote, had "murdered innocent & unoffending persons without provocation." He claimed he had pursued and investigated these groups, although he made no arrests. If there had been any doubt in General Griffin's mind as to Helm's real purposes, he added: "I have been, an[d] am now activated solely by a desire to discharge my duty as an officer, and to see justice done."[28]

Individually these two men may not have earned the unde-
sirable reputation they did, but working together they began
a reign of terror across not only South Texas but other parts
of the state as well, with the Taylors prime objects of their pursuit. They claimed to be working for law and order, ridding
the country of desperadoes and outlaws. Some citizens, however, considered them worse than the men they were pursuing.
Helm frequently made use of the columns of various newspapers
to explain and justify his actions, suggesting that he was fully
aware of what some citizens thought of him and that he was
overly sensitive to criticism. One notable example appears in
Victor M. Rose's study of the feud, the earliest effort at recording its history at any length. Helm claimed that about June 1,
1868, the military authorities, through Captain Bell, summoned him "to assist in arresting desperadoes in Texas known
as the 'Taylor party.'" They found several near Creed Taylor's
ranch and attempted to arrest them. One man, Randolph W.
Spencer, was wounded, but the others escaped. Helm and Bell
then went to Austin where they received "emphatic orders to
arrest the party." He then returned to DeWitt County and
discovered that now "about forty had collected, in open defiance of law, determined to resist the legal authorities of the
State." Helm then explains how he included DeWitt County
sheriff James F. Blair among his posse, adding that the sheriff's life as well as his own had been threatened by them. Upon
learning that Helm was in charge of a posse, the forty or more
desperadoes separated "in squads of from five to fifteen." Helm
went in pursuit of the "strongest of these bands" commanded
by "Jim Bell," no doubt James C. Bell, who he describes as a
"noted desperado of DeWitt County." Helm claims to have
captured Bell and several others who were afterward "*killed
in attempting to escape* from the authorities." Following the
killing of Bell and the others Helm continued his work and
told of it at some length.[29]

During the next months a wave of terror did engulf South Texas. How many men Jack Helm and C. S. Bell and their posses did kill in the mistaken belief that their victims were horse thieves or desperadoes, as the near fifty were in their mind, remains unknown. The summer of 1869 may have been the bloodiest time yet. In neighboring Goliad County, Sheriff Andrew J. Jacobs was "waylaid and killed" on June 3, 1869. Brothers Christopher and Madison Peace were charged with the killing.[30] Gen. J. J. Reynolds, now replacing General Griffin who had died from disease, appointed Sergeant N. W. Jenkins, Company H, 4th Cavalry, to assume the duties of the late sheriff. When Sergeant Jenkins arrived in Goliad with a squad of soldiers there was a "salutary effect upon the community" and some individuals who had broken the law actually came in to give bond for their appearance at a future court date. Somehow the word spread that the Peace brothers had killed the sheriff for the sole reason that he "showed partiality in making arrests."[31] Certainly there was more behind the killing than his showing partiality, but the full reasons are today unknown.

Action against the Peace brothers followed quickly, but not by Sergeant Jenkins. Lt. William Thompson, 4th U.S. Cavalry, commander of the post at Helena, investigated and determined at the inquest over Sheriff Jacobs' body that "it was proven" that Goliad County citizen James S. Stapp had "induced Jacobs over to his house the morning he was killed." There, Jacobs had inquired of Stapp if he knew where the Peace brothers were, that they had threatened to kill him, the sheriff. Stapp indicated he had no knowledge of the whereabouts of the Peace brothers, which was not believed as there was evidence they had been there that very morning, the third of June. At the inquest it was determined that Stapp was as guilty of the sheriff's death as if he had squeezed the trigger. With this knowledge a posse arrested the Peace brothers. J. S. Stapp sympathized with the brothers and volunteered to accompany them, offering to assist in obtaining bail if necessary. Lieutenant Thompson learned that on the twelfth of June the seven or eight citizens started in the direction of Goliad with their prisoners, but not one of them reached their destination. Four miles from his house, Stapp was "perforated with balls." The Peace brothers escaped, although Matt Peace was "severely wounded in the melee and has since died." The only witness to the vigilante party was Stapp's widow, and she could not recognize any of them.[32]

On June 22, Lieutenant Thompson received news of the Taylor brothers. "I have the honor to report," he began, "that Hays Taylor, Doughboy Taylor and Ed. Glover, desperadoes," had organized a band of twenty-five men for the avowed purpose of liberating two men by the name of Wofford, then in confinement in the Clinton jail. He also had learned that the group intended to kill a Mr. Tumlinson of Karnes County as well as three men of DeWitt County: James W. Cox, "Doc" White, and Bill Sutton. The "Mr. Tumlinson" was certainly Captain Joe Tumlinson, and the others were James W. Cox, J. P. "Doc" White[33] and William E. Sutton. Thompson, with no apparent wonder at what he had been told, reported that he had learned Cox, White, and Sutton had been "driven from their homes and are now living in the woods, and do not dare to approach their homes through fear of being killed." Although Thompson was gullible in believing Bill Sutton and the others were afraid to stay in their homes, he at least was recognized for some leadership qualities, as he had been "called upon by the Citizens of the two Counties" to aid them in arresting the Taylors and Glover. Thompson was short-handed however, as he had but seven men for duty and knew his command would be reduced even further in the very near future. In conclusion Thompson requested that troops be sent to headquarters at Helena due to the "present condition of affairs."[34] Through the remainder of June and the summer months Thompson continued working in the area to capture fugitives.

A correspondent to *Flake's Daily Bulletin* in Galveston, who signed his name simply as "DeWitt," noted that on July 2, 1869, "two noted characters" whom he identified as Jim Bell and Bill Morrel "were shot on the Coletto [*sic*: Ecleto], in the lower part of Dewitt [*sic*: DeWitt] county." He concluded by writing that many rumors were "afloat of others in different directions being killed, but owing to the dread existing, men say but little. Soon a terrible list of killed will be footed up."[35] The vigilantes caught up with and killed James C. Bell in or near the little community of Weesatche in Goliad County. A twenty-eight-year-old wife and six children survived.[36] Census enumerator Edward S. Roberts who compiled the 1870 mortality schedule for Goliad County, wrote in his ledger regarding Bell: "Shot by vigilance committee—homicide."[37] Helm later claimed that Jim Bell "commanded" the "strongest" of the bands of desperadoes, and that he was "a noted desperado of DeWitt County." Helm "succeeded in capturing him and more, who were afterward *killed in attempting to escape* from the authorities."[38] The "terrible list" would eventually include a number of Taylors and their friends or relatives.

The posses under Helm and companion C. S. Bell came to be known as "Regulators." In Goliad County, southwest of DeWitt County, Rutland Jones and Tobias Poole were killed "at their houses" early on the morning of July 16 by these Regulators. Rutland Jones left a widow and two children to mourn his loss. Widow Mary Jones was probably a sister of the man identified only as Fulcrod who was also killed by Helm's Regulators.[39] Local lore relates that Poole and Jones had stolen a team of mules from a "Jew peddler." A man named Parks found the team in Jones's barn and the owner was able to recover his animals. Shortly thereafter a stallion belonging to Parks was shot and killed. Suspicions fell on Poole and Jones. They were immediately gathered up by the Regulators and taken to a place called the Post Oak Water

Hole, north of Goliad. Jones was hanged first, but while this was taking place, Poole spurred his horse and escaped the hangmen. Other Regulators managed to shoot down Poole.[40]

The Regulators also killed a man named Lunsford, who "for a long time" was confined in the county jail at Clinton "not long since." Supposedly the killings by the Regulators were done "for depredations on the stock of the country, and had no connection with politics."[41] Census taker Willis Fawcett identified the victim as James W. Lunsford, fifty years old and married, whose profession was given as wagoner. The coroner's jury determined his corpse had been found on July 13 with "two six shooter balls in the head, and two in the Jaw, and six Buckshot wounds in the body by persons unknown."[42]

The work of the Regulators was not kept secret, as rumors were common regarding the organization of the vigilance association of DeWitt and Goliad counties, organized under the auspices of the military. Rumor had it that the Regulators had lynched "five or six men supposed to be horse thieves in late July." This report of lynching had been provided to the editors of the *Galveston Daily News*, by one who signed his missive only by the letter "R."[43] As the *News* was widely read in all of settled Texas and elsewhere, the group was becoming notorious.

C. S. Bell and Helm worked together and created a wave of terror throughout the area. On August 16 at "Cox's Ranche," no doubt the ranch of James W. Cox, Bell prepared a list of over a dozen men killed by the Regulators under the command of Jack Helm. The list included Rutland Jones and Tobias Poole who had been killed early in July, seven miles from Goliad. Charged with horse stealing, they were "killed after being taken." A James Bell (possibly James C. Bell or a man with the same name) was also killed in July, charged with "killing his brother in a church at Middle town, Goliad Co. A bad man." At the same time Charles Moore was killed; he was "charged with being a thief and conspiring against Tumlinson and others with intent to kill them" and killed as he "tried to run after capture." Perhaps this was the same as the man identified as Morrel. George Blackburn and Reuben Purcell[44] were both at their homes when taken, charged with "stealing and treachery" and were both shot to death after their capture. No explanation was given as to what "treachery" they had committed. James Stapp was charged with being an accessory to the murder of ex-sheriff Jacobs "and being a thief." Although his body was not found for three days, the Regulators killed James Lunsford on the tenth of July four miles from Clinton, "unresisting and on very vague charges," and ten days later, on July 20, killed James Wills while he was trying to escape in Fayette Creek; he was charged with stealing. Henry Wheaton was killed at the same time and place. Helm claimed that Wheaton "fought but Wills ran." Bell's report also included the Choates as well as Frank Skidmore, although Skidmore did survive. The name of Sam Kirkman concluded the list of vigilante victims. Another list of men killed in Goliad County included Matt Peace, Andrew McCarty and William Bell, killed at the same time as James Stapp.[45]

Some rumors and reports of the Regulators' actions were incorrect or exaggerated but reports of killings in San Patricio County were factual. John Choate and his cousin Crockett Choate were now the victims, and both were friends of William P. "Buck" Taylor. Initial reports provided much for the rumor mill, as headlines in the widely read *Galveston Daily News* reported that Jack Helm was "on the War Path!" and that at the fight near San Patricio five men were killed. Helm indeed was on the warpath, but five men were not killed at the Choate Ranch raid. The *Goliad Guard* of August 7 first reported the news of the raid, and although it contained errors it reflected the attitude of many in that region, that Helm was acting beyond the law's legal limits. All that can be positively determined today, amidst the conflicting reports, is that the two Choates had been killed; F. O. Skidmore was badly wounded but did survive. The mail carrier between Goliad and San Patricio, some fifty miles away if the news was delivered in a straight line, reported to the *Goliad Guard*. His knowledge may have been second-hand, but he reported that John Choate, Crockett Choate, one Skidmore, another man whose name he had not learned, and a U.S. soldier had all been killed as well as another man wounded. Worse for the reputation of Helm's command, was that, at least as it was initially reported, Choate's *rancho* was "broken up" and the men who needed fresh horses simply took what they wanted from Choate's *caballada*, or horse herd.[46]

Friends of Buck Taylor and Dick Chisholm, among them Crockett and John Choate, were highly critical of Sutton and his friends. Crockett Choate was especially strong in his denouncement of Sutton and it was for this reason that Crockett Choate was singled out "as another victim to levy vengeance upon" according to Jack Hays Day.[47] By this time Bill Sutton was considered part of the Helm-Bell team of Regulator leaders. Day recalled that "the Sutton gang" went to Choate's "solitary ranch house and surrounded it" and then a drunken member of the gang, "following instruction," stepped upon the porch and yelled out, "Schoate meat for breakfast!"[48] Whether or not there was a drunken member of Helm's party—as far as known Sutton was not directly involved—Day was only reciting what he had either created or had heard second-hand. And whether the drunken member of the posse, if indeed there was one, yelled out such a play on words, remains speculative.

Other news reports included conflicting statements. A Goliad County "gentleman," in correspondence to the *Galveston Daily News,* stated that the fight occurred during the first week of August—it occurred on August third—and that a battle was between the "regulators" and "desperadoes," the latter having barricaded themselves in a house of one of the band. Loopholes had been made in the walls "and every preparation for a desperate fight made." Further, after the Regulators had "charged upon the house and captured it" they took out six men and shot them in front of the house, the two Choates and Skidmore. None of the Regulators were hurt. Further, perhaps to add additional color to the letter, the correspondent wrote that "[s]ome women were also in the house with the desperadoes and aided them in the fight." Eight "double-barreled shotguns and revolvers, a keg of powder, lead, &c. was found in the barricaded house."[49]

Since there are numerous conflicting accounts of the Choate-Helm gun-battle it is necessary to learn how Jack Helm himself considered the events of that engagement. He prepared a "card," which at least in his mind justified every action he had taken. The card first appeared in the *Victoria Advocate* of August 19, then was reprinted in the *Galveston Daily News* of the twenty-fourth as well as *Flake's Daily Bulletin* and the *Dallas Times-Herald*, of the same date, and perhaps other newspapers. In so doing Helm's name was becoming well-known throughout the state.

Helm felt unjustly criticized for his actions, and believed that his explanation would calm the critics. Curiously, Helm wrote of himself in the first person and also in the same communication wrote of himself in the third person. It is a fascinating document from the leader of the vigilante organization, or, as the *Galveston Daily News* termed him, "The leader of the Regulators":

> As an erroneous impression has, through the misrepresentations of certain journals of the State, gotten abroad, respecting Jack Helm and those co-operating with him, to arrest and bring to justice thieves and desperadoes who have been holding high carnival for years in our midst, I take this opportunity of saying

to the people that Jack Helm is acting under the highest authority in the State, (orders from Military Headquarters.) He seeks to molest no one. To the honest, law abiding citizens he offers protection. For those thieves who have been depredating upon the stock interests of the country with impunity, he has orders to arrest and bring them to justice. That this will be done, and effectually done, there is no doubt.

Fellow citizens, this is the last resort. Grand juries have failed to accuse, and the law has been impotent to convict in multitudes of cases. As citizens of the country, we are interested in the suppression of crime, whether we are stock raisers or not. That you will respond with alacrity to assist me, I ask no further guarantee for the future than your conduct in the past.

My men are kept under control, and no [good] citizen can complain of the least injury at our hands. I labor for the supremacy of the law, without compensation or reward; and when the robbers are brought to justice, the majesty of the law vindicated—when honesty and industry can receive the fruits of their labors, I will be repaid for all, in the knowledge that I have done my duty.[50]

This self-eulogizing card did not favorably impress everyone. Editor Ferdinand Flake of Galveston printed the card as well, but added this note: "Without knowing anything positive of the facts, our impression has been that 'Jack Helm' was an outlaw of the Bickerstaff order."[51] Comparing Helm to the notorious Ben Bickerstaff of northern Texas, an associate of Bob Lee and Cullen M. Baker, would have greatly disappointed Helm if it had been brought to his attention.[52] Perhaps Flake was somehow aware of Helm's activities in North Texas during the early 1860s.

Helm felt compelled to justify much of his work in South
Texas and provided a report that appeared in the *Victoria Advo-*
cate, and no doubt other newspapers. He wrote that about
the first of June Captain C. S. Bell had summoned him and
requested his assistance. The two together intended to arrest
members of the Taylor party. After making a raid on the Creed
Taylor ranch, they altered their efforts in order to capture the
Peace brothers, accused of the killing of Goliad County Sheriff
Jacobs. Helm learned that the Peaces were at the John Choate
ranch and hence proceeded to that location. Helm related a
strange tale about Choate having gone to Joe Tumlinson to
try to convince Tumlinson he should join up with him (Choate).
He claimed Choate informed Tumlinson that "the Yankees had
offered twelve hundred dollars reward for him." The reward
was supposedly offered because Tumlinson had killed Stapp
during the attempted capture of the Peace brothers. Choate
then went to Jim Bell's house and obtained the effects of the
Peace brothers which had been left there, taking all to his
own house in San Patricio County. There he met with some
forty-two "known desperadoes ... many having indictments
against them for thieving." Besides Jim Bell there was Fulcrod,
the Broolans, Doughtys, Gormans, and Perrys. Choate then
warned them all that "Jack Helm would be upon them" and
that "they must prepare for a fight."

Helm stated, and the estimates are surely exaggerations, that
he had "one hundred and twenty-five of the best citizens of
the country" with him. He believed the large force was necessary as he expected there were at least one hundred desperadoes who would resist his efforts to capture or kill. He arrived
at the Choate ranch just after sunrise and "immediately proceeded to carry the house by storm." Here one of his men was
killed and two wounded in the attack. Of those attacked,
cousins Crockett and John Choate were killed. Helm himself
claimed one, boasting that Choate "perfidiously attempted to

shoot me after he had surrendered, and was killed by myself in defense of my life." Another curious claim by Helm is that he "made all necessary preparations for interring the dead, which was done." He further claimed that the statements that he or his men had disturbed any of Mrs. Choate's property or the property of anyone else were "lies."[53]

How much of what Helm recorded or dictated was factual, and how much was his own self-aggrandizing interpretation of what happened at the Choate ranch, will never be definitely determined. When he stated that he made preparations for interring the dead, perhaps he meant for Kuykendall's interment, his own man, as it is not likely that he cared that much for the men who had fought against him. The Choates were buried in Rockport Cemetery in Fulton, Aransas County, in above-ground tombs. Since the exact location of the Choate ranch is undetermined, one can only guess how the bodies were transported some sixty or seventy miles to their final resting place.[54]

What exactly did happen no one will ever know. Someone gave an account to the *Gonzales Inquirer* which leaves questions unanswered, stating that when they called John Choate to come out of the house, which he did, "they shot him down." Then Crockett Choate ran out of the house and shot down a Mr. Kuykendall, one of Helm's men, and wounded another named Russell. Then Crockett Choate was shot down and killed, while two men in the house were wounded.[55]

Following the Choate engagement, Helm encamped in the neighborhood of the community of San Patricio—or perhaps had his men make camp near there—and then conferred with a Captain Smith at Corpus Christi, Nueces County. Following the Smith conference he and his men traveled to Yorktown in DeWitt County, some fifteen miles from Clinton, to make out a report that he sent to Helena, the military post. There he reconnoitered with C. S. Bell. He disbanded his force until he could determine what his next move would be. Helm spent three days there and somehow learned where Hays and Doboy Taylor were last seen; he then gathered up twenty-five of his men and went to the forks of the San Antonio and Guadalupe rivers. There he succeeded in arresting the Hogans, "who were members of the same party" and sent them to Helena, Karnes County.

Helm failed to specify what charges he had against the Hogans, but curiously they were not "killed while attempting to escape." Again the Taylor brothers had eluded him. Camping at Yorktown, Helm then detailed fifteen of his men to go with Bell, while he remained in camp with the rest, "to attract attention while Bell could operate." Helm now disbanded his men, "after complimenting them for their orderly conduct, gentlemanly bearing, and devotion to the laws of the country."

Throughout this missive Helm's style suggests he is impressed with his own qualities and is above reproach. He is always ready "to act with the legal authorities of my country in the enforcement of law and suppression of crime" and is "opposed to mob law" and is "ready to give my assistance to the authorities ... either in Texas or any other part of the United States, regardless of all threats, knowing that the law-abiding citizen is my friend, and the desperado my enemy, which is the only guaranty that I desire to know that I am right."[56] No matter how Helm viewed himself, the Taylors and many others, as well as history, would view him as a "bad seed" which "he unquestionably was."[57]

Lt. William Thompson had as yet accomplished little, but still continued in his efforts to capture fugitives. As late as September he met with "a posse of citizens" from DeWitt County who had "been ordered to assemble there, at a prior date." Thompson and a posse that included Capt. Joe Tumlinson headed for Columbus, Colorado County, on the evening of October 1. The group arrived there on the third and remained for two days, collecting information about the probable where-abouts of the Peace brothers, both still alive in spite of earlier reports that one of them had been killed. Some of the information gathered proved to be false, although Thompson obtained a clue that Christopher Peace might be in Galveston, as his wife lived there. Some of the posse returned home as he took with him only Joe Tumlinson, W. W. Wells, and Doc White. At Galveston he informed chief of police E. McCormick[58] of the nature of his business, and, according to Thompson, McCormick then informed Peace. If this was true then McCormick was in sympathy with the Peace brothers, not surprisingly as he was related to Mrs. Stapp, a relative of the Peaces. Thompson blamed McCormick for informing Peace and his companion, another "desperado" named Fulcrod, that they were in the city in pursuit. "I would have been successful, at least, in securing the arrest of Mat Peace, and also of a desperate character, _____ Fulcrod of Goliad County, who has eighteen indictments against him," reported Thompson.[59]

Francis Osborn "Frank" Skidmore, who survived the battle between the Regulators and the Choates. *Courtesy Steve Schiwetz.*

CHAPTER FOUR

The State Police—
"Murder Most Foul"

"E. J. Davis is responsible before God and man for the murder, by Jack Helm's party, of Henry and William Kelly. He cannot escape this responsibility, because he knew the character of Helm and his gang when he commissioned them to do this murder most foul."
—A. H. LONGLEY, EDITOR, *Weekly Austin Republican,*
NOVEMBER 9, 1870

pecial Officer C. S. Bell sought out Helm knowing his special abilities in dealing with so-called desperadoes. In late April 1869 Bell left Austin in pursuit of an escaped convict, James W. Weaver. He first proceeded to the plantation of Helm's father-in-law, named Crawford, some "twenty miles south of Gonzales" near the DeWitt and Gonzales county line, where he "secured the assistance of Jack Helm," a noted "scout and guide." Bell and Helm gathered three other men and "immediately commenced trailing for Weaver." The quintet scouted through Bastrop and Caldwell counties before ascertaining that his probable whereabouts were farther west in Gillespie County. Bell reported in great detail his actions to Captain C. E. Morse of the 5th Military District. At one point the pursuit led to the Blanco River in Hays County where Weaver was believed to be only a few hours ahead. Bell, however, failed to capture Weaver, but he learned Helm was a good man to have assisting him.

"Mr. Helm," he wrote, "acts as my guide, is perfectly familliar [*sic*] with places and men from the Rio Grande to Red River. He is invaluable as a scout, and is personally a man of great bravery." Bell was not through with his praises, as he informed Captain Morse that Judge Wesley B. Ogden, of the 10th Judicial District, "endorses him highly, as he has done more to arrest and bring to trial thieves and murderers, than any single man in Texas." As deputy sheriff of Lavaca County in 1868, Helm "to my knowledge has done much for the suppression of crime." Bell was aware of the possible connection between Weaver and the Taylor clan because, as he later informed Morse, Weaver frequently used the alias of Jim Taylor. In conclusion Bell requested a list of the worst criminals, "from the official list of 'Persons evading justice.'" Bell, a man extremely confident in his abilities as a man-hunter, further wrote that "in our moving about, I frequently meet and could arrest [wanted fugitives] without extra expense or duty." In spite of Bell's supreme confidence, he had to admit he could use some good help. He recommended that his assistant, Jack Helm, be allowed a regular salary, as "I find it difficult to cope with Texas criminals single handed, as they invariably travel in company, and if I apply for a detail of cavalry, escape before I can reach them."[1]

Helm quickly became as notorious as Charles S. Bell in covering South Texas searching for alleged desperadoes. In July 1869 there was "some excitement about Yorktown" when Helm made his appearance with a squad of picked men. He summoned a large number of citizens but this time the only result was confusion and tired horses. Nothing "was undertaken, or at least accomplished against the parties whom the people imagined Helm was after." Helm later learned the parties he was looking for had already left the area. Helm then headed for Goliad. "Subscriber," who wrote of these events in DeWitt County, did report that five or six men were "Suddenly taken off" but, with tongue in cheek perhaps, "by whom, this deponent knoweth not, nor does he know what particular ailment they had." Helm and his posse may have tracked down these men and killed them but unfortunately no names were recorded. All Subscriber knew is that those men who "came to a sudden end" were said to "have borne unenviable characters."[2]

The attack on the Choate Ranch and the killing of several men in DeWitt County resulted in Helm, Bell, and their Regulators becoming notorious. Some believed the Choates, if not actually thieves, did in fact harbor thieves.[3] Although the latest killings may have been justified in the eyes of their superiors, many citizens considered the pair of Helm and Bell no different from leaders of a murderous mob.

Although some considered Helm no different from outlaw Ben Bickerstaff, some praised him. The editors of the *Daily Austin Republican* made frequent mention of the activities of the Regulators, identifying "the bands of lawless men, thieves and murderers" that Helm opposed as being headed by the Taylors. But in this "good work, Mr. Helm, Deputy Sheriff of DeWitt county, has taken the lead."[4]

No doubt Helm appreciated the plaudits in the press, but it was his partner Charles S. Bell who finally caught up with Hays and Doboy Taylor. Bell and his posse secreted themselves at the ranch of Creed Taylor, on Ecleto Creek in Karnes County on the morning of the twenty-second of August 1869. The Taylors refused the demand to surrender; in the resultant gunfire Hays Taylor and a man identified as Henry Westfall were shot, Taylor dying instantly and Westfall severely wounded. Doboy escaped, although he too received wounds. Bell quickly notified authorities to be on the watch for those who had escaped: "Dobe" Taylor, James Cook, and George Kellison. He believed the "desperadoes" were "making for Some points in northern Texas." One of his men, Charles Maddox, had received a slight wound.[5]

Galveston's *Daily News* editor Alfred Horatio Belo commented that all accounts agreed that "the Taylor gang" was a "most desperate band of outlaws, who had made their very names a terror to that section of the State." Further, a correspondent of the *San Antonio Herald* stated that with this latest fight "a general feeling of satisfaction prevails in consequence of Capt. Bell's success in crushing these dreaded outlaws." Ironically, a statement that originated in the *Courier-Journal* of Louisville, Kentucky, appeared in the same issue of Galveston's *Daily News*: "Helm's party in Texas seem[s] to have full sway, and the military and civil authorities alike [are] powerless to check his lawless career." Obviously there were varying degrees of satisfaction with Bell's and Helm's methods of dealing with alleged desperadoes and outlaws.[6]

But at least authorities could take some pride in the fact that one of the slayers of Major Thompson and Sergeant McDougall was now dead, and the other perhaps mortally wounded. From "Campbell's Ranch above Helena" Bell made out his report. He had left Yorktown on August 18, having been delayed due to heavy rains and high water. On the twenty-first he and his party arrived at Campbell's Ranch, taking cover in a "dense thicket near this place." From that dense thicket he made a scout alone and secretly, as Bell "*trusted no man*, past experience having taught me that *secrets* can not be kept by Texas people." He even had difficulty in keeping his own men quiet, as they would laugh and talk, thus "running a risk of betraying our presence." In the evening Bell moved his command to a "dense thicket" in Creed Taylor's pasture, about a half mile from the Taylor house.

Early the next morning he approached close enough to call Mr. Taylor out and converse with him. Bell asked to search his house, and Taylor assured him that neither of his boys was at home, although he admitted they had been there the previous day. Bell suspected that the boys would return and confined all—"black and white"—in one room. He placed his men around the house in the weeds, and awaited the arrival of Hays and Doboy. Soon after sunrise the posse heard the "tramp of advancing horsemen," the visibility poor "while a heavy fog hung over the earth." Bell's orders were that no one was to fire until he fired first. The two Taylors with Henry Westfall rode to their father's house, unaware that their home was surrounded. There they were as close to Bell as ten feet, and unknowingly covered with shotguns and revolvers. Something did give the secreted party away, perhaps a cough or sound of a weapon being cocked, as one of the Taylors realized the situation and reached for his weapon.

"My rifle spoke," explained Bell. "I shot Dobe Taylor through the shoulder and his arm dangled at his side." Instantly, the others fired, "from every quarter" producing a "withering fire." Taylor and Westfall fled, "pierced with numerous wounds." Bell and his men pursued them, and Hays fell, "with his skull smashed in, scarce two hundred yards from the house ... instantly killed." A dead horse was found another hundred yards further, along with two wounded horses. The injured Westfall was then taken. No coward or weakling was Westfall, as he actually inspired a degree of admiration in Bell. Westfall, "wounded in three places—although his wounds must prove mortal ... ran, *on foot*, over a mile" wrote Bell. "Such tenacity of life is remarkable."[7] Bell learned that Doboy Taylor was later seen some two miles away, "with a broken shoulder, and *spitting blood*." Bell was confident he could capture Taylor that day, and would take him in "regardless of his wounds." But Doboy Taylor would elude the posse again.

Bell's men then carried Hays Taylor inside his father's house and placed the corpse in the passageway. Creed was not allowed to mourn his son peacefully, as he was immediately taken to Helena as a prisoner. According to Bell, Creed Taylor was "the *worst living man* in this country. His life has been one of robbery and murder." Without noting any specific charges against the grieving father and Texas hero, Bell stated that his intention was to deliver him to Austin, to be held "for future action."

Bell was confident that even though there were several others with Hays, Doboy, and Westfall when the shooting began, who had fled at the sound of gunfire and were still on the loose, there would be "peace throughout this region, now that the Taylors have been crushed." Bell added a postscript, that Helm had been operating in the "northward for several [weeks?] past" with about one hundred men, chasing horse and cattle thieves.[8]

On the twenty-third of August 1869, Bell reported in writing to Brevet Major General J. J. Reynolds, informing him of the killing of Hays Taylor and the wounding of Doboy, stating that he hoped "to take him" that very day. Bell was now concerned with collecting the reward offered for the dead Taylor, asking General Reynolds to inform Gov. E. M. Pease that he claimed the state reward, and would bring in the necessary papers with him when he arrived in Austin. Bell certainly intended to collect the $500 blood money for the death of Hays Taylor, but gave no indication as to how he would share it with the other members of the posse.[9]

Bell did deliver Creed Taylor to the authorities, but nearly a month later he was still in custody in military headquarters at Helena, Karnes County, not in Austin as Bell had originally intended. Friends of Taylor met with attorney Thomas H. Stribling asking him to contact General Reynolds about Taylor's plight. No charges had yet been brought against him, although it was surmised he was being held due to "some suspected complicity with the '*Taylor Boys*'—his sons." Stribling admitted that the father may have done some things in relation to protecting Hays and Doboy that may have been illegal, but this was done only because he was their father. Stribling stated that he did not believe nor had he ever met any one "that did believe that Creed Taylor *was ever in any manner* a party to their crimes." Stribling further pointed out that Creed was "now old and in bad health" and "broken in fortune and in spirit" and seemed "to be an object of pity."[10] Stribling was obviously overstating Creed Taylor's condition, as he was only fifty years of age and lived another quarter of a century.

Whether Stribling's appeal had any impact on the military is uncertain, but what is certain is that C. S. Bell had the best intentions of catching up with the rest of the Taylor party. He left Austin with a detachment of eleven men of the 4th Cavalry and four citizens on the night of August 26, in quest of Randolph W. Spencer. Bell believed Spencer was hiding in the house of Coryell County citizen Jake Miller, although he gives no indication of how he learned this information. At Miller's he arrested four men, but Spencer was not one of them. Bell finally did catch up with Spencer, arresting him some twelve miles northeast of Denton, north of Dallas, on the morning of September 26. Bell's posse consisted of Sheriff B. F. Greenlee and several citizens. Bell gained entrance to where Spencer was sleeping and placed the barrel of his shotgun in his face, and Spencer immediately surrendered.[11] Bell took Spencer to Austin in irons, arriving there on the evening of October 2. The prisoner freely confessed that he was with the Taylors in Mason on the day Major Thompson was killed, and that he had left the scene with them, but said that he immediately thereafter left "the Taylor party" and had since avoided them.[12] Whether Bell believed him or not is unknown; it would be difficult for him to completely stay away from the Taylors as his brother William Addison Spencer had married Caroline Hephzibeth Taylor, a sister of Hays and Doboy.[13]

Officer Bell had little time to rest after his traveling to North Texas, for later that month he again was in DeWitt County. He now had to report on more killings, that of highly respected citizen Captain Henry Gonzalvo Woods (one of the two men who had escaped the Dawson Massacre in 1842), and William Faust "who were with me in my affair with the *Taylors*." He seemingly contradicts himself in the next statement, however: "I will just state that the death of these men was *not* in any way connected with any previous affair." Deputy Faust had a *capias* for Chris Kerlick Jr. who resided four miles southwest of Yorktown. Kerlick was charged with killing a man in Houston the previous month. The posse surrounded the Kerlick house and searched it, but found no one they wanted. As they were preparing to leave, five men appeared, who were identified as Chris Kerlick Jr., William Kerlick, Chris Kerlick Sr., John Kerlick, and George Kerlick. Gunfire erupted. Who fired first is unknown, but posse member Captain Woods fell mortally wounded. Chris Sr. and George Kerlick fired their weapons as they dashed through the posse, but hit no one. Meantime Deputy Faust was struggling with John Kerlick, the result leaving both men wounded. At dawn a search was made and William and Chris Kerlick Sr. were captured and both taken to Yorktown. "Late in the evening under a strong guard the prisoners were sent off," Bell reported, "it being the design to take them to Clinton and put them in jail." However, when a short distance from Yorktown "a large crowd of men fully disguised took the prisoners from the guard and shot them to death."[14] Little else is known of this affair, whether it was an isolated incident of vigilante "justice" or if the masked men were somehow convinced the Kerlicks "needed killing" because they may have associated with "the Taylor party" and thus felt obliged to perform their Regulator duty.[15]

In November Bell began an association with James W. Cox[16] and Henry Ragland,[17] two men who remained in the background for a while but later earned prominence in the feud. Bell must have loved to travel as he reported to Captain Morse that he left Austin on October 27 in search of desperado Jim Wright, his destination the ranch of Peter Tumlinson, brother of Captain Joe, some miles north of Pleasanton in Atascosa County. There he learned that his prey had left for the Rio Grande, but was expected to return soon as his wife on November 1 was "daily expecting to be confined." Bell was delayed when he lost his horse, but then recovered it, and continued his search for desperadoes. Among others he hunted but did not find were the noted Bill Thompson, wanted for the killing of Lt. William Burke in Austin, a clerk in the Adjutant General's office, as well as Sam or Drew Hensley, both accused of murdering a soldier in Bell County the previous year. Thompson was "in company with Ben Hinds an old grey-headed gambler." Thompson, the Hensleys, and Ben Hinds were not connected to the Taylor party in any way. Their names were among many others who were fugitives for alleged crimes. Several other desperadoes were reportedly "moving about" in the country between the Nueces and the Rio Grande. Bell joined forces with Cox and Ragland as "interpreters and guides" although it is difficult to see why Bell would need either. His letters suggest he was so full of confidence in his own abilities he would have need of no one else. Writing from San Antonio, Bell reported that he, Cox, and Ragland had "armed ourselves with a shot-gun and two revolvers each and in the character of cow-hunters we are going on a three weeks scout in the chaparal [*sic*: chaparral] south of this point." Bell intended to "visit all notorious places from Edinburg on the Rio Grande to Eagle Pass." Bell promised he and his party could "go unquestioned where soldiers could do nothing." Whenever they would come across fugitives, and he had a "complete list" now of outlaws living in the brush between the Nueces and the Rio Grande, he intended to "*take them at all hazards. I have men with me who are afraid of no danger* and will follow wherever I will lead." Bell further explained his plans, that he avoided taking soldiers with him because "*finesse* as much as force" was needed "to move with secrecy." With only Cox and Ragland with him Bell felt totally confident that outlaws would not think of them as a threat, their "false security" being their "strongest ally." Bell concluded his report by indicating he was aware of where Doboy Taylor and Jim Cook were and he intended to "at once go on their trail."[18] Bell was indeed serious in his undertaking, although his intentions seem incredible. Investigating those "notorious places" would take several months at a minimum, as the distance to be covered—if they stayed along the river—would approximate nearly three hundred miles. Searching for those outlaws on his "complete list" between the Nueces and the Rio Grande would be impracticable. The area, known as the "Nueces Strip," covers parts or all of some twenty modern-day Texas counties. Searching this amount of wild and dangerous land on horseback would be an insurmountable undertaking. But C. S. Bell, if nothing else, had confidence in his abilities.

Over a week later Bell reported on his activities. He had learned that perhaps the Peace brothers, accused of killing Goliad County Sheriff Jacobs, and Doboy Taylor were in the vicinity of Oakville, Live Oak County. Further, his "supposition was strengthened" when he learned that Martin Luther Taylor, a cousin of Doboy, "had recently been on a trip to *Creed Taylor's* ranche." Bell determined to arrest Martin Taylor as well as William B. "Dave" Morris, his father-in-law,[19] and "examine them."

Martin Taylor and Morris lived on the San Miguel River three miles below the Fort Ewell road in McMullen County. According to Bell, Taylor was regarded by his neighbors as "very dangerous," as he had been indicted two years before in DeWitt County for assault with intent to commit murder. James W. Cox was on the grand jury that had indicted him. Bell reminded Captain Morse of how Hays and Doboy Taylor had driven some seven hundred head of cattle from the San Miguel country to market the previous April and May. Of that number, only seventy head were registered, the balance "being *stolen outright.*" According to Bell, who based his statement on hearsay, Morris, Martin Taylor, Hays and Doboy Taylor, Ed Glover, and Jack Wright had stolen the cattle, but no one was brave enough to do anything as people "had such a terror of the Taylors that no one ventured to oppose them."

Bell determined that stolen cattle were being held at the house of a Mr. Hill, and that Taylor and Morris intended to move them to a market very soon. Bell "seized Hill's house" at dawn and waited, over the protests of Mrs. Hill and their daughters who warned Bell he would be killed as "Taylor and Morris were desperate men—would not be taken." On the twenty-third of November 1869, an hour after sunrise, Martin Taylor, Morris, and three others approached, with Bell, Cox, and Ragland in the house. With the quintet twenty yards from the house "we all rushed out with cocked pieces, and demanded an immediate surrender." Taylor "blanched white, and slid off his horse." An hour later, presumably with Taylor and Morris in chains or some other form of restraint, the party set out "for a favorite haunt of *Dobe Taylor's on the Nueces* [River]." Doboy Taylor was not there. On the night of November 23 Bell set out with his prisoners, his stated intention to deliver them to the authorities at Pleasanton, the seat of Atascosa County. He reiterated in his report that the charges against them were "being members of the Taylor clan, cattle-stealing," and in Martin Taylor's case, "assault with intent to murder."

But Bell's plans were "frustrated by a most lamentable occurrence." According to Bell, a dozen or more armed men met them on the Oakville-Frio road, some twenty miles west of Oakville. Bell could not "distinguish their features" since the moon was "partially obscured by clouds" but "instinctly" (*sic*: instinctively) he "divined their object." Bell placed himself in front of his prisoners, who "seemed also to apprehend the worst" as they "instantly turned to run." Bell preferred his prisoners to escape, rather than be killed by a mob, and "endeavored to check the progress of the latter" but the disguised men dashed past him "with savage oaths" and then "commenced rapidly firing their weapons." Due to Bell's apparent opposition to the mob's intent he was "*struck over the head*" and nearly knocked off his horse. The mob then ordered him to leave and say nothing, that good people appreciated his actions, and "safety demanded the death of such men" as those he had captured. As he, Cox, and Ragland rode away, they heard several shots out on the prairie. Bell regretted that his prisoners had been taken from him "in so unjustifiable and lawless a manner" but he could place no blame upon himself, no "dereliction of duty," for he did "run some personal risk in opposing the mob," and he had a blow on the head to show for it. Bell concluded his lengthy report by pointing out that he condemned the cowardice of the mob in "avenging themselves upon unarmed and helpless prisoners, who, whatever their crimes, were under the protection of an officer of the government responsible for their safety."[20]

In reality neither Bell, Cox, nor Ragland displayed any such heroics when the mob took their prisoners and then murdered them. In spite of Bell's self-righteous claim of trying to protect his prisoners, one senses clearly that it was merely for the sake of appearances. Bell claimed he did something to resist the mob, but makes no mention of Cox or Ragland attempting to help. Did they merely observe what was happening, doing nothing? Kinsman Jack Hays Day grew up hearing of how the Sutton gang persecuted the Taylors, and wrote of this incident in the 1930s: "There was no quenching the Sutton gang's thirst for Taylor blood," he wrote. "Martin Taylor [had] settled on a ranch between Tilden and Oakville. ... Led by Joe Tummilson [sic], an old member of the gang, ... several of the desperadoes trailed him down. Mart's place was near that of Dave Morris, his father-in-law. Going first to the Morris home, they captured Dave. Tying him on his horse they went to Mart's house. ... Facing the point of guns, captured, Taylor knew full well what was going to happen to him. 'Don't shoot me here,' he requested manfully. 'My wife is in bed with a young baby. It would frighten her to death.'" Day concludes his description stating that Taylor and Morris "were carried into the woods and shot down like dogs." Day points out that no one ever stood trial for the killing of "these two innocent men" and the only excuse was that they were relatives of Buck Taylor.[21]

There are problems with both the report of C. S. Bell and Jack Hays Day's version of the deaths of Taylor and Morris. Because it makes no mention of Cox and Ragland, Bell's description of resisting the mob lacks verisimilitude. A different version is preserved in the *San Antonio Express*, although again it is an older man's reminiscences of an experience when he was a youth. Judge Andrew Dilworth recalled that as a boy he learned the Regulators first rode to Morris's place and arrested Martin Taylor, informing him they would take him to Oakville to jail, at that time the county seat of Live Oak County, but also the only court in the district serving McMullen County. Morris volunteered to accompany them and act as Taylor's bondsman. As the party passed the Dilworth ranch, young Andrew gave them water to drink. He did not know the men in charge, but they were not masked; nor did he know that his act of kindness would be the last act of mercy the men would receive. The following day some Dilworth cowhands, out looking for cattle, found the bullet-riddled bodies of Taylor and Morris.[22] Judge Dilworth, in his research into the deaths of these two men, learned of another, slightly different, version of how they met their deaths: the Dilworth cowboys, out looking for cattle, "found the bodies hanging to the only big mesquite tree thereabouts." They were first buried where they fell.[23]

Four men named Taylor and several kinsmen, had now died violently at the hands of a vigilance committee, none having the benefit of a trial. Bill Sutton, Joe Tumlinson, Jack Helm, C. S. Bell, Doc White, and Jim Cox were involved in their deaths, as well as others. But killing prisoners and then claiming they were killed "attempting to escape" was not believed by everyone. A new decade was about to begin, and perhaps the murderous Regulators would be eradicated. On the horizon was the creation of the Texas State Police.

In spite of the apparently successful partnership of Bell and Helm, in early 1870 there were strains in the relationship. In mid-June 1870 DeWitt County Sheriff Helm wrote to Governor Edmund J. Davis, in answer to a letter from him dated June 9, in which he first told of a murder "on the person of one of the best freedmen in the County" but did not provide a name or cause. In addition he explained he had just sent a report of all the murders committed in DeWitt County "for some time past" to the chairman of the Committee on Militia. But Helm had a matter of concern which he felt necessary to bring to the attention of the governor. "I feel a great delicacy in so doing, but I think it is my duty," he wrote. He was concerned about his partner C. S. Bell. Several of the best citizens were "constantly writing" and "stating that he is passing through the Country under different names and collecting money under false pretenses representing to be agents for certain publishing establishments." Helm admitted that he had been working with Bell but he did not wish to work with him any more until he cleared himself of such charges.

Helm also felt supremely capable and knowledgeable. "Civil [law] alone is not sufficient [as] about one man in fifty will help and that is about the way of the state at large and I know as well as any one could know for I have worked almost all over the State and we must have law at all events." Helm had heard of several men killed near Victoria and was now waiting for orders "to raise a squad of about 10 men" intending to put down lawlessness. Helm also requested a territory of "about 10 counties" to work in, and with this he would "soon show the Citizens law and order fully restored."[24] Helm firmly believed that the existing court system was only nominally working, and thus justified his own vigilante action.

Governor Davis responded by asking for particulars. Helm answered on the twenty-sixth, stating that the men who had made those charges against Bell were James Cox and his father-in-law, James Crawford. "Mr. Cox is a good man and has always been a friend of Bell," wrote Helm. Crawford was a good man as well, but, complained Helm, he did not know how they got their information. Helm explained that he liked Bell, as "I and him have worked together and encountered difficultys [*sic*] and hardships together that places us almost like brothers and I am ready at any time to say to the world that I believe Bell to be a gentleman and strictly honest" and further, he believed that "the whole matter" was the "work of bad men."[25]

Presumably both Cox and Helm were aware of the developments taking place in Austin to institute not only a State Militia but a State Police force as well. At the first session of the Twelfth Legislature in April 1870, Governor Davis had declared that radical changes had been made in the Constitution of 1869. Most important for his administration was the matter of law and order and the punishment and repression of crime. To secure both of these goals, a two-step process was necessary. First he would create a state militia that would require membership of all males between the age of eighteen and forty-five years. A tax would be levied on all men in that age bracket and those who paid it would be exempt. The militia would be used only in extreme emergencies. Secondly he would create a State Police force. One individual would head this organization, the Adjutant General, and all local sheriffs, constables, and their deputies would be part of the force. The State Police would assist greatly in destroying lawless organizations. Martial law would be declared only when absolutely necessary. The lawless would be intimidated, the crime rate would be lowered, and offenders would be punished. Money from fines would be used to help build jails and courthouses where necessary.

On May 10, 1870, Senator Phidello W. Hall introduced a bill entitled "An Act to Establish a State Police, and provide for the regulation and government of the same."[26] Many no

E. J. Davis, Civil War veteran and Texas governor, whose term was marked by the early years of the Sutton-Taylor Feud. *Courtesy Texas State Library and Archives Commission.*

doubt welcomed its creation but also many feared this act granted the governor too much power. With the passing of the police bill, law enforcement became centralized in the state; sheriffs, marshals, deputies, and constables were now subject to state supervision. James Davidson, a native of Scotland who had served in the British army as well as the U.S. Army for four years, was nominated to head the force. He had maintained a close association with prominent Republican politicians, which resulted in his selection as police chief.[27]

Davidson divided the state into four districts, each of which would have one captain, two lieutenants, five sergeants, and fifty-six privates. He selected M. P. Hunnicutt, E. M. Alexander, Leander H. McNelly, and John Jackson "Jack" Helm as captains.[28] All officer positions were filled as of August but there were problems in finding enough competent men to fill the positions of privates.

Within a month, the State Police had arrested forty-four murderers and felons, five of whom had been killed resisting arrest. About August 12, Jack Helm reported arresting "Buck" McCrabb and W. M. Sutton, each charged with murdering a freedman in Victoria County. Buck McCrabb was in reality John F. McCrabb, and certainly his associate was William E. Sutton, not W. M. The two were turned over to the DeWitt County sheriff.[29] The police were apparently working from a circular dated July 1, an aggregate of names provided by the county sheriffs. Although not all counties had complied as requested, 108 counties did report, resulting in a list of 2,790 names of fugitives from justice in those counties.

James Davidson was, if not well-received, at least acceptable to most Texans as adjutant general. He was "widely known for his thorough, energetic, executive talent in Eastern Texas."[30] It is unknown how Davidson selected his officers; it would be especially valuable to know how he determined Helm warranted the powerful position of captain. How much did Davidson know of Helm's background? Possibly he made the selections based on the recommendations of men he trusted. On a visit to Gonzales, the editor of the *Gonzales Index* interviewed Helm and expressed concerns about the men who would become policemen. The editor pointed out that Helm had received a commission as "senior Captain in the Police force" and had permission to operate in any portion of the state. The editor courageously informed Helm some civilians felt "utter abhorrence of the law under which he was appointed to act" but Helm assured him that he would "receive none but good men." He claimed to select men for his company from his entire district, two or three from each county. Helm was perhaps in Gonzales County to select a few good men. Helm declared he would receive "none indicted for crime" and since his men would be performing service detached from the main body, he would receive none "who have not [the] business capacity to make a report—hence the ranks will not be filled with ignorant negroes."

Further, the *Index* informed its readers, as long as the force confined its operations "to the letter of the law in carrying out its ostensible designs" rather than oppressing the innocent "or for purpose of private revenge, as such organizations have been used in other States, no one can answer for the consequences." Besides being aware of such groups who had carried out private revenge, no doubt in that particular area of the state, the editor did encourage his readers "to give no cause, or even pretext for any violence." Even though the police bill was "passed by fraud, is unnecessary, and would, by any judge with a thimble full of brains, be pronounced unconstitutional"—in spite of that, the editor wrote—"let us give to the world one more evidence of our forbearance by submitting to it." Any resistance to the bill would "but lengthen the days of the tyranny which the law was designed to perpetuate, but which is now in its last gasp."[31]

In mid-1870, another vigilante action took place in Matagorda County, and again Jack Helm was involved. There were four Lunn brothers, all working for cattleman Abel Head "Shanghai"

Pierce, at one time, along with "All-Jaw" Smith, so-called due to the unusual shape of his face. The Lunns supposedly had been hired by Pierce some time before, and possibly they were stealing from his herds as well as from those of other cattlemen to build up their own. Suspected of theft, they were "arrested" by a mob and taken to a grove of trees. Taken with them were three men: a man named Grimes, All-Jaw Smith, and Ike Hewitt. After lynching them the mob fired a volley of shots at the hanging figures. A bullet shattered the rope holding Hewitt who fell to the ground, more dead than alive. After dark Hewitt crawled away, was then found and given aid, and cared for by James C. Hatch.[32]

Shanghai Pierce's biographer, Chris Emmett, related basically the same incident, only stating that it was Jack Helm who found evidence of the Lunn brothers and their cattle-stealing operation. Along with Helm, Joe Tumlinson was "riding the range in search of suspicious characters." The result in this instance was that three of the Lunn brothers, Smith, and a stranger were caught in the act and lynched.[33] Although Helm and Tumlinson both may have been somehow involved in the lynching in Matagorda County, contemporary sources failed to mention their names. Also there were apparently only three men lynched: Benny Lunn, Eddy Lunn, and John B. M. Smith. The gang had successfully eluded one "posse" after an exchange of gunfire, which resulted in the death of Regulator Edward Anderson as well as gang member Joe Grimes. Apparently there was no official law officer in the group, merely "a squad of citizens, who are laudably engaged in ridding the country of brigands and murderers" as correspondent "Trespalacios" described them. The lynching took place on June 20, 1870, at Newel's Grove near the Matagorda-Jackson County line.[34] This deadly incident was essentially ignored by the contemporary press, no doubt due to its isolation. In contrast, the killing of two young men named Kelly, related to the Taylors through marriage, resulted in great public outcry. The double murder resulted in much negative publicity for the newly created State Police force, and ultimately led to Captain Jack Helm's downfall and dismissal.

The Kelly family had emigrated from Mississippi, bringing nine children with them; one more was born in Texas in 1855. In 1870 the youngest child, Mary Elizabeth or Mollie, married James C. "Jim" Taylor, son of Pitkin B. Taylor.[35] The Kellys first settled in Lavaca County. When the Civil War began all the sons who were old enough to serve did so in one capacity or another, regular cavalry or assigned to Home Militia, at Sweet Home, their duty to protect women and children and property. Then came Reconstruction and tragedy enveloped the Kelly clan. In 1868, in Clinton, Tobe Kelly, son of Robert Kelly's half-brother William and his wife Margaret Ann, along with Lewis S. Delony, witnessed the murders of Buck Taylor and Richard Chisholm. But it was the incident involving brothers William, Henry, Wiley, and Eugene Kelly that resulted in the greatest tragedy for the family.

The four Kelly brothers were accused of shooting up a circus in Lavaca County in August of 1870. Some of the performers and audience were allegedly wounded in their wild shooting. State Police Captain Jack Helm determined to arrest them. Four men were deputized to arrest William and Henry: Bill Sutton, C. C. Simmons, "Doc" White, and John Meador. Helm himself intended to arrest Wiley and Eugene. Presumably, once the arrests were made the two groups would all meet at a predetermined spot and continue to county seat Hallettsville together, where the prisoners would be turned over to the authorities.

Sutton, Simmons, White, and Meador had reached their destination early on the morning of August 26. The four stopped at the home of Henry Kelly, while Helm and Sutton continued, stopping at the home of William Kelly, whose house was only a quarter of a mile away. Simmons and his men approached

Mary Elizabeth "Mollie" Kelly Taylor, wife of James C. Taylor. *Courtesy E .J. Thormaehlen.*

the Henry Kelly home, apparently not proud of their action as their hats were pulled down over their faces as if to conceal their identity. Amanda Kelly, Henry's wife and the daughter of Pitkin Taylor, saw the men on horseback at the front gate and informed her husband. Henry went out to see what they wanted, only to be informed that he was under arrest and was to be taken to Hallettsville. He was not allowed to take his six-shooter, belt, or scabbard, nor did he have on his spurs. The actual arrest was without incident.

In the meantime, Sutton and Helm had arrested William Kelly and were approaching the others. When Sutton and his prisoner were within a hundred yards of them, John Meador dropped back to join Sutton. Shortly thereafter Doc White also dropped back and took a double-barreled shotgun from Meador, then returned to Simmons. Simmons held his progress to now allow the others to catch up with him, so now the four-man posse was together with its two prisoners. No doubt both brothers believed their being taken to Hallettsville would only be an inconvenience, and they would be released on bond to answer the charges against them.

What the policemen did not know was that they were being observed by members of the Kelly family: Amanda Kelly, Henry's wife; Delilah Kelly, the mother of the prisoners; Louisa Kelly Day, sister of the brothers; Pitkin B. Taylor, Amanda's father; John W. Day, and F. K. Hawks. When the brothers were arrested, the family members became gravely concerned and followed, unobserved.

The parties halted in an open place, surrounded by thick bushes and trees, perhaps conversing just how to best commit their act. Henry Kelly was on horseback close to White and Simmons; William Kelly was also astride his horse, closer to Sutton. John Meador was some distance away. It was in this open place that the posse chose to commit murder. William Kelly was a pipe smoker, and he cut up some tobacco to fill his pipe, then dismounted. He took out a match, and while in the act of striking it on the bottom of his boot, was shot by Bill Sutton. Amanda Kelly witnessed the movement of Sutton suddenly raising his gun, pointing it downward in the direction of her husband, and firing. William Kelly immediately collapsed. At nearly the same time Doc White raised his gun and shot Henry Kelly, who was still mounted. He fell to the ground, and then the three men all fired at the Kelly brothers on the ground and smoke clouded the scene. As Amanda Kelly screamed and ran towards her husband, the trio fled in the brush. She found Henry still, apparently dead; William Kelly showed some sign of life but did not speak. William's clothes were smoldering, the gun blast had been so close. His mother put out the flames.

The two other brothers accused of the circus shooting, Eugene and Wiley, were arrested without incident.

Initial reports indicated that brothers William and Henry had attempted to escape and were thus killed. Wiley and Eugene were turned over to civil authorities. The *State Journal* of Austin, reporting the killings as well as arrests of several other "notorious" individuals, stated that there had been fifty-four arrests, in addition to those in Lavaca County, men "all charged with various crimes." And, the "good citizens turned out unanimously to aid the police, which is fast becoming popular."[36] That was unlikely, as various communities expressed the opposite view.

The killing of the Kelly brothers was a tragedy for the family and their friends, but it also drew attention to the troubles in DeWitt County as no other incident had before. Senator Bolivar Jackson Pridgen was especially troubled and gathered affidavits from witnesses, which were printed in the influential *Daily Austin Republican* of November 1, 1870. Pridgen stated that the killings had taken place near where he lived, and that the general conduct of the policemen was "unwarranted, inhuman, and outrageous." He criticized policeman

C. C. Simmons—who nominally had the brothers in charge—for failing to make any kind of report, and more disgusting still, had abandoned their bodies "(as prisoners generally are who are killed by the notorious Jack Helm, or his crowd) to the mercy of buzzards, wolves, and hogs." He further accused Helm of having "the country completely terrorized" and said that he knew "nothing about the laws of the State, and less about the rights of its citizens." The statements of the Kelly family gathered by Pridgen told of the double killing in great detail.[37]

Lavaca County District Court records list a variety of relatively minor charges against numerous Kellys. Wiley Kelly was fined $25 for disturbing public worship; Henry Kelly was charged with "Robbery and theft" but the prosecuting attorney reversed himself to *nolle prosequi*, a decision to discontinue prosecution. A charge of assault with intent to commit murder against William Kelly was reduced to simple assault resulting in a fine of $5.00. Other charges included "Gaming" against Wiley Kelly, which was dismissed by the state, but on another charge he was fined $25 for gaming. A charge against Wiley of carrying a pistol was also dismissed by the state.

In District Court in August 1867, Henry Kelly, Thomas Franks, and George Skipton were charged, that on July 10 they had "at the Baptist church on Mustang Creek near Sweet Home unlawfully and willfully did disturb a congregation then and there assembled for religious worship ... against the peace and dignity of the State." For this charge they were found guilty and fined $5.00.[38]

It was thus on August 26, 1870, that peace officer C. C. Simmons from Hallettsville held a warrant for the arrest of the Kellys, wanted "for a disturbance at Sweet Home, being accused of shooting out the lights at an entertainment there." From there Simmons contacted DeWitt County authorities, and with Sutton, White, and Meador went out to make the arrests.[39] None of the charges recorded in the Lavaca County District Court Index show a charge for disturbing anything resembling a circus. Perhaps the disturbance that resulted in the arrests of the Kellys was their reckless shooting at Sweet Home. The "Record of Arrests" showing arrests made, by whom, and other details, reveals that on August 26, 1870, the four Kelly brothers were arrested by Jack Helm and C. C. Simmons. The remarks by the names of William and Henry are "Killed in attempt to escape by guard [in] charge of C. C. Simmons." For Eugene and Wiley Kelly the remarks show they were turned over to the sheriff of Lavaca County. The charge against all four: "Disturbing performance of Smiths Circus at Sweet Home," which charge does not appear in the court records.[40] One Gabe Lewis was also arrested by Helm for "shooting in Smith's circus at Sweet Home."[41]

Jack Hays Day offered a justification for the action of the Kellys, that Henry and William Kelly were at Sweet Home "attending a show [which] turned out to be of the indecent variety and Henry proceeded to shoot out the lights." Further, Day complained of the unequal treatment given the Kellys: Captain William E. Jones, soon to be sheriff of Gonzales County, was with the Kellys at the time of the "indecent variety" show but even though he had as much to do with the shooting as the Kellys, Jones was not named in the indictment.[42]

Day wrote that the "gang claimed they killed the Kelly brothers because they had tried to make a get away."[43] Eddie Day Truitt agreed, stating that the State Police, "and in particular one of their captains, Jack Helm, was behind the killing of the Kelly boys." Helm sent Sutton, White, Meador, and Simmons "to do his dirty work [arresting Henry and William] while he was out trying to arrest two more Kelly brothers, ..."[44]

The *Daily Republican* of Austin offered no apology for devoting a great amount of space to the "exposure of the recent tragedy" of the Kelly killings. It reminded its readers that White and Sutton who "figured so prominently in the arrest and murder of the Kellys" stood charged in Bastrop County with the murder of Charles Taylor and the killing of two citizens, and reminded them that they had "plundered Taylor of his clothes and fine saddle."[45]

The men responsible for the shooting deaths of the Kelly brothers were charged with murder. Jack Helm was not indicted for the murder of the Kellys. Nevertheless, some considered him guilty as well. Highly respected Civil War veteran John R. Baylor wrote that "it is time that the career of this man [Helm], who is a murderer and professional cut throat, should be stopped. It is the duty at least of every one to hold up to public gaze his infamous acts."[46]

In case the citizens of South Texas did not realize that a dangerous feud between two separate factions was becoming a bloody reality during the early 1870s, events following the Kelly tragedy would definitely impress that as a fact upon their collective minds. The Kelly murders remained a topic for guarded conversation for some time. The sense of tragedy was deepened when it became known that of the four Kelly brothers arrested for their alleged disturbance at Sweet Home, the two survivors who were turned over to Hallettsville authorities did stand trial and were acquitted.[47] The significance of the killing was not only that two more of those considered members of the Taylor party had been killed, but that the manner of their death became newsworthy. Some editors, however, treated the subject callously. A report from Lavaca County reached the desk of the editor of the *Honey-Grove Enterprise* in northeast Fannin County, nearly four hundred miles from the scene of conflict. Although the editor's feelings were not specifically expressed, his intent was clear, "Some young men that disturb a circus by firing pistols, resist the sheriff sent to arrest them, and get two of their number killed by the operation. The others are tried and acquitted."[48]

Criticism of the State Police increased. The *San Antonio Daily Herald* facetiously called the force a "delectable body of men" reminding its readers that Governor Davis had promised that only good men would be allowed in the force. But in full irony, the editor continued:

> If good men are known by their actions we scarcely agree that there are many of that class in the State Police. Good men do not steal horses, good men do not kill people on sight, good men are not recruited from desperadoes, law abiding men do not commit violence on unprotected females, neither do they go sloshing around searching private houses, forcing farmers from their work, nor do they imbibe ben- zine [sic] and insult unoffending citizens.[49]

In Gonzales, the *Index* editor pointed out to its readers that Adjutant General Davidson was a soldier, and by reputation "a good one." As chief of the police, upon him "devolves ... the responsibility of the acts of his subordinates." There could be no excuse for the shooting of prisoners, "especially where the offense charged against the prisoners is one not punishable by death under the law." To this editor, shooting prisoners who "endeavored to make their escape" was simply not acceptable.[50]

About this same time Henry Westfall was reported killed near the Nueces River by Helm and the State Police. Again reports were that he was killed "while resisting arrest."[51] Jack Helm was not the only policeman receiving criticism for his actions: Captain M. P. Hunnicutt, commander of the State Police in the Waco district, suffered for his actions. He was removed "for inefficiency and general worthlessness" and his removal was not the only one, as "others are impending."[52]

The hue and cry against Helm, although he hadn't personally squeezed the trigger on the Kellys, reached Adjutant General Davidson and as many wished for, Helm was removed. He was allowed to resign his position as captain of police, but he was still the sheriff of DeWitt County. His police resignation was accepted November 30, 1870; Robert F. Haskins replaced him on December 1, 1870.[53] Helm had other concerns as well: at the same time an indictment was brought against him for robbery in Bee County, as well as charges against him in other counties.[54]

On the last day of 1870, Adj. Gen. James Davidson concluded his annual report, which covered the period from June 24 through December 31, 1870. He wrote a few paragraphs about the State Militia, the State Guard, the Frontier Forces, the Ordnance Stores, and three paragraphs entitled "Miscellaneous." Then he devoted over six pages to the police department. He told of how at first he had experienced great difficulty in finding names and getting the services of "reliable, energetic and efficient men." Above all, the men he wanted had to have "courage and nerve" as, he pointed out to Governor Davis, the state was "overrun with desperadoes and refugees from justice." He had always, "as far as possible, satisfied myself before recommending an applicant that he possessed courage and nerve." Davidson was proud of the number of arrests the force had made. His figures showed 978 persons had been arrested and turned over to civil authorities. With that number of arrests made in the force's five and one-half months existence, "it is reasonable to suppose that in my next annual report I will be able to show that but few offenders are at large."

In his final paragraph, Davidson wrote that during the previous five and one-half months, seven persons were killed and two wounded while resisting the police by force of arms, and three killed while trying to escape after being arrested.[55] Two of the persons killed while "trying to escape" were the Kelly brothers, and one was married to a Taylor woman. And William E. Sutton was on the scene.

By the end of 1870 Sutton had been directly involved in the deaths of Charles Taylor, William P. "Buck" Taylor, Richard Chisholm, and William and Henry Kelly. Martin L. Taylor and W. B. "Dave" Morris had earlier been killed. Knowing those Taylors were killed with Sutton's involvement, could the Taylor men have done anything but declare outright war on William E. Sutton and those who rode with him?

P. G. "Doboy" Taylor had been on the run since the killing of Major Thompson in Mason back in 1867. On April 18, 1871, he courageously rode into the town of Sutherland Springs, Wilson County, intending to surrender to the authorities. Someone in the State Police force recognized him; fortunately for him the person in charge knew Taylor and it was a peaceful arrest with Doboy offering no resistance, merely handing over his pistol. The *Daily Herald* commented that he should never have surrendered, no doubt anticipating his being killed "while attempting to escape." Doboy had changed so much while a fugitive that "his most intimate friends would not have recognized him." Taylor employed the well-known attorney Trevanion T. Teel to defend him.[56] His arrest was reported differently in Austin from in San Antonio. The *Daily State Journal*, the official publication of the Davis administration, stated that the "last and the worst of the murderous Taylor gang ... was recently arrested in Wilson county by policeman [W. W.] Black." He had been hiding out in Alabama, and he had just returned, as was reported. Commented the *Journal*, "The State police follow on the trail of these cut-throats and desperadoes with a perseverance that is deadly, unremitting, and crowned with the most surprising success."[57] Perhaps. But Taylor had turned himself in, so the claim of the police bringing him in was hardly a result of their deadly perseverance. He later stood an examination in Wilson County where there were five indictments against him, and provided the bond required. He and Attorney Teel then went to Mason to answer to the charge of murder.[58] They did reach Mason, where he was able to give bond of $1000.[59]

But Doboy Taylor never did stand trial for the Thompson killing. Released on bond, later that year he and cattleman

Simpson Holstein quarreled in Kerrville. Words led to the inevitable gunplay, although Holstein was not armed. Taylor fired twice at Holstein but missed; Holstein then grabbed Taylor's gun away from him and shot back. Two balls struck Doboy Taylor, who then ran towards his house calling on his friends for help. He collapsed when another shot from Holstein struck him. His friends were prevented from doing anything to assist him. Taylor lived six hours and died at 11 o'clock that night, "sensible to the last" and cursing the man who had shot him. How his trial would have ended, that long after the Thompson killing, is speculative. There was a reward of $500 for him. He perhaps would have been cleared of the charge against him.[60]

J. B. Polley, then of Floresville, Wilson County, wrote that the killing had happened in Kerrville, Kerr County. "Holstein was one of the bravest men that ever lived on the frontier," concluded Polley.[61] Little else is known of Holstein. Son of King and Elizabeth Holstein, he was born in Louisiana about 1847. By 1870 the family was farming in Gonzales County. Simpson then was raising stock with his younger brother Henry F., then a student.[62] By 1871 he was in charge of Company H of Frontier Protection men, stationed at Rancho Station, Gonzales County. Among other names on the list appeared that of Brown Bowen, who would in the decade of the seventies become involved in the feud. What had drawn Holstein to Kerr County is unknown; after leaving Gonzales County he remained in the cattle business, as in 1873 he was driving herds north to Ellsworth, Kansas.[63]

In the meantime, the trio who were charged with the killing of the Kelly brothers had stood their trial in DeWitt County. On October 4, 1871, the trial of White, Sutton, and Simmons, charged with murder, ended with a "Not Guilty" verdict.[64] No doubt the Taylor family as a whole pondered the number of men killed by Sutton, and resolved that something had to be done.

John Wesley Hardin, from the original tintype made in Abilene, Kansas, in 1871. *Courtesy the Robert G. McCubbin Collection.*

Creed Taylor's home in Kimble County, where he later lived to escape the feud after the death of a son. Creed is the figure with the white beard. *Courtesy the Western History Collections, University of Oklahoma.*

CHAPTER FIVE

Rampant Killings

"I am pained to informe you that they is a verry bad State of affairs in our County[.] our Sheriff Capt. Jack Helm was Killed a few Days Since ... I held an Inquest on the bodies of James Cox & John Crisman [sic]."
—Justice L. B. Wright, JULY 24, 1873

The man who made a huge difference in the events of the feud entered onto the stage in 1871. He was John Wesley Hardin, the second-born son of Rev. James G. and Elizabeth Dixon Hardin, and he was named for the founder of Methodism. Born on May 26, 1853, in Fannin County, he grew up learning to distrust and hate authority and the federal government. Although his parents dreamed of him becoming a minister of the gospel, Hardin grew up learning to handle knives and guns of all types, seemingly in all cases using a pistol or shotgun or a knife to solve any problem. In a school yard fight in 1867, he knifed his opponent, but not fatally. In 1868, at the age of fifteen, he killed a former slave in Trinity County. It was the first of his many killings, which numbered anywhere from twenty to perhaps forty. After this first killing he became a fugitive, with his father's blessing. In Hardin's mind he was fleeing from the unjust rule of the federal government then occupying the South, not from justice. "To be tried at that time for the killing of a negro meant certain death at the hands of a court, backed

109

by Northern bayonets," Hardin recalled many years later in his memoirs. "Thus, unwillingly I became a fugitive, not from justice be it known, but from the injustice and misrule of the people who had subjugated the South."[1] Hardin killed several more men during the early years of Reconstruction.

The creation of the State Police acted as a magnet for his acts of violence; his autobiography relates numerous escapades involving policemen. Even though he was captured several times, he always managed to escape, usually by outwitting his guards and killing them. On January 22, 1871, he killed a state policeman named James Smalley near Marshall.[2] In February of that year, State Policeman General Bell was killed at Waco. Although Hardin does not specifically take credit for this killing in his memoir, he relates an incident "between Belton and Waco," in which he killed three policemen, whom he identified as Smith, Jones, and Davis. In all likelihood he magnified the killing of Policeman General Bell into the trio of policemen killed.[3]

To escape the bounty hunters, Hardin seriously considered relocating to Mexico. He stopped in Gonzales County, where he visited his cousins, the Clements brothers: Emanuel "Mannen," John Gibson "Gip," Joseph Hardin "Joe," and James "Jim." Instead of continuing southward, Hardin joined his cousins and headed north to the cattle markets in Kansas. The young cowboys experienced excitement and danger on the trail, not only from nature's heat and dust and storms, but also from potential cattle thieves. Hardin killed over half a dozen individuals between South Texas and Kansas for various reasons, always thoroughly justified and necessary in his mind. In Abilene he and City Marshal James Butler "Wild Bill" Hickok confronted each other but neither backed down, despite what Hardin later claimed in his self-serving autobiography. After Hardin returned from the Kansas cattle drive, on October 19, 1871, State Policemen Green Paramore and John Lackey attempted to arrest him; Hardin killed Paramore and wounded Lackey. Thoroughly frightened but alive, Lackey

Gonzales cowboys of the 1870s. Several of these men feuded with the Sutton party. Seated figure center is Joseph Hardin Clements. Standing left is James M. "Doc" Bockius. Second from left standing is perhaps John Gibson Clements. Seated left is perhaps James Clements; seated right is Frank Smith. Tentative identification provided by Ed Bartholomew. *Courtesy Mrs. Ray Caffall.*

lived to tell how he survived a gunfight with Wes Hardin.[4] The young Hardin, not yet twenty-one years old, was becoming the most dangerous man in Texas.

In spite of constantly being on the run, Hardin found the time to court Jane Bowen, the sixteen-year-old daughter of Gonzales County rancher Neill Bowen. On February 27, 1872, Hardin married the rancher's daughter.[5] Marriage did not pacify the young fugitive, and his lifestyle of killing continued. Jane's brother, Joshua R. "Brown" Bowen, frequently found himself in trouble and usually brother-in-law Hardin helped him out. Now, near the geographic center of the feud, with his cousins the Clements siding with the Taylors, Hardin became a valuable ally. He was not related to them as has frequently been written, but Hardin provided the fighting capabilities that the Taylors needed.[6]

Hardin was aware that Sutton, Cox, Ragland, and Tumlinson, leading forces of the Sutton party, were members of the State Police, an organization that he viewed as destroyers of "life, liberty and property." Hardin and his friends "all knew that many members of this State Police outfit were members of some secret vigilant band, especially in DeWitt and Gonzales counties."[7] This is how Hardin and his friends perceived the police force: vigilantes led by Bill Sutton.

The dismissal of Jack Helm from the force may have brought some satisfaction to the Taylors and Hardin, but Helm retained considerable power because he was still sheriff of DeWitt County. On August 5, 1872, Helm easily provided a new bond as requirement for remaining in office, with Bill Sutton, Joseph Taylor, James P. Beck, Joseph Tumlinson, James W. Cox, and Richard B. Hudson serving as sureties. These men provided a bond of $10,000 so Helm could remain in office. J. B. Tucker and R. W. Thomas—perhaps the "Bob" Thomas of the bloody Bastrop affair—acted as witnesses. Presiding Justice O. K. Tuton approved his oath and bond the following day.[8]

Not long after Jack Helm renewed his bond for county sheriff, Hardin, with several friends and relatives, gathered at the William M. Billings store near Nopal in the northwestern corner of DeWitt County. There was no known reason for their gathering; apparently they did not need a reason to celebrate, but racing horses, eating, drinking, and carousing occupied their time. Present at the store that day, December 17, 1872, were the store's proprietor William MacDonald Billings, his son John, commonly called "Mac," John Wesley Hardin, Brown Bowen, Gip and brother Jim Clements, Rockwood Birtsell, George C. Tennille, and Thomas J. Haldeman. There may have been others.

Three feudists cleaned up after a cattle drive to Abilene, Kansas, in 1871. From left: John G. "Gip" Clements, Eph. Baker, and Fred Duderstadt. *Courtesy Mrs. Francis Hartmann.*

In late afternoon, a drunken Haldeman lay down under a tree to sleep. It was then that someone quietly approached the man and shot him in the head.[9] The motivation for Haldeman's murder has never been discovered. Brown Bowen was accused and arrested for the murder, and although he denied the charge, he provided a clue to the motivation. Bowen maintained that Hardin killed Thomas Haldeman, "for the only reason that he was afraid of him being a spy" working for Joe Tumlinson, Jack Helm, and W. W. Davis, in other words, former state policemen and followers of William E. Sutton. Bowen maintained that he and Haldeman were "personal friends" and he of course would not kill Haldeman. In fact he claimed to have prevented Hardin from killing him several times before the actual deed was done. Further, Bowen claimed that Hardin had actually gone to the dead man's father, David Haldeman, and told him that Bowen was the man who had killed his son. On the basis of Hardin's false accusation Bowen was arrested and jailed.[10]

Helm's deputy, Richard B. Hudson, arrested Bowen for the killing, although no details have been preserved pertaining to how this arrest was accomplished. Hudson was a long-time resident of the area, and later said, "I was called on at different times to come to Gonzales for the protection of life and property. On one occasion I arrested Brown Bowen and brought him to the Gonzales jail."[11] Bowen was indicted for murder on February 10, 1873, as Cause Number 1163. Not being able to raise the bail amount of $2,500, he was ordered held in the Gonzales County Jail by Judge C. C. DeWitt. Although the Bowens hired an attorney to defend their son, he escaped when the opportunity was offered. On March 22, brother-in-law Wes Hardin and a dozen friends, "all armed with Winchester guns and six-shooters, rode into the town of Gonzales, and delivered the county jail of all its prisoners, threatening the guard with death if they made any alarm."[12] Although there is no definite record of those who aided Hardin in liberating the jail, among them were probably the four Clements brothers, George C. Tennille, and perhaps Jim Taylor and cousin Bill Taylor. After his deliverance, Bowen wisely relocated to Alabama where relatives lived.[13]

On April 4, 1873, two weeks after liberating the Gonzales jail of its prisoners, Hardin was in Cuero when he and John B. Morgan, described as an occasional deputy for Sheriff Helm, had a difficulty.[14] This was one instance in which Morgan was clearly the aggressor and Hardin the would-be victim. According to Hardin, the pair argued over drinks in a Cuero saloon, Morgan wanting Hardin to treat him to a bottle of champagne. Hardin refused and forgot about the situation. But outside the bar a short time later Morgan again confronted Hardin, foolishly believing he could intimidate him. The words led to gunplay: Hardin shot and killed Morgan, and then rode out of town.[15]

The following year, Ranger Lieutenant T. C. "Pidge" Robinson, stationed in DeWitt County, learned of the killing and of Hardin's reputation and described him as "a whale among little fishes." Pidge wrote that Hardin "was more dreaded than any desperado in the State of Texas." Of the Morgan killing Pidge sarcastically wrote that Hardin had "killed a man in Cuero because he took his hands out of his own pockets when he (Wes.) told him not to do so." Pidge knew that Hardin's killing of Morgan was justified, as it was clearly self-defense, but certainly not all the killings in DeWitt County were of that nature. "We can all understand how men, when goaded by passion, or with deep wrongs to avenge, can take the life of a human being, ..." he wrote. Pidge warmed to his subject and continued, writing of the feud situation, "the good citizens of this county, of whom there are many, deeply implore the lawless deeds done in it, and which have made it a synonym for crime and desperadoism over the whole State. To a want of moral courage in denouncing wrong may be attributed some of it."[16] Pidge was well aware of men "goaded by passion" and having "deep wrongs to avenge" in DeWitt County.

A significant killing, which was not goaded by passion but a cold-blooded assassination, was the killing of Alabama-born Pitkin Barnes Taylor, a veteran who had survived the earlier wars against Mexicans and Indians. As a Texas Ranger, he had served under the noted Captain John Coffee Hays.[17] On December 13, 1846, Pitkin married the widow Susan Day; three children were born to their union: an infant who died at birth; Amanda Jane, born August 1, 1848; and a son, James Creed Taylor, commonly called Jim, born January 15, 1851.[18]

Amanda Jane Taylor married Henry P. Kelly on June 25, 1868. She lost Henry and his brother Will at the hands of Sutton and members of the State Police in 1870. Because of these deaths Pitkin advocated prosecuting William Sutton and the others who he believed had coldly murdered his relatives. According to Jack Hays Day, Pitkin "did all he could to have the murderers brought to justice. This so enraged the gang that they decided to put him in his grave."[19] As Day recalled the event, Sutton and four others stole the bell off one of Taylor's oxen. Then one of them sneaked into the corn field and rang it, knowing Pitkin would come out to investigate. It was then that they shot him. Pitkin's daughter, the widow of Henry Kelly, heard the shots and went to assist him, probably guessing that it was her father who had been shot. "She climbed the rail fence and, as she leaped to the ground on the other side, she almost fell on one of the desperadoes crouched with a gun in his hand." She then ran to the home of her half-brother John Day. After rousing the family, some of the men attempted to capture those who had shot Pitkin, "but the gang was gone." Old Pitkin Taylor was carried inside and given whatever first aid was available. He was then taken to the home of Delilah Kelly, near Sweet Home in Lavaca County. The date of Pitkin's shooting remains unknown, but Day explained that "he lingered for about six months." If Day was

Victim of the feud Pitkin B. Taylor and his wife Susan Day Taylor. Ambushed at night, his killing placed their son James Creed into the leadership role of the Taylors. *Courtesy the Western History Collections, University of Oklahoma.*

correct then the shooting occurred in October or November of 1872, as his headstone in the Taylor-Bennett Cemetery gives his death date as March 1873.[20]

An even more dramatic telling of Pitkin's shooting comes from the Kelly family. Betsy Birdwell, the great-granddaughter of Amanda and Henry Peter Kelly, recalled how her father related the event to her. When Pitkin went out to investigate the sound of the cow bell, a shot rang out. Daughter Amanda Jane heard the shot from inside the house. She "picked up the baby and went outside to see about her father. She found Pitkin and she put the child down beside him, then drug him a little ways towards the house; then she went back and picked up the child and moved him up by where she had dragged Pitkin, put him down again and pulled Pitkin a little closer to the house. These actions were repeated until she had Pitkin and the baby safely back in the house."[21]

The shooting and subsequent death of Pitkin Taylor was not widely reported; at least contemporary accounts of his death have not been found. John Wesley Hardin did allude to it, believing that Taylor had fallen victim to vigilantes led by Jack Helm. Hardin identified Helm's "most able lieutenants" as deputies Jim Cox, Joe Tumlinson, and Bill Sutton. "Some of the best men in the country had been murdered by this mob," Hardin wrote, and included Pitkin Taylor among them. Taylor had been lured from his home and shot down because "he did not indorse the killing of his own sons-in-law Henry and Will Kelly by this brutal Helms' mob." In fact, according to Hardin, anyone "who did not indorse their foul deeds or go with them on their raids, incurred their hatred and it meant death at their hands." Hardin estimated their number at about two hundred and were "waging a war with the Taylors and their friends."[22]

At the funeral of Pitkin Taylor his son Jim emerged as the recognized leader of the Taylors. Jack Hays Day was there and witnessed the oath that guaranteed the feud would continue. "It was a grim and tragic scene," wrote Day, recalling how the

A youthful James C. "Jim" Taylor, killed in 1875 along with ex-McNelly Ranger A. R. Hendricks and Mason Arnold. *Courtesy E. J. Thormaehlen.*

little cemetery was near the Guadalupe River on "a shaded knoll" where the family had gathered. Which family members were there is undetermined, since Day identifies only the deceased's son Jim by name, but added there were also five other youthful kin of the slain man. "In hideous contrast to this grief-stricken group, across the river while the funeral services were being conducted Bill Sutton assembled his cut throat gang in bold mockery. With raw drink and coarse jest and wild firing of guns they celebrated the death of Pipkin [*sic*] Taylor while he was being lowered into the grave."[23]

Jim's mother, who up to this point had controlled her grief, "broke down and wept." It became clear in young Jim's mind what he had to do about the slaying of his father. "If ever a man [was] provoked into taking the law into his own hands Jim Taylor was justly provoked; if ever a man had reason to see that Justice was meted out, Jim Taylor was inspired by that reason."

It was here that Jim Taylor made his vow. Putting his arms "protectively about his mother" he said, "Do not weep, mother. I will wash my hands in old Bill Sutton's blood!" The "five other youthful relatives likewise pledged themselves to the same cause."[24]

They may have indeed sworn vengeance on Bill Sutton there at the funeral of Pitkin B. Taylor, but he proved to be a hard man to kill. How many attempts were made in the following months is difficult to say, but according to Jack Hays Day, Jim Taylor soon "had his first chance to carry out his vow." Taylor was informed by an unidentified friend that Sutton and "six of his gang" were in Cuero playing billiards in a saloon. Taylor and Alfred C. Day, a brother of Jack Hays Day, armed themselves with double-barreled shotguns. Sutton stood facing the door when he spotted Jim Taylor and was shot down before he could react. The lights were extinguished; there was confusion within the saloon, and with Sutton writhing on the floor the would-be assassins believed they had killed their man. Sutton's injuries were not mortal however, and he was taken to Burns Station to recuperate. Day recalls that in about two months Sutton was up and about and filed charges against Alf Day and Taylor. (J. H. Day first identified the assailant as Jim Taylor, then a few lines later Scrap Taylor.) Perhaps it was Rufus P. "Scrap" Taylor, as Day indicated that Sutton "knew it was a 'kid' who had fired on him because the gun kicked the boy down." Day further states that while recuperating and under guard by members of the gang, Sutton remarked: "We must kill these damned

Alfred C. Day as he appeared in the early 1870s. His ultimate fate remains a mystery. Although occasionally identified as "Alford," family sources give his name as Alfred. *Courtesy Western History Collections, University of Oklahoma.*

little devils as soon as they leave the cradle. The first thing they learn is how to shoot a gun. They will have their revenge and they will kill all of us." Day does not explain how he learned Sutton had made this remarkable statement.[25]

A contemporary version of the assault was recorded by Victor M. Rose. Headlined "Attempted Assassination," the *Victoria Advocate* reported that Sutton was shot in Cuero "by some party or parties unknown. Sutton was sitting in a billiard saloon when someone from the outside fired two shots at him in rapid succession, one of which took effect in his left arm and breast, inflicting a serious wound, shattering the arm badly."[26]

The young men tried again on or about the sixteenth of June. They were identified by Day as Jim Taylor, "Bud" Dowlearn, "Scrap" Taylor, Alfred Day, Bill Taylor, and one other, who probably was Jack Hays Day himself.[27] The young men were over anxious and excited: Sutton and his friends saw where they were hiding, chose to run instead of fight, and thus saved their lives. Thus, explained Day, Jim Taylor's vengeance was "postponed for the time."[28]

Someone wrote a letter to a friend in San Antonio, who shared its contents with the *Daily Herald*. He wrote that there was "great excitement" in Cuero because of "some trouble between the Taylor and Sutton parties." On June 16, Sutton, Horace French, J. P. "Doc" White, John Meador, and Addison Patterson began a trip to Clinton to attend "the examination of Scrap Taylor, charged with the shooting of Sutton some time ago." Seven men fired into the Sutton party on the road to Clinton. French's horse was killed and two other horses wounded. Meador was slightly wounded in the leg. Men sympathetic to Sutton grouped together and pursued the assailants, but failed to catch up with them.[29]

At about this time John Wesley Hardin became a more aggressive leader of the Taylor party. As he recalled it—or at least wanted posterity to believe—he met Jack Helm somewhere on the road between San Antonio and Cuero, only some seven miles from the latter. Hardin recalled the meeting was by chance, and that he did not know who Helm was, believing Richard B. Hudson was the county sheriff. Helm attempted to get Hardin to join his vigilance committee. Hardin declined, of course, as "the people with whom he was waging war were my friends." Hardin informed Helm that he wished to remain neutral. They agreed to meet again, however, and did the next day, where Helm again invited Hardin to join his "vigilant company, of which he was captain."

Since there is now no way of knowing when Helm and Hardin had their conversation, it is unknown if it preceded or followed Hardin's killing of John B. Morgan, who may have been a deputy of Sheriff Helm, although no official document corroborates this. The adjutant general recorded that this killing occurred on April 4, 1873, and Morgan's slayer was using the alias of Fred Johnson.[30]

After the attempted killing of Sutton in the Cuero billiard room, the country was in a state of chaotic uncertainty. Hardin, Mannen Clements, and George Culver Tennille met with Helm at the home of Jim Cox to discuss matters. Still, according to Hardin, if he wished to have the numerous charges against him dropped, he as well as Clements and Tennille would have to join the vigilance committee and do some killing for the committee. Hardin refused, since some of the men marked for death were his friends. Following the conclusion of this strange gathering, Hardin shared with Clements and Tennille his belief that "the murdering cowards" would raid their homes within a week.

Hardin gave the date as about April 23 when Helm and a posse inquired about him, Clements, and Tennille in their neighborhood. Not finding them, they insulted their women. Helm was especially abusive toward Hardin's wife because she would not reveal where they were. On learning of this insulting treatment Hardin sent word to the Taylors to meet him at Mustang Motte, "to concoct a plan of campaign."

There, just off the present Cuero-Victoria highway, Hardin, Clements, and Tennille met Jim, John, and Rufus P. "Scrap" Taylor. There, these men "agreed to fight mob law to the bitter end, as our lives and families were in danger."[31] Of course we have only Hardin's interpretation of these activities, recorded at least twenty years after the event, when nearly all the others mentioned were dead.

If indeed there is truth in Hardin's memoir, he could easily have solved his legal problems by joining the Helm-Sutton-Tumlinson group. In March of that year, about the time Pitkin was being laid to rest, the reward for Hardin's capture was significant—$1000.[32] He had "committed sixteen different murders" according to Adjutant General Britton's report to the governor.

With John Wesley Hardin now acting as the chief of the Taylor party, violent events quickly escalated. In mid-July another ambush was planned, perhaps by Hardin himself. Jack Hays Day recalled that it was now "open war." As evidence he described how Jim and Scrap Taylor, Alf Day, and Bud Dowlearn, while returning from a horse buying trip, "sighted and recognized Jim Cox, Joe Tummilson [*sic*] and three more of the Sutton outfit." Jim Taylor opened fire and the fight began. Two men "toppled dead from their horses." Jim Taylor "rode over to the dead bodies of his enemies and shook his head regretfully when he discovered that he had failed to kill Tummilson who had done so much injury to his family."[33]

Hardin tells the story differently, of course, stating that "not long afterwards near Tomlinson [*sic*] creek" Jim Cox and Jake Christman were killed. Contemporaries described Hardin as the leader of this fight, which was simply an ambush, but, as he later coyly recalled, "as I have never pleaded to that case, I will at this time have little to say, except to state that [they] met their death from the Taylor party about the 15th of May [*sic*], 1873."[34] Riding along with Cox were several men, who have been identified as W. C. Wallace, Henry Ragland, Joe

Tumlinson, and J. L. Griffin.[35] Confusion has been created by contemporary errors in reporting just who was killed with Cox. Day, who should have known, identified the other victim as J. L. Griffin.[36] The *Victoria Advocate* headlined the event as a "shocking double murder" and placed the ambush as between Helena in Karnes County, and Yorktown in DeWitt County. Cox and "Cresman" were ambushed by "unknown parties" and killed. Cox was found with "nineteen buckshot in his body, and his throat cut from ear to ear." The *Advocate* further explained that Cox had been with Helm in his "Regulator depredations, and no doubt he was killed to avenge some injury inflicted then."[37] Further, the "unfortunate" Christman, spelled here Cresman, "was a stranger in this section, and not a party to the feud" while Tumlinson and Ragland were riding "a few yards to the rear when the volley emptied the saddles of their companions, and thus warned, saved themselves by a hasty retreat."[38]

The *Advocate's* informant was wrong on at least one account. Christman was not a stranger to the feud. His real name was John W. S. Christman, and perhaps he was called Jake or Jack. He had been in Texas at least six years, as in 1867 he and Mary E. Prather were married in DeWitt County. James W. Cox was one of the men who witnessed their marriage. Christman was about forty years old at the time of his death, and was a native of Indiana.[39] Cox was about fifty years of age. He had married Arrena Wofford in 1848, and after her death he married Laura A. DeMoss Hanks on August 22, 1872. He left six children from his first wife; his last child was born the year he was killed, whether before his death or shortly after is unknown.[40]

Little else has been learned of this killing. A report appearing in the *Herald* of San Antonio stated they were killed on their return from attending court in Helena, Karnes County. They were with Joe Tumlinson "and two other men." Further, and it is difficult to accept this as accurate, the *Herald* reported the "party who did the shooting numbered 16 men, and [their victims] were ambuscaded at the crossing of Tumlinson's creek." Cox was reportedly under indictment for a Karnes County murder but the case had been continued. Naturally the supposition was that the shooting "was done by relatives and friends of the man who was murdered by Cox." The *Herald* concluded, "Where the matter will end no one can possibly conjecture."[41] What the *Herald* did not point out was that James W. Cox had several sons who could carry on the feud by avenging his death.

Now, by mid-1873, residents of the violence-wracked area became openly concerned. On July 24, Justice of the Peace L. B. Wright of DeWitt County, who also dealt in dry goods, groceries, boots, shoes, and country produce in Yorktown, reported on local affairs to Gov. E. J. Davis. He had seen the bodies of Cox and Christman, and "was pained" to inform the governor that there "is a verry [*sic*] bad State of affairs in our County[.]" He reported that he had conducted an inquest on the mutilated bodies "a few Days Since they were ambushed by 10 or 12 men and Killed ther bodes [their bodies] ware mutaleated [*sic*]."[42] Wright was "pained" not only because he was a concerned citizen, but because his father-in-law Joseph Tumlinson had been a target of the Taylor ambushes. L. B. Wright had married Ann Tumlinson, daughter of Joseph, on November 4, 1858.[43]

Whereas the death of Pitkin Taylor was essentially ignored by the Texas press, the opposite is true of the killing of Jack Helm. Helm became notorious by his actions not only as a captain in the State Police force but prior to his DeWitt County residency. He had been involved in vigilante activity during the Civil War in northeast Texas.

As a recognized leader of the Sutton force, or at least one of the top members, Helm naturally became a target for Taylor and young Hardin. They caught up with their prey in the little community of Albuquerque, just inside the Gonzales County line. Helm was working in a blacksmith shop, no doubt tinkering on his patented invention he called a cotton worm destroyer. Two men rode up, recognized Helm, and challenged him. Helm was totally unprepared for any type of confrontation, apparently having set aside his guns in order to work on his invention and being among friends. The only weapon on his person was a large knife. With Hardin and Taylor intent on his destruction, both armed and ready to kill, Helm could only run. Shotgun and six-shooter balls ended his life.

Since Hardin was closest to the final moments of Helm's career it is only fair that we consider his version of the event first. Hardin claimed that he was to *meet* Helm at a little community named Albuquerque, which he placed in Wilson County but actually was on the western edge of Gonzales County. Presumably, their discussion concerned how Hardin could get the charges against him dropped. Hardin chose to take with him "trusted friend" Jim Taylor. They were both well armed of course, Taylor with a pistol and Hardin with a shotgun, an English-made W. & C. Scott & Son 12-gauge side-by-side.[44] Hardin explained how he and Helm, apparently off by themselves to discuss serious matters, failed to come to any agreement. Helm even threatened to kill Taylor, this to the face of Hardin, which casts considerable doubt on the wisdom of Helm or else the truthfulness of Hardin. At any rate, Hardin explained to his trusted friend that Helm intended to "shoot him on sight because he had shot Bill Sutton and because he was a Taylor." Taylor asked to be introduced to Helm, another surprising statement by Hardin as presumably Jim Taylor would by now know one of his arch enemies by sight.

Hardin relates that at this point he went to a blacksmith shop to have his horse shod. Helm followed him there, and as he was preparing to leave, Helm called to him: "Hands up, you d— s— of a b—." Hardin looked around and saw Helm

THE KILLING OF JACK HELMS.

The death of Jack Helm, as drawn by San Antonio artist R. J. Onderdonk, and first published in *The Life of John Wesley Hardin*, 1896. Onderdonk erred in the spelling of Helm's name. Census records and his marriage license show the name clearly as Helm.

advancing on Taylor "with a large knife." Someone yelled, "Shoot the d—d scoundrel." Hardin then unintentionally provided some humor in his account, stating that it appeared to him that Helm was the damned scoundrel, so he grabbed his shotgun and blasted away, as Helm "was closing with Jim Taylor." Then he covered the crowd and made one fellow put up his gun. In the meantime, Taylor was emptying his pistol, shooting Helm in the head, "so thus died the leader of the vigilant committee, the sheriff of DeWitt, the terror of the country, whose name was a horror to all law-abiding citizens, meet his death. He fell with twelve buckshot in his breast and several six-shooter balls in his head." The killing of Helm occurred in the midst of his friends and advisors, according to Hardin.[45]

Another version comes from Jack Hays Day. He learned of the killing second-hand but probably from either Jim Taylor or Wes Hardin, and recalled that Taylor and Hardin were "[o]n a hunt for members of the Sutton gang" and located Helm in a blacksmith shop in the country. As they dismounted, Taylor informed his friend to "keep the dogs off" while he disposed of Helm alone. Helm, apparently not recognizing the young men approaching, asked several persons close by who they were but nobody seemed to know them. As Taylor walked up to him, Helm "became terribly excited at his approach." Taylor informed him that he was the man he was after. Helm started "running crazily around the shop. Taylor circled with him, shooting until Helms [sic] fell dead. Like the rest of the gang, Helms couldn't face a gun. Used to taking to his heels, there was no avenue open this time for cowardly flight. No one interfered with Jim and Wes, who calmly remounted their horses and rode back from whence they had come."[46]

Victor M. Rose, for an unknown reason, gives very little space to this important killing, merely recording that Helm was killed "a little while afterwards" after his election as sheriff of DeWitt. He was at work on his invention in a blacksmith shop "near the northern line of the county" when two young men "supposed to have been friends of the Taylors" rode up and "announced through the throats of their revolvers the implacable message of fate."[47]

The contemporary press, on the other hand, gave considerable attention to the Helm killing. The *Daily Herald* of San Antonio gathered its report from "a gentleman just up from Helena," and identified the victim as "the notorious Jack Helm," killed "while standing in the door of a store on Sandies [Creek], by a man named Hardin, and others."[48] The *Daily Express* of San Antonio printed the news in a one-line item on July 25: "In DeWit [*sic*] County a desperado by the name of Hardin with several others of the same stripe rode up to the blacksmith shop of Jack Helm, while he was engaged at his work and riddled him with bullets."[49] News of Helm's death was also reported in the *Houston Telegraph*, but not quite as accurately: "Jack Helm, Davis' ex-State policeman, was shot to death, in DeWitt county, while riding along the highway."[50] A few days later the *San Antonio Daily Express* provided a greater description of the action, having been given an account of it by a "gentleman" from neighboring Guadalupe County. He was almost certainly an eye-witness, and his version provides an explanation of why Helm would seemingly attack Taylor armed only with a knife. According to this report, Helm was sitting under a tree near Samuel L. McCracken's grocery store with another man whose identity was not given. Two armed men rode up and initiated a conversation. Suddenly one of the strangers inquired, "Are you Jack Helm?" and with an affirmative answer, the stranger remarked "that he was the man he was looking for and presented his revolver." Three times the stranger [Taylor] fired at Helm but the caps snapped. Helm "was solicitous of reaching a neighboring tree, against which his shotgun was leaning." Realizing it was impossible to reach the shotgun, Helm drew his bowie-knife "and endeavored to defend himself." In the meantime the second stranger [Hardin] had obtained possession of the weapon and "shot Helm in the shoulder knocking him over." The "first murderer then dispatched him at his leisure with his pistol." The pair then went to a neighboring blacksmith shop where they remained for several hours while their horses were being shod, "after having enquired of the friend of Helm if he wished to take it up, &c."[51] This account, by an apparent eye-witness, has a much greater tone of accuracy than the version left by Hardin.

The Gonzales newspaper also provided details not printed elsewhere. Here one learns that McCracken, Helm, and Hardin "were sitting engaged in friendly conversation, when a stranger rode up, and walking up behind Helm attempted to shoot him." As the man's pistol misfired Helm turned, but at that point the pistol did fire and Helm received a shot in the breast. Helm, wounded, then rushed at his assailant, "attempting to grapple with him." At that moment Hardin fired at Helm with the double-barrel shotgun, "shattering his arm." Helm attempted to get into the shop but "the stranger" pursued him, shooting him five times about the head and face. Helm fell dead, and Hardin and "the stranger"—Jim Taylor— mounted their horses and rode away together "remarking that they had accomplished what they had come to do." This would indicate that Hardin was marking Helm for death, Jim Taylor possibly not knowing Helm by sight, but knew that Hardin would be conversing with him when it was time for the killing. The *Gonzales Index* editorialized after reporting the account from Mr. McCracken, pointing out that Helm "had many charges laid at his door while in command of the Police," and certainly "had incurred the mortal hatred of many surviving friends said to be hunted down and killed by him and his party." While "nominally" sheriff of DeWitt County, he had for a long time left the duties of shrievalty "to be performed by efficient deputies."[52]

Justice L. B. Wright had scarcely recovered from examining the bloody mess of Cox and Christman and now had an additional concern to give him pain. Jack Helm's death was significant: it proved the Taylors were becoming more efficient in their killing. Wright's *angst* over Helm's death was equaled only by the elation that the Taylor and Hardin party must have felt with their own success. After all, Helm had been the head of the vigilance committee who murdered prisoners "attempting to escape"; he had been a captain in the State Police and had insulted the wives of various members of the Taylor force, including Hardin's.[53] Helm perhaps had suffered from a feeling of invincibility, but now he was a corpse.

Justice Wright began his letter of sadness describing the "verry bad State of affars in our County" noting that "our Sheriff Capt. Jack Helm was Killed a few Days Since" by one who he understood was John Hardin, only days after holding an inquest on the mutilated bodies of Cox and Christman. And not only had these three men been killed, and all three friends of his father-in-law, but a freedman named Robert Taylor had been killed, and from what he had learned Brown Bowen was guilty of the murder.[54] Bowen, the brother of Hardin's wife, had only recently been released from the Gonzales jail, although Wright probably did not know who was responsible for that accomplishment. Wright continued, pointing out that the civil authorities were wholly inadequate to restore peace and bring the parties to justice. Even though the identity of the jail breakers and killers was well known, the officers had not even attempted to make an arrest. Since the State Police had been "Dispenced with" Wright felt "wholy Powerless." Justice Wright concluded his mournful missive to the governor by admitting, "I am wholey destitute of Power to inforce the Law. I have done all that I Can [.] our best Citizens ar[e] being Killed Evary few Days."[55] Very distressed and subject to hyperbole was Justice L.B. Wright.[56]

The July 1870 creation of the Texas State Police, which promised to reduce crime within the state's borders, may have been productive in certain quarters, but in the DeWitt County area its effectiveness was minimal. Bill Sutton and his followers and the Taylor clan produced many fatalities. The body count was indeed impressive once John Wesley Hardin entered the scene: John B. Morgan, James W. Cox, John W. S. Christman, Jack Helm, and Thomas J. Haldeman were among the dead on the Sutton side. Hardin was directly involved in these killings. Bill Sutton and John Meador had been wounded in Taylor ambushes. The Taylors had been more careful in their movements, as only Pitkin B. Taylor had lost his life. But those on both sides who had fallen had friends and family who naturally had no choice but to carry on the feud. The State Police did have success in some respects, but it became and remained unpopular among the average Texans, in part due to former slaves now being in positions of power, with badges and guns. It also was the creation of unpopular Governor Davis. On April 22, 1873, the Legislature ended the State Police by repealing the law that created it. Ironically, in the following year Governor Richard Coke created the Frontier Battalion, or Texas Rangers, which became and has remained a popular force, although its major function began with establishing law and order, as the State Police force had failed to do.[57]

As the body count mounted, Detective Charles S. Bell disappeared from the geographical area of the feud. In April 1870, he was busy in Hays County investigating the death of fugitive Randolph Spencer, wanted for his participation in the killing of Major Thompson in Mason. He determined that Spencer had been killed by a stroke of lightning while working cattle on Patton's Ranch near San Marcos, county seat of Hays County.[58]

Two months later it was reported in the press that Bell had been killed in a gunfight with five men near the Guadalupe

River in DeWitt County. Correspondent "Clinton" wrote that Jack Helm was informed of a body in the river and investigated, finding not only Bell's body but also his silver-handled pistol with "C. S. Bell" engraved on it. Five chambers had been discharged, indicating he had put up a worthwhile fight.[59] But not long after the reported death of Bell he was seen on the streets of Austin, so the "death reports" were obviously bogus.[60] J. G. Tracy, in response to a query regarding Bell's character, responded that Bell had desired the newly created position of Adjutant General of the State Militia and State Police, and since he received nothing, not even a position in the force, he became an embarrassment to the Republican Party. Tracy further wrote that Bell, on learning he would receive no position in the militia or police force, then began to initiate a scheme by which he would blackmail "certain Capitalists [*sic*], office holders, and legislators." Enough men decided it would be simpler to pay him to leave the state, and bribed him with $500 to "convey his person and extraordinary talents beyond the boundries [*sic*] of the State of Texas" and if he did not, he would have to "abide the consequences."[61] Apparently this was the real reason Bell left the state. If he had remained and continued hunting down those who in his mind were outlaws, thieves and murderers, he would no doubt have met up with John Wesley Hardin and followed Jack Helm to the grave.

Although exactly when Bell left Texas is unknown, he did ultimately work his way through the South until locating in the Washington, D.C. area. Meanwhile authorities in Texas were busy. A Grand Jury in Live Oak County in February 1872, indicted Bell, James W. Cox, and Henry Ragland for the murder of Martin Taylor.[62] By then a detective, James F. Cunningham, began his pursuit of Bell, now himself a fugitive from justice. Cunningham did capture Bell in 1877 in Mississippi, but Bell was released when the presiding judge decided the requisition papers for his arrest and delivery to Texas were fraudulent. In a letter dated May 24, 1878, written to Texas Gov. Richard B. Hubbard, Bell attempted to explain how Martin Taylor was killed, for whose death Bell was indicted. He wrote that Taylor and Dave Morris were "killed by men acting under my orders but not while I was present." After Taylor and Morris were arrested, they were "killed that night by men who overpowered the *posse* I sent out." Further, he claimed that the indictment for the death of Taylor in Live Oak County was prepared "as an effort of spite on the part of the friends of the men killed."[63] To gain further sympathy, Bell accused the state's agent, James F. Cunningham, of being an ex-convict from Mississippi. For this very reason, although Bell may not have appreciated the irony, Bell feared that if Cunningham were to deliver him back to Texas, traveling through various states, he would be killed, *while attempting to escape.* Bell, by early 1879, was no longer the proud, confident, arrogant detective he once was. He was suffering from consumption, and after failing to find relief in Arkansas, became a resident of the Soldiers' Home in Dayton, Ohio, and died there on February 18, 1879.[64]

James Creed "Jim" Taylor, head of the Taylor party after the death of Pitkin B. Taylor. From the original photograph, attributed to Hickman of Mason, Texas. *Courtesy the Robert G. McCubbin Collection.*

CHAPTER SIX

Treaties of Peace

*"The matter of dispute between the two contending parties
... was ... amicably settled without injury or bloodshed ..."*
—*Cuero Weekly Star,* JANUARY 3, 1874

J uly of 1873 was deadly for the followers of William E.
Sutton, as Cox, Christman, and Helm all fell before the
guns of the Taylor party. Clearly, John Wesley Hardin's
expertise in planning and executing ambushes had produced
positive results. Historian Robert C. Sutton Jr. believed that it
was at this point that a "pattern of pre-meditation" emerged,
which is borne out by the dates: Sutton was ambushed in early
April; Hardin then met with the Taylors at Mustang Motte where
they agreed to "a war of extermination." Sutton suggests that
perhaps Hardin's cousins, the Clements brothers, "asked him
down. ..."[1] The meeting at Mustang Motte was perhaps a gathering to plan strategy. It was as safe there, if not safer, than any
of the homes of the Taylors. Perhaps the Taylors did import
Hardin, contacting him directly or through his cousins to join
them. Or possibly Hardin simply decided that by joining the
Taylors he had better protection against lawmen anxious to
earn the significant reward.

Assuming that Hardin planned the deadly work of eliminating
Sutton's men, then the next logical target—other than William E.
Sutton himself—was Capt. Joseph Tumlinson. Captain Joe's first

137

wife, Johanna Taylor, had died sometime during the 1830s; if she had survived would Captain Joe have been a Taylor ally? But she died leaving Joe a widower, with no children. Joseph Tumlinson was married a second time to Elizabeth Newman in 1840; this union produced three children. Their daughter Ann Elizabeth married DeWitt County Justice of the Peace L. B. Wright; their son John J. "Peg-Leg" married Isabelle Cresap whose husband participated in the feud; their daughter Martha E., commonly called "Matt," married feudist William W. Wells. To complicate the family matters even more during the feud, Captain Joe's first wife Johanna was a sister of William Riley Taylor who had married Elizabeth Tumlinson, Captain Joe's sister. In 1870 Captain Joe claimed $4000 in real estate and $5000 in personal estate in DeWitt County. He was fifty-nine years old and gave his occupation as "Stock Raiser."[2]

After years of fighting Indians and Mexicans, Tumlinson now fought Anglos, essentially the Taylors. Ranger-correspondent Pidge wrote of Captain Joe and his involvement in the last Indian fight in DeWitt County in 1844. He continued that after that "he has been fighting whites ever since, ..." [3] Feudist Joseph Tumlinson, like Bill Sutton, Henry Ragland, and Jim Cox, had also been a member of the State Police, but was dismissed in April 1871 for refusing to obey orders.[4]

Hardin and Jim Taylor, now co-leaders of the Taylor forces, determined to attack Joe Tumlinson and as many of his associates as possible, all in one dramatic engagement. It probably was Hardin's idea as he had exhibited his ability to plan and execute a successful ambush; but setting up an ambush on some lonely country road to kill an enemy had proved generally unsatisfactory, as too many variables entered into that type of killing. The plan, at least on paper (if the feudists had drawn up a plan on paper) was simple: surround the Tumlinson house, set it aflame, then shoot all those attempting to escape. The pair gathered men of like spirit: Brown

Three feudists in the early 1870s. From left: Ed. J. Glover, James C. Taylor and Ed Harris. *Photo made at Powder Horn, Calhoun County. Courtesy E. J. Thormaehlen.*

Bowen, George C. Tennille, the four Clements brothers, Ed Glover, Joshua "Bud" Dowlearn, Alf Day and his brother Jack Hays Day, John Milam Taylor, and E. A. Kelly, brother of the murdered Kelly brothers, and an unknown number of others. Hardin had a justifiable reason to end the career of Captain Joe other than his desire for a good fight, at least in his mind. He had learned that a short time before, Tumlinson and some fifty of his men had gone to the Clements home place in Gonzales County looking for him, no doubt intending to end his effectiveness as a leader of the Taylors—permanently. Mrs. Hardin no doubt informed her husband of the ill treatment administered her, with perhaps some embellishment. This may have been the real reason Hardin developed his grand plan. In all likelihood, Tumlinson had gathered his forces intending to wipe out a few of the Taylors in revenge for the deaths of Cox, Christman, and Helm.

Towards mid-August Hardin now led his guerrilla army to the Tumlinson house near Yorktown. Besides their rifles, shotguns, and side arms, they had "turpentine and balls," swatches of grass or hay which when dipped in oil and lighted could be thrown into a building. The 1870s equivalent of the Molotov cocktail would be used if gunfire did not accomplish their mission. The Hardin party arrived near Tumlinson's house around two o'clock in the morning of the tenth of August. The murderous plan fell apart almost immediately, as the arrival of a few dozen men on horseback at that time of the night disturbed Tumlinson's dogs, which alerted Captain Joe and all the others, those sleeping on the gallery as well as those inside. The barking dogs effectively ruined any chance for a surprise attack, and the situation soon developed into a siege.[5]

Whether someone inside the Tumlinson house managed to sneak out or if neighbors became aware of the situation, someone got the word to authorities in Clinton of the serious situation. Justice L. B. Wright, son-in-law of Captain Joe, was at the court house when word reached him early that morning. Judge Daniel D. Claiborne was on the bench, no doubt ready to call the court to session when disturbed with the news. He ordered deputy sheriff David J. Blair to summon a posse of citizens to go to Tumlinson's relief. Nine men answered Blair's summons, including rancher Lazarus Nichols and his son Morgan O. Nichols.[6]

The posse hurried to Tumlinson's and found the house surrounded. Some of the Hardin group, not surprisingly, refused to allow any of Blair's party to approach, holding them virtual hostages to prevent their interference. Before the Hardin-Taylor party could adjust to this new development, as apparently they had no quarrel with Blair, other citizens now arrived on the scene as well. By now there were about seventy-five men siding with Hardin's group, against the Tumlinson fifty, according to his estimates. The newly arrived citizens convinced the opposing forces that signing an agreement to preserve the peace was preferable to shooting each other, although no one recorded for posterity the details of just how this was effected. By now there were perhaps as many as one hundred or more men in the immediate area of Tumlinson's house: Hardin and his group, Tumlinson and his men, the Blair posse, and the citizens who arrived to prevent the battle.

Hardin was effectively the leader of the Taylors, with Jim Taylor playing a secondary role. In spite of Hardin's relishing the idea of a good fight, he admitted that the citizens, probably from Yorktown and Clinton both, "were the means of preventing a collision, and through their efforts a treaty was made which each and every one of both parties signed."[7] "[E]ach and every one of both parties," however, did not sign the treaty, as only forty men in all stepped up to record their names. Hardin's ability to recall dates accurately was weak, as he dated the siege as taking place May 18–20, when it was actually in August.

We can overlook Hardin's errors in dates, as he was dictating his memoirs years after the fact. DeWitt County Justice of the Peace Wright, son-in-law of Captain Joe, recorded his worries as they occurred and thus must be considered more accurate. He shared with Gov. E. J. Davis details of the dreadful events happening in his area. On a Saturday, August 16, just days after the siege had been lifted, he wrote the chief executive, stating that since the murders of Cox and Christman a party of about forty men headed by John Wesley Hardin, Brown Bowen, George C. Tennille, Lazarus Nichols, and his son Mack had surrounded Tumlinson's house and held the occupants virtual prisoners for two days and nights. Wright had no further details as to the reason for the siege, only that the Hardin party wanted to kill Tumlinson and several others, men who had been members of the State Police. How long the agreement to respect each other's right to life would last was a reasonable concern, and Wright assumed it would not last long. He named specifically Hardin, Bowen, Tennille, and the four Clements brothers as part of the besieging group.

When the two forces arrived at Clinton to sign the treaty, they all still wore their six-shooters and carried their guns, meaning rifles or more than likely shotguns. Amazingly, at least some members of the Hardin party went into Judge Daniel D. Claiborne's court and took virtual control. Someone introduced Hardin to the judge, or possibly Hardin himself handled that token of respect, and explained the situation. Wright does not suggest Tumlinson or any of his men were allowed to explain their side of the event, but after Hardin's talk with the judge, he sent them all on their way. Wright's explanation was that there were simply too many to arrest, but more likely the judge was intimidated by John Wesley Hardin and the friends who had crowded into the courtroom with him. To add to the problem, according to Wright, some of those in Hardin's party lived in neighboring Gonzales County, but the authorities there didn't enforce the law any better than in DeWitt County.[8]

A copy of the treaty of peace was preserved and passed down through Tumlinson's descendants, finally to E. A. "Dogie" Wright who presented a copy to Robert C. Sutton Jr. If the copy was accurate, Joseph Tumlinson made his mark first. Others signing on the Tumlinson side of the ledger include C. C. Simmons, former policeman at the killing of the Kellys, Joe's son Peter C. Tumlinson, W. N. Templeton, Henry Ragland, Oliver K. Tuton and his son H. H. Tuton, Reuben H. Brown, and W. C. Wallace. In all, eighteen men signed following Captain Joe.

In opposition appeared the name of Lazarus Nichols and his son Morgan, George C. Tennille, Ed J. Glover, the four Clements brothers, Hardin, Patrick H. "Bud" Dowlearn, Alfred C. Day, John Milam Taylor, and E. A. Kelly, a surviving brother of Henry and William Kelly, both victims a few years previously of Helm's vigilante party. Twenty-two men stepped up and signed on the Hardin side. All signed in the presence of Hugh B. Boston, DeWitt County Clerk. The only Taylor signature is that of one J. M. Taylor, certainly John Milam Taylor. Jim Taylor could not agree to the terms of the treaty and did not sign. The "preamble" reads as follows:

> Be it known by those persons whose names are here-to signed, that we severally recognize the fact that disputes and controversies of a nature likely to result in blood shed have existed between the undersigned. Those whose names are in the left column hereto of one party, and those whose names are in the right column of the opposite party, and for the purpose of promoting peace and quiet and order in this community, We each for himself, here promise on honor, to abstain from all hostile acts, or demonstration calculated to create a breach of peace or to induce any one to suppose that any violence is intended. And be it further more [known we] severally promise on honor that we will not connect ourselves with any organization of any armed character contrary to the spirit and meaning of above agreement. And we further promise and agree that should we or either of us at any time

know of any organization being in existence for the purpose of doing violence to any man whose name is hereto signed, that we will as soon as is our power give notice of such organization to the party so threatened. To which we hereto sign our names, this the 12th day of August, A.D. 1873.[9]

The news of the compromise was spread over the land. The *Daily Express* of San Antonio reported that the "hostilities" between the Hardin and Tumlinson "crowds" in DeWitt County had "been brought to a close by the sheriff, and that an armistace [*sic*] had been agreed on." Another report came from "a gentleman, recently from that vicinity" stating that Tumlinson had been besieged in his house with some twenty of his friends for over thirty-six hours by "a force of about 60 men" before the siege was raised by the sheriff and his posse. "We know nothing of the merits or demerits of the parties to the guerilla warfare," editorialized the *Express*, "but one thing we do know, and that is the state of affairs existing in DeWitt county never was heard of until the State Police was abolished."[10] The *Express* believed that the State Police had been a positive force in reducing the amount of lawlessness, but with its abolition violence had increased.

Bringing the feudists together to sign a peace treaty was a significant accomplishment for the citizens of DeWitt County. No doubt many breathed a huge sigh of relief. Obviously Hardin's estimates of the numbers involved in the siege were highly inflated for his literary purposes, for only a minority of those involved did in fact sign, the others not caring to affix their name to anything.

In spite of the treaty of peace, assassinations continued. Just after Christmas, four months following the treaty, a group of men shot to death Wiley Washington Pridgen while he was standing in the doorway of his brother's store in Thomaston, a small

community on the Cuero-Victoria highway. Five men rode up,
hitched their horses and "presented their pistols at the breast
of Pridgen" telling him he had not a minute to live. Shot through
the heart, he fell, screaming, "I'm a dead man." They then shot
him again through the head and arm. Pridgen lived a few minutes, but was unable to indicate who his assassins were or give
a reason as to why he should be killed. Possibly the simple
fact that he was Senator Pridgen's brother was reason enough.
Day identified the murderers as John Goens, Jim Mason, Bill
Sutton, Doc White, and his brother Jeff White, but failed to
indicate how he determined these men were the guilty ones.[11]
None of their names appeared on the treaty of peace.

By now attempts at killing were so common that they received
little notice. In spite of the Christmas season, the hatreds of
the feud erupted and feudists exchanged shots, this time prac-
tically in the heart of Cuero itself. The killing of Wiley Pridgen
resulted in the recent treaty being ignored, and the feud resumed.
The Taylors ambushed some of the Sutton party on the road
but they failed in their purpose. The ambush became a skirmish
between two groups, and now both sides took the fight to within
the city limits of Cuero. Shots were exchanged near the lumber
yard, but there were no casualties. The Sutton party took over
the Gulf Hotel, the Taylors a building on the corner of Main
and Evans streets. During the two days and nights while the
feudists cleaned their weapons and planned their options, some
families near the scene left their homes for safety's sake. About
noon on Saturday, the third of January 1874, the opposing
forces withdrew from town, perhaps for a fight where no innocent people would be hurt. But again, some citizens intervened
and convinced the leaders to put aside their weapons and sign
another treaty of peace.

With the fighting forces in the town itself a reporter for
Cuero's *Weekly Star* could observe the events first hand. Editor
Kleberg headlined the report "War at Home" and described

how a "formal war reigned for two or three days in and about our town last week," how a war between two groups "known respectively as the Sutton and Taylor parties were arrayed against each other for some old feud." The sheriff, noted the newspaper report, "was powerless." With the sheriff considered ineffective, some citizens considered forming a "strong organization to sustain the officers of the law and to protect themselves."[12]

Justice O. K. Tuton provided a copy of the document, dated January 3, 1874, to the *Cuero Weekly Star*, introduced as a "treaty of peace between the two contending parties." This treaty bore a much briefer preamble than the one of August:

> We the undersigned, individually and collectively, do pledge ourselves, and solemnly swear to keep the peace between each other, and obey the laws of the country, now, henceforth and forever: furthermore, we pledge ourselves nevermore to engage in any organization against any of the signers of this agreement.[13]

Again Lazarus Nichols signed first, and his son Morgan Oliver signed as well. Eighty-seven men signed this treaty. Signing on the Taylor side were the Clements brothers, brothers Alfred and Lodwick Tuggle, blacksmith Martin V. King, Richmond Anderson, George Culver Tennille (again), John Milam Taylor, and Jack Hays Day along with his brother Alfred C. Day. Jim Taylor signed as "J. C. Taylor" as well as his cousins Rufus P. "Scrap" Taylor, and William R. "Bill" Taylor. Curiously John Wesley Hardin did not sign, although he certainly was present.

On the opposing side, William Sutton now signed, along with Deputy D. J. Blair, as well as John J. Meador and his brother William L. Men who had heretofore remained in the background in the battles now came forward and signed their names, indicating that their sympathies lay with Bill Sutton: Joe Sitterle,[14] Christopher T. Hunter, Addison Kilgore, Hugh Boston Jr., Frank

Fred Duderstadt (left) and brother-in-law Tom Tennille, feudists and trail
drivers. *Courtesy Mrs. Francis Hartmann.*

Cox, son of the slain Jim Cox, Addison Patterson, John J.
Tumlinson, John Gyns (Goens? Guynn?). W.J. Ragland, and
Gabriel Webster Slaughter. Several names were badly misspelled,
no doubt due to the inability of the signers to write their own

name legibly. The eighty-seven men who did sign swore their oath on January 3, 1874, before Justice of the Peace Tuton to preserve the peace.

Editor Robert J. Kleberg was pleased with the announcement and added several comments in the same issue. "Considering the late disturbance, holidays, etc., business is livelier than we expected. Cotton is beginning to come in like usually. 'Let us have peace!'" Many of his readers could appreciate the allusion to the statement of Union General U. S. Grant to "Let us have peace!" during his speech accepting the nomination for the presidency. Kleberg further commented on the fine weather and "[e]very thing is quiet again" but just in case, he noted that the "citizens are determined to sustain the officers of the law in case of another disturbance." Yet in contrast to these encouraging comments, in the same issue he wrote that lawlessness "seems to be the order of the day, not only in Cuero, but in many portions of our State." Perhaps, and hopefully, the next Legislature would pass an act that would "conduce directly to the rigid enforcement of our penal code. Such an act is imperatively necessary." Kleberg finally provided a paragraph describing the deadly feud as a "matter of dispute between the contending parties" which was "amicably settled without injury or bloodshed, on Saturday last." Both parties numbered about one hundred "well armed and equipped." He hoped this treaty would endure.[15]

Editor Kleberg was not the only businessman concerned with the local situation. Robert J. Clow, an outsider, happened to be in DeWitt County at this time. Clow had obtained a leather-bound memo book in Port Lavaca on the December 5, 1873, in which he began to record various notes about business matters as well as family concerns. His entries are basically separated by dashes rather than periods, indicating his journal may have been intended for simple notes to prompt more detailed entries later. In the entry for New Year's Day 1874 he wrote of the recent agreement to end hostilities: "The Hostile forces had a skirmish in suburbs of the town—no one hurt—both parties Stopped all night—One at B & Bro's Hotel [Brown Brothers, more commonly known as the Gulf Hotel] & the other in Lumber Yard[.]" That he was aware of the celebrity status of John Wesley Hardin is confirmed in the entry dated January 2 in which he continues describing the situation in town: "Night *very quiet*—both parties still in town—The Forces Mustering—Hardin has arrived—Expect fight this evening—Very warm[.]" Then Clow commented on two ladies who had arrived, pointing out that one of them disliked Cuero. Then he returned to the subject that really concerned him: "The hostile forces are still in town—Took possession of Brown's Hotel— ... Dark— No fighting yet—Things look gloomy—Every body complaining—don't know what will be the result[.]"

On the fifth of January it snowed five inches and his wife Alice went sleighing. That night it froze; on the sixth the day was cold and clear.[16] Perhaps on these nights the members of the feuding factions were more concerned with physical comfort for themselves and horses than their animosities against their enemies.

The winter months may have been used to good advantage in keeping creature comforts and planning strategy. After the treaty of peace was signed, calm apparently reigned over the distracted "kingdom of DeWitt." Citizens finally did take some action for their own protection, no doubt realizing that if the sheriff were as "powerless" as the newspaper proclaimed, they would have to fend for themselves. Some men did form a committee for mutual protection, naming their organization the "Home Protection Club." The *Indianola Bulletin* learned of this and commented that they were "glad that the citizens of Cuero have formed themselves into a committee for mutual protection, and we know ... that they will be sustained by the good citizens of the surrounding counties." Continued the *Bulletin*: "The scenes that have transpired in and around Cuero, in which boys have participated, encouraged by their elders to do so, have been outrageously disgraceful. Children should not be ... permitted to act like savages; and now ... we shall look for better times in that neighborhood."[17] And apparently the existence of the Home Protection Club did some good, at least on the streets of Clinton and Cuero.

But for the Taylors, the feud was very much alive, in spite of what Editor Kleberg said, or the preamble, or who signed it, or whatever the temperature was outside. William E. Sutton was still alive, his name still on the list of those who "needed killing." John Wesley Hardin and the Taylors had failed in getting Joe Tumlinson, but the more important target was Sutton himself. The treaties of peace were now ignored.

The Taylor network somehow learned that Sutton was preparing to leave Texas for Kansas. Not all cattlemen trailed their herds, as it was much more convenient to travel to the Kansas markets via steamer and railroad, and this was Sutton's plan. The Suttons—he was taking his wife with him to be close, as she was four months pregnant—took the train to Indianola where they would board a steamer to go to New Orleans. From there they would be transported to Kansas via the railroad.

Exactly how the Taylors learned Sutton would be in Indianola that eleventh of March is unknown, but there are several theories. As Hardin recalled, it was about the middle of February 1874 that he returned from a visit to Comanche, Comanche County, where his parents and other brothers and sisters lived, one of whom was older brother Joseph G. Hardin. John Wesley was aware that "the Sutton party" had "violated their pledges" and on several occasions had maliciously turned loose cattle belonging to the Taylors. Further, he had learned that Sutton was gathering his herds to send them north to Kansas markets, but he intended to go by rail to Wichita. At this point John Wesley Hardin reminisced about their efforts to kill Sutton: "We had

View of a busy Indianola street during the time of the feud. William Sutton and Gabriel Slaughter were killed here. *Courtesy Robert W. Shook.*

often tried to catch him, but he was so wily that he always eluded us," he complained. "Jim Taylor had shot him and broken his arm in a saloon in Cuero. He had a horse killed under him in a fight on the prairie below Cuero and he had another killed while crossing the river below there." Sutton was "looked upon as hard to catch and I had made futile efforts to get him myself. I had even gone down to his home at Victoria, but did not get him."[18]

Hardin probably stayed with his father-in-law, Neill Bowen, who lived in Gonzales County, as he recalled that at this point brother Joe and cousin Alec Barekman[19] came down from Comanche to visit. Hardin got the pair to go to Indianola, informing Joe that Sutton was a deadly enemy and would be going to Kansas soon. "I told him to find out when Sutton would leave Indianola so that I could tell Jim Taylor and go at once to Indianola to kill him, as it was a life or death case whenever either I or Jim Taylor met him." Thus Joe Hardin and cousin Alec Barekman went to Indianola where they first attended to Hardin's "shipping interests" and in so doing learned when Sutton would leave, and that he would leave on the steamer *Clinton*. With this important news John Wesley Hardin, who probably wished to be in on the kill but for some reason stayed clear of Indianola, alerted Jim and Bill Taylor who went to the port city. There they obtained good horses for their "get away." Hardin recalled that there were "six or eight brave men ready there who stood in with the play." Unfortunately he provided no identification of these six or eight "brave men" and no witness mentioned seeing a group of men who could be considered accomplices.

Another view of how the Taylors learned of Sutton's plans appeared in the history of the feud by Victor M. Rose. He wrote that Bill Sutton had some business in Cuero prior to his departure, and it was perhaps there that a careless word was overheard by someone in sympathy with the Taylors. That careless word then was relayed to the Taylors who acted upon it. That may well be true, or it may be nothing more than speculation on the part of Rose.[20]

At Indianola, on March 11, 1874, the Suttons took a hack from the Indianola depot to the wharf where the steamer *Clinton* waited for passengers. Stockman John N. Keeran,[21] Ed McDonough and Gabriel W. Slaughter rode together with Bill and Laura Sutton. McDonough and Slaughter went on board first, then waited for Mr. and Mrs. Sutton. As the Suttons walked on board, two men who had only moments before approached the hack but remained out of view, followed. They were Jim Taylor and his cousin Bill Taylor; they had been there since the previous week and the wait was now paying off. As the Suttons approached their cabin, Jim Taylor, now on the deck, drew a brace of pistols. Sutton, completely taken by surprise, "gasped" out "Hell is in the door, Gabe. Yonder comes Jim Taylor." Sutton then grabbed his gun but instead of standing and shooting back, he ran. Sutton collapsed with bullets in his breast and head.

While Jim Taylor finished Sutton, Bill Taylor engaged Slaughter. The original plan focused on killing Bill Sutton, but Slaughter was there, armed, and thus became a target as well. He drew his pistol but managed to fire only once at his assailant. Bill Taylor fired at least two shots, one of them hitting Slaughter in the face. When the first shots were fired the dozen or more other persons on the deck scattered. In spite of numerous witnesses, apparently no attempt was made to prevent the killing or the escape of the killers. In the confusion Jim Taylor picked up Bill Sutton's pistol as a souvenir. John Keeran, over his shock and surprise, picked up Slaughter's pistol—noted it was half cocked, with one barrel having been fired —and strangely, gave it to Mrs. Sutton. The other witnesses, after their initial shock, approached her as she screamed and wept over the lifeless form of her murdered husband. She had attempted to shield him from his enemies, to no avail.[22] They also observed the corpse of Gabriel Slaughter, Bill Sutton's friend, who may have done nothing more than be a friend to Sutton. But he had signed the January treaty of peace on the Sutton side, and by signing his name on that side of the treaty, he became a feudist aligned with Sutton.[23]

William R. "Bill" Taylor, who avoided punishment for his killing of Gabriel W. Slaughter. *Courtesy the Eddie Day Truitt Collection.*

John Wesley Hardin was not present on the deck of the *Clinton*, but he learned of the killing first-hand from the Taylors. As he recalled, Gabriel Slaughter observed the Taylors first and called out to warn his friend: "Look out, Billy." Bill Taylor then turned on Slaughter, saying, "Look out yourself, you d— s— of a b—." Bill Taylor fired on Slaughter "who was drawing his pistol, and Slaughter fell with Sutton, a pistol in his hand and a bullet in his head."[24]

Jack Hays Day left an explanation that is less credible as to how the killings were accomplished. Day stated that on the tenth of March, a banker in Victoria wired Sen. B. J. Pridgen that Sutton was planning to leave Indianola on a boat the next day. Pridgen then wired Jim Taylor, who with Bill Taylor that night boarded a train and arrived in Indianola sometime late on the night of the tenth. Jim made arrangements with a livery stable owner to have the two best horses saddled and ready to ride near the wharf.[25] Then the two Taylors went there and waited. Day's account is suspect for two reasons: the Victoria banker who supposedly wired Senator Pridgen about when Sutton would leave is not identified; getting the word to the Taylors who then had to get to Indianola quickly is also difficult to accept. Also, according to witness John N. Keeran's later court testimony, the Taylors had been at Indianola the week preceding the shooting. One thing Day said, however, is plausible: after the killing, the Taylors "went to the horses, mounted calmly and rode away." Finally, "Jim had avenged the murder of his father."

Mrs. Sutton arranged for both her husband and his friend Gabriel Slaughter to be buried in Evergreen Cemetery in Victoria, their graves but a few feet apart. With their killing, the Taylor cousins now became wanted fugitives. Governor Coke offered a reward of $500 for their arrest and confinement, and in addition, during her mourning period the widow Sutton arranged for a $1,000 reward to be offered. She was not only made a

Grave marker of William E. Sutton in Evergreen Cemetery, Victoria. *Courtesy Robert W. Shook.*

widow, but a widow carrying a child who would be born five months later. The Biblical admonition "Vengeance is mine; I will repay, sayeth the Lord," may have been ringing in her ears, but she was going to do what she could to hasten that vengeance along. Three months after burying her husband the reward was publicized, first appearing in the *Victoria Advocate*. The notice reminded all potential bounty hunters that she saw James Taylor "shooting my husband in the back with two six-shooters" while Bill Taylor killed his companion Gabriel Slaughter. The word "alleged" did not appear. The reward would be paid to anyone who could "arrest and deliver him inside [the] jail door of Calhoun County, Texas"; she clarified as well that her reward was in addition to the $500 offered by the State of Texas. If there were any doubts

Grave marker of Gabriel Webster Slaughter in Evergreen Cemetery, Victoria. *Courtesy Robert W. Shook.*

as to her ability to pay, she referred them to Brownson's Bank of Victoria.[26]

Day alluded to a big celebration at B. J. Pridgen's house following the killing of Sutton, and in fact there may have been a celebration, similar to the one held by the Suttons across the Guadalupe River from the Taylor cemetery when Pitkin Taylor was being interred about a year before. John Taylor, the uncle of Bill, later testified that a few days following the killing, or March 15 or 16, he was at Senator Pridgen's home along with Jim and Bill Taylor, among others. After spending the night, John, Jim, and Bill Taylor "started off together, and had gone up the road a piece" when Jim told Bill that he had forgotten the pistol, meaning Sutton's, and that if he—Bill—would go back and get it he would make him a present of it. While Bill Taylor was going back to retrieve the pistol, Jim told John that it was the Sutton pistol, and that he had taken it off Sutton when he killed him. John Taylor described it as a white-handled Smith & Wesson.[27]

When the immediate excitement of the Sutton-Slaughter killing had died down, Joe Hardin and Alec Barekman returned to Comanche. John Hardin, the four Clements brothers, and Ed Glover decided to start another herd. Jim Taylor, not wanting to stay in the area with so many of his friends going up the trail, wisely joined them. Bill Taylor chose to remain in DeWitt County.

Hardin, the Clements, and others, within a two-week period, "had complied with the laws and had started another herd of about 1000 head," Hardin recalled. He placed Dr. James Monroe Bockius[28] in charge with instructions to take the herd to Hamilton, Hamilton County. Hardin and Jim Taylor would be in Comanche, and when the herd reached Hamilton Bockius was to alert them and all would proceed north to Kansas together. Around April 23 Wes Hardin and Jim Taylor left Gonzales for Comanche, their plans then to continue to Wichita, Kansas.[29]

James Monroe "Doc" Bockius. He narrowly escaped death from a lynch mob in Clinton. *Courtesy Mrs. Ray Caffall.*

What occurred between the twenty-third of April and the twenty-sixth of May of that year is uncertain, except perhaps it was a matter of Hardin visiting family and friends as well as preparing for the drive north to Kansas. His father as well as older brother Joe lived in Comanche. His father, Methodist minister James G. Hardin, was no doubt highly respected, but brother Joe had had his own legal problems, mainly dealing with false bills of sale for land and cattle. But in spite of all the potential problems and surrounded by family members, John Wesley Hardin must have felt secure in Comanche.

On May 26 Comanche celebrated—although exactly what they were celebrating has never been determined—and it was also Hardin's twenty-first birthday. Naturally it was a day of drinking, betting on fast horses, and in general enjoying themselves. Hardin claimed he was lucky at the race track, as he and his friends "won everything in sight. I won about $3000 in cash, fifty head of cattle, a wagon or two and fifteen head of saddle horses."[30] The friends, besides Jim Taylor, feeling much safer here than in his home county of DeWitt, included his brother Joe, two cousins, brothers William A. "Bud" and Thomas K. "Tom" Dixon, cousins Alexander Hamilton "Ham" Anderson and his brother Doctor James T. L. "Jim" Anderson,[31] and another cousin Alexander Henry "Alec" Barekman.

John Wesley Hardin's birthday was indeed an enjoyable one. He was among family members, surrounded by friends, winning handsomely in all his gambling, yet the day turned to tragedy when Deputy Sheriff Charles M. Webb from neighboring Brown County approached. Why Webb was outside his jurisdiction is subject to debate: Hardin maintained that he was there "with fifteen men to kill me or capture Jim Taylor for the reward." But no other record indicates Webb had anywhere near fifteen men with him; this must surely be nothing more than an error on Hardin's part. That Webb was merely visiting Comanche to see his lady friend has also been suggested, but that may be just another unfounded rumor. Webb may have been there merely to enjoy the celebration.

Although it is uncertain why Webb was in Comanche, he and John Wesley Hardin did meet in front of the Jack Wright saloon on the north side of the town square. Hardin was with Jim Taylor and cousin Bud Dixon when Webb approached. Several other men were close enough to hear the conversation that passed between them. Although Webb no doubt was a brave man, having served honorably only a few months before with the Brown and San Saba County Rangers, he made a serious error in judgment in the next few moments. As the group apparently were all going to enter the Wright Saloon for a final drink, Webb foolishly drew his pistol, intending to either shoot Hardin or make a peaceable arrest. But Bud Dixon saw Webb's movement and yelled out a warning to Hardin: "Look out, Jack!" Charles Webb and Hardin shot at each other, perhaps simultaneously, with Hardin receiving a wound in the side and Webb receiving a bullet in the left cheek. Hardin's shot proved fatal, but Taylor and Dixon also shot Webb, who managed to fire a harmless shot into the ground as he collapsed. Hardin had now added another victim to his kill list; Jim Taylor and Bud Dixon were accessories. What was to be a memorable celebration in Comanche had turned into a tragedy. Jim Taylor's efforts to leave the feud behind him proved useless. The trio managed to ride out of town with a mob forming quickly behind them.[32]

The *Comanche Chief* reported Webb's death, mourning its "sad duty to chronicle one of the most painful affairs that ever occurred in our midst." The affair was described as "a difficulty" between Hardin and Webb, resulting "in the almost instant death of Mr. Webb." Bystanders informed the *Chief* reporter that Hardin, Taylor, and Bud Dixon did the shooting, that Webb received one ball through the body, one through the right jaw that passed down his neck, and several through the hat. Webb supposedly shot three times, and in all "about a dozen shots were exchanged." Hardin did receive a wound in the side from Webb's pistol.[33]

Within hours, Joe Hardin and other family members were gathered together and placed under what amounted to house arrest. Bud Dixon chose to take his chances in town and left his companions. He and his brother Tom were captured and confined. Four other Hardin friends in Comanche that day were arrested on suspicion. They were James Anderson, Thomas Jefferson Waldrip, William Green, and Dr. J. M. Bockius.[34] The local authorities isolated Hardin and Jim Taylor when they confined their family and friends. Perhaps they would be forced to surrender to the citizens of Comanche.

By midnight on the night of Sunday May 31, the guards at the two-story rock building that served as Comanche's jail were disturbed by an armed mob demanding three prisoners: Joe Hardin and the two Dixons. Whether the guards cooperated and meekly surrendered the trio to the mob, or the three were taken forcibly, is uncertain, but the mob took the three they wanted. They were taken a few miles outside of town and lynched. The next morning the bodies were taken down and buried not far from Reverend Hardin's home. No other prisoners were harmed. The *Comanche Chief* expressed confidence that no citizens of Comanche nor "any one living in this county took part in it"—probably because the parties were disguised, and in so reporting could maintain a degree of "objectivity."

The lynch mob was composed of Brown County men who knew and liked deputy Charles Webb, but some Comanche citizens may have joined. No one believed that Joe Hardin was directly involved in the shooting of Webb, as it was by then common knowledge that it was his brother John and Bud Dixon, along with Jim Taylor, whose bullets had killed him. But the Brown County mob wanted revenge; clearly, they wanted blood, and if they could not hang John Wesley Hardin then his brother would have to do. Bud Dixon had also shot Webb, and as he and his brother Tom were there in that rock house jail, then that proved to be a bonus. Joe Hardin and Bud and Tom Dixon paid the price.

The *Cuero Weekly Star* printed the tragic news, picked up from the *Comanche Chief*. Now all of DeWitt County knew where Jim Taylor and John Hardin were, and what had happened following the killing of Webb.

Comanche County was in turmoil. Even as a mob was forming, citizens also were preparing a petition asking Governor Coke to send help. Over two dozen men signed their names, claiming that the county was "infested with a band of Murderers & thieves headed by the notorious John Wesley Hardin and Jim Taylor" who made the lives and property of peaceable citizens unsafe. Deputy Webb, they claimed, had come to Comanche "peaceably and quietly attending to his private business." Now they requested twenty-five or thirty men of Captain John R. Waller's Texas Ranger company to be stationed at the town, to be "specially charged with the capture of the said John Wesley Hardin & Jim Taylor and their coadjutors" and further that a reward be offered "commensurate with the crime."[35]

Although the Comanche County citizens and friends of Webb from Brown County formed mobs intent on vigilante justice, Charles Webb cannot be rightfully included among the victims of the feud itself, only peripherally. In the aftermath, however, the Sutton forces took advantage of the situation and it became part of the feud. Mob justice became the order of the day; in the weeks following the Webb killing eight of Hardin's friends and relatives paid the supreme price.

Hardin had earned the reputation of a killer, his kill tally far outnumbering Jim Taylor's and the others combined. But Captain Waller had his orders and the cooperation of many citizens of the area. His Rangers were divided into squads who scoured the countryside in search of Hardin and Taylor. Captain Waller began his scouting at Comanche on the twenty-eighth of May, two days after the Webb killing. Three-fourths of his company were constantly in the saddle until the twelfth of June, during which time he made over twenty-two arrests. Waller sent seven of the men arrested to DeWitt County. The others were turned over to sheriffs of various other counties. Waller proved to be an effective leader and placed himself in the field along with his men. He saw dangerous action and reported:

> Barekman & Anderson two [of] Hardins gang fired on Some of my men and Several Citizens. My men returned the fire Killing both Barekman & Anderson. I exchanged Several Shots with John Wesley Hardin & Jim Taylor wounding Hardin in the Shoulder but he made good his escape being well mounted.[36]

The death of Anderson and Barekman was only indirectly a result of the Taylor-Sutton Feud, but ironically they had left a different feud behind in their home country, which had started with the death of Dr. William N. Anderson, shot to death by William M. Love in early 1855. The widow Anderson, pregnant at the time, vowed to raise her son to kill the man who had killed her husband. The Anderson son grew up to avenge his father, after which he and cousin Barekman left their home in Navarro County to seek refuge with John Wesley Hardin in Comanche County.[37] There they met their deaths.

What happened at Comanche brought not only statewide attention to the lawlessness in certain areas, but the Texas Rangers as well. Captain John R. Waller did his best to capture or kill Hardin and Taylor, but failed. What he did accomplish was to drive Hardin out of the state, as the man-killer now chose to leave Texas and relocate in far-off Florida where relatives of his wife lived. He left behind a dead brother, four dead cousins, and the herd of cattle kept in Hamilton County. But vigilante justice was not yet complete.

Comanche County Representative John D. Stephens gathered a posse and rode out to the Hardin-Taylor camp and arrested those herders present. They had done nothing in Comanche or Brown County, but were merely cowboys tending the herd in Hamilton County. Whether the cattle were actually stolen stock or purchased legally, or whether the men were driving them for their rightful owners, a common practice, was never legally determined. Whether the mobs acted out of anger over Webb's death, or simply believed the Hardin-Taylor crowd were rustlers, was also never determined. But their reaction was swift and deadly.

The herders arrested by Stephens were James M. "Doc" Bockius, John Elder, G. W. Parkes, Thomas Bass, Rufus P. "Scrap" Taylor, James White, and Alfred "Kute" Tuggle. Captain Waller now sent a squad of twelve rangers under Sergeant J. V. Atkinson with orders to deliver them to Clinton. Arriving in Austin on June 14, Atkinson, or else one of his men, was interviewed by a reporter of the *Daily Democratic Statesman*. The reporter learned that the prisoners had been captured in Hamilton County, southeast and adjacent to Comanche County "while in possession of seven hundred stolen cattle and thirty three horses." J. D. Stephens, representative from Comanche County, was in charge of the "capturing party." Prisoner Bockius was also interviewed. Bockius "graduated from a medical school in Philadelphia. ... [He] appears to be well educated, and is gentlemanly in his manner and deportment. He says that his supposed connection with the cattle thieves is all a mistake." But the reporter concluded by pointing out that his captors claimed they could prove he was a partner of Hardin, then believed to be fleeing to Kansas. Further, the prisoners were being sent to Clinton, "where they are under indictment."[38] Purportedly there were warrants sworn out by DeWitt County resident Richard B. Hudson, claiming that the herd in question had been stolen from him.

From Hamilton County to Austin, where they spent the night, was a three-day ride. On the fifteenth of June Governor Coke met with Valerius C. Giles who was to continue with the prisoners. Coke's message, dated June 15, gave Giles the necessary letter of introduction. "The bearer ... will deliver to you the following prisoners, that we have in arrest [giving names]. The above named prisoners you will hold subject to the orders of the Sheriff of DeWitt County, or until discharged by due course of law."[39]

It is obvious that Governor Coke was very concerned with the situation in DeWitt County. He shared his concerns with his adjutant general, William Steele, who gave orders to Sergeant Atkinson: "You will proceed by the most direct route with the prisoners now in your charge to Clinton DeWitt County and deliver Said prisoners into the custody of the Sheriff of that county." Steele explained, assuming that Atkinson was unaware of the volatile situation there, that there "exists a state of lawlessness in that section of the state" and because of that he needed to guard against attempts to take the prisoners, either by their friends to liberate them, or by their enemies to kill them. As soon as he accomplished his mission he was to return to Austin to report to General Steele. On the same day Steele informed DeWitt County Sheriff William J. Weisiger that the prisoners were leaving with a detachment of "frontier forces" that day and he was to "be prepared to take charge of them."[40]

From Austin to Clinton was perhaps a three- or four-day ride, assuming the group traveled through Lockhart, through Gonzales and on to Clinton. The Rangers and prisoners did arrive in Clinton without incident, but due to the jail being already full they were placed under guard in the court house, "where they were held to prepare for an examining trial."[41] Sergeant Atkinson and his men could not immediately leave

Clinton, as they had to rest their horses and the sheriff requested their presence in guarding the prisoners.

The night of June 21–22 was dark and stormy at Clinton, "a perfect time for a deed of darkness" as one historian described it, when a mob surrounded the court house about one o'clock in the morning. Four prisoners were taken out: Tuggle, Taylor, White, and Bockius. Bockius, who was a Mason, gave the traditional Masonic distress signal and fellow Mason Joseph Sunday saw it. Joe Sunday was an extremely large man, and fortunately Bockius was small; Sunday managed to get the smaller Bockius up on his horse and away from the mob before they knew it. Bockius survived that night of terror, but the other three did not. George Boston, one of the guards, told the sheriff that he ought to protect the prisoners; Weisiger, who obviously had more concern for property than for human lives, responded by saying that if the prisoners were not released to the mob, they would burn the court house down to get them. Jim Wofford, another guard, also attempted to protect the prisoners. Standing at the head of the stairs he bravely announced, "I will shoot the first man who comes up these steps." But he surrendered after a voice from behind told him he would fire but one shot. As the mob took complete control, White and Taylor begged for their guns so they could at least protect themselves, but this was denied them. The mob rushed in, took the quartet out, Bockius somehow making his escape, and then hanged the other three near the Clinton cemetery. Jack Hays Day wrote that the trio "died game" telling the mob, "You are murdering us for nothing, but we have plenty of friends and some of you will be in hell in a few days."[42] Of course no real effort was made to determine the identity of the mob's members. DeWitt County citizens could hardly be blamed, for they were in disguise, perhaps wearing hoods over their faces in the manner of the Ku Klux Klan. One report indicated it was a "large body of disguised men" and the prisoners were taken to the Clinton cemetery where they were executed. There the bodies "hung until next morning when they were taken down by their relatives and interred."[43] Rufus P. "Scrap" Taylor's remains were taken to the Taylor cemetery, laid to rest not far from the grave of his uncle, Pitkin Taylor. Whether White and Tuggle were buried there as well is unknown. No stones bear their names either in the Clinton Cemetery, or the Taylor-Bennett Cemetery where Scrap Taylor's remains lie.

Sergeant Atkinson and his men were back in Austin on the twenty-fourth, apparently unaware of what had happened to the prisoners he had safely delivered. He was so ill from the journey that he could not leave Austin as he wished, but did manage to write a brief note to Adjutant General Steele. He had delivered the prisoners, he said, "into the custody of the sheriff" and at his "Solicitations I remained in Clinton thirty six hours for the purpose of guarding his prisoners."[44] After Atkinson and his Rangers were safely out of sight, the mob had formed to do its work.

Although John Wesley Hardin had been a definite asset to the Taylors, bringing death to several important members of the Sutton force, his action in Comanche resulted in unforeseen and terrible consequences. The wrath of mob law forced him to flee the state; he lost relatives and friends to lynch law. And to add to the sorrow of the immediate Taylor family, one of the victims was young Rufus P., commonly called "Scrap."

Rufus P. "Scrap" Taylor, one of three men lynched by a mob of Sutton sympathizers in June 1874. *Courtesy the Western History Collections, University of Oklahoma.*

Ranger Captain L. H. McNelly, in early 1873. From the original cabinet portrait made by James Inglis in Montreal, Canada. *Courtesy the Albert and Ethel Herzstein Library, San Jacinto Museum of History.*

CHAPTER SEVEN

McNelly and the Rangers Arrive

*"This is also a family feud, and they are arrayed against
each other in the opposing parties, from children of the
same parents down to fourth cousins and step-neighbors-in-
law, there are* a great *many strangers, too, among them, ..."*
— *"Pidge,"* OCTOBER 13, 1874, FROM CLINTON

The June lynching of the three young men in Clinton, as
well as the double killing of William E. Sutton and companion Gabriel Webster Slaughter on the deck of the *Clinton* in March, brought statewide attention to the feud. The death
of Sutton should have marked the end of the feud, allowing
the Taylors to claim victory, but such was not the case as now
Cuero's City Marshal Reuben H. Brown replaced the deceased
Sutton as leader of the opposing party. Brown was the son of
P. T. and Miriam Keneday Brown, both Tennessee natives who
had migrated to Texas sometime in the mid-1840s. Their first
three children were born in Tennessee, the oldest, Jesse K., in
1834; daughter Josephine followed in 1841; Basil J., in 1845.
Joseph, born in 1849, and the youngest, Reuben H., born on
November 28, 1851, were Texas-born. Where Reuben attended
school is unknown, but Victor Rose, who wrote of him as if he
knew him well, described the now "acknowledged head of the
Sutton party," as a young man, "liberally educated, and almost
a perfect specimen of physical manhood."[1]

Details of the upbringing of the Brown children are unknown, but Reuben earned sufficient respect of his peers to earn him a place as city marshal of Cuero. He pinned on the badge in the summer of 1873, certainly realizing it was a dangerous position to hold in a dangerous time and place. Among his first concerns was lining up the feudists to sign the first treaty of peace in August. Brown was one of the men signing, and from the placement of his name among those of Joseph Tumlinson, C. C. Simmons, and other Sutton sympathizers, he proved to all he was clearly a member of the Sutton party. In early 1874 Marshal Brown was forced to defend himself, resulting in the death of James Gladney "Gladden" McVea, a young farmer originally from South Carolina.[2] Details are scant, but Jack Hays Day claimed Marshal Brown had locked McVea up for drunkenness, then took about $100 from him but refused to return it. The pair argued and Brown shot and killed him, then placed a small pistol on his body to "prove" it was a case of self-defense.[3] According to another version printed in the *Cuero Star*, however, the difficulty occurred in McGanan's bar room, with McVea killed instantly. Judge O. K. Tuton held an inquest and determined the killing was justifiable. The cause of the tragedy remains controversial, but the more objective *Star* learned that McVea had struck a blow to Marshal Brown's head, who was "still suffering from the wounds he received" by the time the newspaper went to press.[4]

Brown's duties included such mundane acts as delivering court papers and shooting stray dogs bothering the citizens of Cuero, but at times he probably entertained the notion of arresting a notorious figure such as Bill Taylor. The opportunity came on April 3, 1874, less than a month after the double killing of Sutton and Slaughter. Considering the notoriety of Bill Taylor, the arrest seems incredibly simple. Was "Rube" Brown such an effective and courageous lawman that Taylor chose not to resist, or was it a mere quirk of circumstance wherein Taylor was caught totally off guard, and Brown had a bit of incredible good luck? Probably

Brown and Taylor were not deadly enemies at all, as they were kin by marriage: Rube Brown's brother Basil J. had married Anna J. Taylor, a cousin of Bill Taylor's.[5]

Bill Taylor must have felt supremely confident in returning to his DeWitt County haunts after killing Slaughter, an attitude just the opposite of his cousin Jim Taylor. Jim had joined up with John Wesley Hardin on a cattle drive, essentially removing himself from the center of the feud, at least for a while.

On the third of April, Brown observed Bill Taylor wearing a pistol in Cuero and determined to arrest him. Taylor had entered a dry goods store intending to purchase a new pair of boots. Brown followed him inside where he observed Taylor with his guard relaxed. As Taylor pulled on a boot, which action placed him at a definite disadvantage, Brown grabbed him from behind and carried him struggling into the street where bystanders helped to subdue him.[6] Brown confiscated Taylor's weapon, the pistol which had earlier been in the hands of Bill Sutton, a white-handled Smith & Wesson, serial number 21418. The pistol meant a great deal to Bill Taylor, as he believed that it had formerly been the property of his uncle, William P. "Buck" Taylor, killed by Sutton back in 1868. Now disarmed, Taylor asked Marshal Brown what would happen to the pistol, and was told it would be sold "for the benefit of the town of Cuero." Bill Taylor asked the marshal to buy it for him, even if it cost $100. The pistol was not sold however, and was turned over to the mayor of Cuero, Otto L. Threlkeld, who then turned it over to the district attorney. Its location, at the time of this writing, if it still exists, is unknown.

Taylor appeared in court preparing to provide bail on the relatively minor charge of carrying a pistol. In the court room, while arrangements were being made, someone handed the marshal a copy of Governor Coke's reward offering $500 for Taylor's arrest. Marshal Brown was now required to follow the instructions "to hold the accused for the charge of murder preferred against him." This suggests Brown was somehow ignorant of the reward offer or else he was at first choosing to ignore it. Recognizing his duty, Brown now called for assistance from various citizens in delivering Taylor safely to jail, and "the citizens responded en mass[e]." The next morning Taylor was taken by train to Indianola, accompanied by enough citizens to protect him from enemies who would mob him, or friends who would rescue him. The citizens were now cooperating openly with law officers.[7]

On two occasions on the road to Indianola, unknown parties recklessly fired shots into the train itself, but no harm was done to Taylor or his guards. An Indianola reporter commented, "Hot times are anticipated if he is kept here." In spite of the concerns of friends and foes, Bill Taylor was delivered safely to the Indianola jail.[8] The case was prosecuted by District Attorney William H. Crain, and Taylor's defense argued by Attorney John H. Givens. Taylor was bound over to the May term of the District Court to stand trial for first-degree murder. Due to the inadequacy of the Indianola jail, and the probability of mob action to lynch or rescue him, he was delivered to the stronger facility at Galveston. Shipping magnate Charles Morgan provided his steamer *Clinton* to use by lawmen to deliver Taylor, the same one in use the day Sutton and Slaughter were killed. Reportedly no other passengers were allowed on board.[9] John Wesley Hardin learned of Bill Taylor's arrest and considered a rescue attempt, but he did not act quickly enough; he could only complain that "Rube Brown had arrested Billy Taylor and had sent him at once to Galveston, so we never had a chance to rescue him."[10]

William Francis "Billy" Buchanan now became the next victim of the DeWitt County violence, shot to death on the seventeenth of May 1874. Billy Buchanan was the son of Francis M. and Nancy Brown Buchanan who farmed in DeWitt County. By the time of his death Billy was in his late thirties.[11] Although the name of former Sen. Bolivar J. Pridgen was connected to the killing, Buchanan's death received little press attention and little is known of the event, other than the account left by Jack Hays Day. According to Day, Buchanan had to be killed because he attempted to lead several members of the Taylor party into an ambush set up by members of the Sutton party. He was "a young sympathizer with the Sutton gang" who intended to act as a decoy in a plot to lead John M. Taylor and some of the Pridgen men into the trap. Buchanan had been absent from the country for a while—long enough for him to grow a beard which he believed would be an adequate disguise. The naïve Buchanan played the role of a relative of Crockett Choate, killed back in 1869, and friend of the Taylors. How Buchanan contacted John M. Taylor and attempted to convince him that he "had the Sutton gang in a trap where Taylor's men could kill them all" is not explained. Taylor, now joined by Augustus W. "Gus" Pridgen and his cousin Bolivar Jackson Pridgen, however, were not fooled by the disguise. Gus first recognized him, and then convinced B. J. Pridgen and Taylor they were being deceived. They now realized that due to Buchanan's treachery he would have to be killed. "Buchanan," wrote Day, "was already very much excited, knowing he was recognized. He started to run and Bolivar shot him." Then the trio rode to the "old Taylor ranch" and told the inhabitants "that there was a dead man lying nearby" and to "notify the officers." An inquest was held the next day. This is how Jack Hays Day recorded the event.[12]

Only two contemporary references to this killing have yet been located, one strangely enough in the popular *Daily Picayune* of New Orleans. The report was a mere one-sentence statement in the Texas news column: "Bill Buchanan was killed recently in De Witt county." Unfortunately, the *Picayune*, obviously thinking Buchanan was sufficiently known to Texas readers, made no further comment upon the killing.[13] The second reference came from the pen of Senator B. J. Pridgen himself. Although Taylor partisan Day clearly stated that Pridgen shot Buchanan,

Senator Bolivar J. Pridgen. *Courtesy the Western History Collections, University of Oklahoma.*

Pridgen himself denied any involvement. Written to the editor of the *Cuero Weekly Star* on the fourth of June from his home on Price's Creek, he began his letter of denial stating he had been "creditably informed that certain malicious persons are connecting my name with the killing of Wm. Buchanan on the evening of 17th of May last, ..." He continued his denial by stating these malicious persons were also connecting his name with "a band of armed men seeking the lives of citizens generally, and particularly that I have made threats against one Thompson Brown," the husband of his cousin Lucinda. Pridgen claimed there was no truth in such statements, no foundation in truth at all. And he was not yet through with his denial: "I have not killed any one or attempted to kill any one; and no living mortal can truthfully say that I ever made threats against the life of any one." Pridgen, seemingly now vying for sympathy, claimed he was merely staying at home, "struggling to make an honest living for myself and orphan children." He denied bearing arms against anyone since January 2, 1874, when the second treaty of peace was signed, "nor have I plotted or plan[n]ed armed expeditions against the life of any one, nor do I contemplate any such lawlessness." Any rumors or statements to the contrary were "mere malicious falsehoods, gotten up by parties of a guilty conscience and evil disposition." Pridgen concluded that it was perhaps Thompson Brown himself who presumed that he meant "evil towards him and those connected with the conspiracy to assassinate me."[14] To make the family feud appellation complete, Thompson Brown was the husband of Lucinda E. Pridgen, a sister of Gus Pridgen; Thompson Brown's sister Nancy Ann had married Francis M. Buchanan, the father of Billy, the man Bolivar Pridgen denied having killed. Even with Hardin and Jim Taylor out of the country, the feud continued. Billy Buchanan's role as a feudist was minor indeed, as apparently his participation was limited to a failed attempt to lead several of the Taylor party into an ambush. He was killed for that one act of treachery.[15]

Although Reuben H. Brown seemingly was effective as Cuero's city marshal, he now chose to quit the position. Was it because he was now the head of the Sutton party, and he feared for his life? Whatever the real reason, he resigned his position on June 8, 1874. What he told the mayor and council members relevant to his resignation is unknown; the newspaper only learned it was due to personal considerations. The *Star* reported he had served "in his office to the satisfaction of all, and it is regretted generally that he resigned." Perhaps the personal considerations involved his brothers and the women they had married, women named Taylor. Whatever the real reason for his resignation, Reuben H. Brown proved he had the potential to reduce the violence by his arrest of Bill Taylor, thus earning as well the sizeable reward.

With Bill Taylor delivered to Indianola as a prisoner to stand trial, so soon after the killing of Sutton and Slaughter, citizens of Indianola became acutely aware of the problems in DeWitt County, and perhaps feared the feud violence would soon be common in Calhoun County. People expected "hot times" to occur when the trial began, hence many felt justified in requesting the governor to send troops. A group of concerned citizens wrote Governor Coke but did not receive a prompt reply. So they wrote to the *Galveston Daily News* stressing the disturbed conditions and bewailing the fact that legitimate business was nearly at a standstill and that businessmen could not show any favoritism, for if they did, "they know not at what moment they may be burned out or assassinated." The remedy, they believed, was to station a company of United States troops at Cuero to assist the sheriff as needed and to preserve order.[16]

Although the specific communication that had reached the desk of Governor Coke has not been preserved, it is clear that Coke realized something had to be done at his level, and soon. Public opinion considered local authorities either unable or unwilling to solve the festering troubles between the Sutton and

Taylor factions. Reinstating the State Police force created by his predecessor Gov. Edmund J. Davis was out of the question, in spite of that organization's best intentions. Instead, Coke's efforts now turned to the creation of a new body of fighting men, a force that would not only provide protection to the frontier counties in the western portion of the state, but would also provide relief to beleaguered interior counties. The Frontier Battalion, composed of six companies to deal with the "Indian problem," had been created in April 1874, but it soon became apparent that in certain areas of the state additional forces were needed. The governor now created the Washington County Volunteer Militia, Company A, and its first assignment was to bring at least a semblance of peace to DeWitt County.

Governor Coke chose Leander H. McNelly to lead the new militia company. He was a veteran of four years fighting for the Confederacy. During the five years after the war he worked his plantation and began a family near Burton, in Washington County. Governor Davis had selected him to be one of the first four captains of the State Police Force in 1870. As State Police Captain he had earned the respect of not only law-abiding people across the state, but also of lawbreakers. McNelly's first assignment as captain of the Washington County militia, after mustering in the men he wanted, was to stop the violence in DeWitt County. Soon the eyes of Texas would be watching to see what he could accomplish.

Word reached the editors of the *Austin Daily Statesman*, who reported on the fourteenth of July, 1874, that "a company is forming in Washington county, under State authority, to assist the civil officers of DeWitt county in enforcing quiet and obedience to law in that desperado ridden section." Editor John Cardwell commented that that was "a move in the right direction."[17] Two days later a follow-up item announced that McNelly was to command the company raised, and that they "will go to DeWitt to assist in restoring order."[18] In McNelly's

Capt. L. H. McNelly, as a State Police Captain in early 1873. From the original cabinet card made in Montreal, Canada, by James Inglis. *Courtesy The Texas Ranger Hall of Fame and Museum, Waco.*

home county of Washington, the county seat newspaper the *Brenham Daily Banner* reported that McNelly was to raise a company of men "for the purpose of enforcing the laws in DeWitt county." *Banner* editor and proprietor J. G. Rankin commented, perhaps with a smirk, that this provided "a chance for courageous young men to show their patriotism and pluck" because the Taylor and Sutton "bands of outlaws, against whom they are to operate, are said to be 'true grit.'"[19] Outside the immediate area of DeWitt, Gonzales, and Karnes counties, many respected citizens considered the feuding men on both sides as outlaws.

Governor Coke had pondered what to do about DeWitt County for some time, but the lynching of the three men near Clinton forced him to act. Only after learning of the Clinton tragedy did the governor take action. He ordered Adj. Gen. William Steele to report to DeWitt County and personally investigate the situation. He was to determine if it was indeed necessary to call up the militia to preserve peace and arrest lawbreakers. Apparently Governor Coke did not consider declaring martial law in DeWitt County, as his predecessor had done in several counties in times of lawlessness. In July, while McNelly was still raising his company, Adjutant General Steele began his investigation, determined to learn first-hand how serious conditions were in the feud country.

Steele arrived in Cuero by stage on July 2, 1874, and began meeting with various individuals. He interviewed citizens of Clinton, Cuero, Victoria. and Indianola. Cuero's *Weekly Star* interviewed Steele as well, reporting that he "made a favorable impression ... , and it is generally presumed that he will pursue a judicious and effective course in the premises."[20] Among his findings, Steele reported that the sheriff intended to resign unless he received help. DeWitt County Sheriff William J. Weisiger, recognizing he did not have the support of the community, was virtually impotent, unable to hire deputies to handle what Steele called the "emergency." A local correspondent, identified only as "DeWitt," wrote that the sheriff's resignation was desired by many, the "good and law-abiding citizens of this county have hoped for this event until they have despaired. There is no such good luck in store for us as the resignation of the Sheriff."[21] This unknown correspondent claimed that the three who had

George Culver Tennille, killed resisting arrest in a Gonzales County pasture in 1874. *Courtesy Mrs. Ray Caffall.*

been lynched were "notorious criminals" and that White was "a bad man—a refugee [fugitive] from justice from Mississippi" and that the hands of two of them "had been stained by the blood of innocent men, and theft had been their occupation for the past year."[22] Typically, DeWitt provided nothing more than the accusation against the victims.

Between Steele's investigative visit to the feud country and his return to Austin the Taylor side lost another man to violence. Missouri native George Culver Tennille, born on December 29,

1825, was twice the age of many of the young feudists. Soon after George's birth the family relocated to Texas with Stephen F. Austin's third colony. Tennille, by 1870, was well established: his real estate valued at $10,000 and his personal estate valued at $2,000. His family consisted of wife Amanda Jane and their five children. In the same household lived Joe Clements, the husband of George's eldest daughter Sarah Jane, then fifteen.[23] Although Tennille may have advised the young feudists in some of their actions, no record shows him actively fighting. In fact, his record shows only one blemish, that of an indictment charging him with the theft of a gelding, and that was in DeWitt County back in 1871. As an essential member of the Taylor faction, he had signed both treaties of peace, indicating his willingness to fight, and that was no doubt the real reason he was marked for death.

McNelly's lieutenant, T. C. "Pidge" Robinson, handled the captain's paper work, and when not on a scout after wanted men he wrote letters from DeWitt County during the second half of 1874. They are most valuable as they provide first-hand accounts of the workings of the feud by one who was there and who recorded his observations almost immediately. His seven letters (and one poem) were written between August 4 and December 5, 1874. The letters were all printed in the *Daily Democratic Statesman* of Austin.[24]

Ranger-reporter Pidge was well aware of Tennille, if not of his influence, then his reputation, as he identified him by name in one letter to the *Statesman* when he referred to the siege of Tumlinson's house back in December 1873. Pidge wrote that it was a "difficult job for the sheriff to get up a *posse*, for was not Wes. Hardin there? And George Tennell [*sic*]? And many more, who in the impressive language of this country, were 'bad ones?'"[25] On his way out of Texas, Hardin and companion Mac Young stopped at Gonzales to say goodbye to a friend, Tip Davis. "George Tennille went part of the way with us," Hardin wrote, "and when we bid him good-bye it was for the last time."[26] Like John Wesley Hardin, and Bill Sutton before him, Tennille considered leaving the country but failed to do so quickly enough. Gonzales County Sheriff Green DeWitt attempted to arrest Tennille on the old charge of theft of a gelding. On the eighth of July, the twenty-man posse found Tennille at the ranch of John Runnels on Five Mile Creek, only a few miles from the DeWitt County line in Gonzales County. Tennille resisted the posse's demands to surrender, no doubt figuring he would be shot to death or lynched and chose to go down fighting. After exchanging a number of shots with the posse, his rifle failed on a defective cartridge. He managed to eject it and was ready to fire again when a bullet hit him, proving to be a mortal wound.[27]

Two days later, on the tenth of July, Steele arrived back in Austin and reported "unfavorably on the position of affairs in DeWitt county." The Taylor party was "hiding in the brush, but may gather head and avenge themselves on the Sutton party." Even though the only Sutton involved in the feud was four months dead, his followers were still considered even by state officials as "the Sutton party." Such reports provided exciting news for area newspapers, such as the *Statesman* of Austin and the *Herald* and *Express* of San Antonio. These reports provided considerable attention to the troubles, giving statewide notoriety to the feudists.

Steele's written report has survived and is most revealing. Having interviewed numerous individuals in various counties he could not help but come to some conclusions as to the cause of the vendetta and its continuation, if indeed there was one single cause. According to Steele, the cause of the feud could be traced back to State Police Capt. Jack Helm, explaining that the *"present state of violence had its origin in the operations of Jack Helm, a sheriff appointed by Gen'l. J. J. Reynolds, and afterward made Capt. Of State Police under Gov. Davis"* [emphasis added]. Steele explained that it was

Tom Tennille, who lost his father, G. C. Tennille, during the feud. *Courtesy Mrs. Francis Hartmann.*

only necessary for an individual to be pointed out as a cattle thief or "bad man" and he would be arrested and started off to Helena, then the county seat of neighboring Karnes County, "for trial by Court Martial; but the greater portion of those who started for Helena never reached that point but were reported as escaped, though never heard of since."[28]

If Governor Coke had any doubts about sending McNelly's Rangers into DeWitt County before receiving Steele's report, they quickly vanished with the conclusion that

> nothing short of an armed force from Some other locality & having no interest in the feuds or quarrels of that county, and of sufficient strength (not less than fifty) to ensure the safety of prisoners against mob violence and to aid in making arrests, will put a stop to the existing state of violence in DeWitt County. At present the courts are powerless against these armed & organized parties. Indeed so great is the fear of assassination that was stated to me, that no information on which to base an indictment could be found in the case of a murder to which there was not less than forty witnesses.[29]

The murder Steele referred to was the brutal killing of one of Senator Bolivar J. Pridgen's former slaves, Abram Bryant, also identified as "Abraham Pickens" or simply "Old Uncle Abraham." The killing took place the night of July 2, 1874, by a mob looking for Pridgen. The old black man refused to divulge the whereabouts of his former master and was taken to the Guadalupe River where he was killed, his body disemboweled and the remains tossed in the water. Twenty-seven men were indicted for this brutal killing, the indictment stating that the conspirators did "fix, tie and fasten, and then and there with the rope aforesaid bind [and] did drag, pull, choke, strangle and dislocate the neck, of which ... Abram Bryant, then and there instantly died. ..." The indicted men were Joseph Tumlinson, Joseph DeMoss, William Meador, Gus Tumlinson, John Tumlinson, Peter Tumlinson, John Meador, Addison Patterson, James E. Smith, W. W. Peavy, "Zan" (Dan or Zann?) Peavy,[30] W. C. Wallace, John Powers, Buck Powers, Ed Parkinson, Addison Kilgore, Christopher T. Hunter, J. W. Ferguson, William Cox, Andrew Newman, Joseph I. Sitterle, David Haldeman, William T. Petit, Andrew Jordan, Jeff White, W. H. Lackie, and James Mason. Among the first actions Captain McNelly took on his arrival was to meet with U.S. Deputy Marshal E. S. Roberts who requested his assistance in serving papers on those indicted for the murder of Bryant. McNelly believed serving the papers had been done just in time. "These writs," he wrote in a communication to Adjutant General Steele, "include all of the leading spirits of the Tomlinson [sic] party and I think have been issued just in time for old 'Joe' has just joined church and I think must be meditating the death of some preacher or some kindred amusement. I have been more on the alert than ever." Nevertheless, no one was ever punished for the murder of Abram Bryant.[31]

McNelly's orders were definite and clear-cut: he was to act at all times in "strict subordination" to the sheriff and civil authorities; he should be accompanied by the sheriff or some other peace officer and have a *capias* or legal warrant from the proper authority in making an arrest; in making an arrest he was to take care not to transgress the limits of the law; peace and tranquility must be preserved. The most rigid discipline was to be maintained among his men, essentially to avoid showing any favoritism to members of either faction. Obviously Steele, keenly aware of the numerous prisoners killed while in custody— most recently during the June 21–22 lynching in Clinton— wanted McNelly's conduct to be exemplary to counteract the harm done by such men as Jack Helm and his associates.

McNelly, at the head of his militia company of forty young men, arrived in Clinton on August 1, 1874, and found that a "perfect reign of terror existed" not only in DeWitt County but in surrounding counties as well. He found that

> armed bands of men were making predatory excursions through the country, overawing the law-abiding Citizens while the civil authorities were unable, or unwilling to enforce the laws framed for their protection. The lives of peaceful citizens who had given no cause of offense to either party, were in jeopardy, as neutrals were considered obnoxious to both factions.[32]

McNelly realized there were two distinct groups, neither one being more law-abiding than the other, in his opinion. He learned of the various treaties, and commented

> From the facility with which treaties of peace and compromises had been broken, confidence in each other's respective promises, was a thing un Known [*sic*]. The Sutton party on my arrival numbered about 100 men (they claimed 150) and were defiant and triumphant. The strength of the opposing Taylor faction could not at that time be definitely ascertained as their main strength lay in the adjoining counties of Gonzales and Lavaca and they Kept up no regularly organized force. They can at this time bring into the field about 100 well armed men.[33]

Captain McNelly certainly realized his small militia would have little chance of success in stopping a fight if the opposing forces entered into a pitched battle, or if either party engaged him. McNelly was there to prevent bloodshed, but would that be possible with only forty men in his command?

John Milam Taylor, subject of a Tumlinson ambush while in Captain McNelly's custody. From the original photograph by E. Nau, Yorktown. *Courtesy the Robert G. McCubbin Collection.*

If indeed the Sutton party was acting "defiant and trium-
phant" as McNelly believed, that may explain why three of the
Taylor party came to his camp seeking protection on the night
of August 5: rancher John Milam Taylor, an uncle of Bill Taylor;
Lodwick "Hun" Tuggle, brother of the recently lynched "Kute"
Tuggle; and blacksmith Martin V. King.[34] After finding protection among the Rangers, for an unknown reason Taylor decided
to leave, perhaps deciding McNelly's small company inadequate
if the Suttons really wanted him, and returned to his home in
Yorktown. Three nights later, on the eighth, McNelly sent out
Sgt. Charles M. Middleton[35] with three privates to take Taylor
to Clinton to give testimony in an upcoming trial. They secured
him with no problem, but returning to camp they rode into an
ambush. About eight miles from Ranger headquarters a party
of fifteen armed men stopped them. One of them shouted out,
"Who are you?" Middleton—with no hesitation—responded in
kind with the same query, "Who are you?" That simple verbal
exchange was enough talk for fighting men. Gunfire erupted;
someone yelled out "*Que dow*" ("Look out") and "here they are
boys give 'em hell."[36] Under fire Middleton and his men quickly
dismounted and sought shelter behind a fence along one side
of the road. Private John Chalk was disabled when he received
a ball through the shoulder. The battle lasted between ten and
fifteen minutes. The attacking party had a distinct advantage, as
they were hiding amidst some trees, "they being in the shade
and my men behind a fence [they] were placed at quite a disadvantage and only succeeded in putting two holes through their
hats and wounding one of their horses." Taylor fled at first fire,
knowing full well that he would be killed if captured, and he
ran off through the trees. The battle subsided, probably because
they had observed Taylor escaping, and then the attacking party
"pretended to discover that it was my men and at once stopped."
They then provided assistance to the wounded Private Chalk
and loaned McNelly's men horses to replace the two that had

been shot. Taylor was taken up by McNelly the next morning, and by then he had determined that the attacking party was commanded by Joe Tumlinson himself. McNelly believed that the principle reason for Tumlinson wanting to kill Taylor was that he could provide damaging testimony against them for the killing of Senator Bolivar Pridgen's former slave, Abram Bryant.[37]

Pidge met Captain Tumlinson, and if not actually getting to know the old Indian fighter, at least became acquainted with his reputation. Pidge, reverting to his mock-epic satirical style, compared him to Robinson Crusoe,

> with a gun on each shoulder and two Smith & Wesson's [revolvers] in his belt. I had the pleasure of seeing this gentleman a few days since; he has the frosts of sixty winters on his head, and green spectacles on his nose, and, it is said, can see with his naked eye farther than any hawk this side the Rio Grande; when he gets on his spectacles there is no telling what he can see, as he magnified five of the company who were traveling the road into an ambuscade of the Taylor party.[38]

Pidge delighted in describing the scene of the ambush by Tumlinson's party: "I was ordered to take a guard and escort John Taylor to what was formerly his home," he wrote, continuing:

> On the route we passed the battle ground; there had been differences of opinion among us as regarded the weapons with which Tomlinson's [sic] mob were armed, but all doubts are now removed; from the appearance of the fence behind which Taylor and his small guard took refuge, I should say they are provided with Gatlin guns. ... You ought to behold a few of the double-barreled ducking pieces which are carried by those

who own the strongest horses; they have barrels about
the size and length of the smoke stack press room
engine, and when they go off they wake the dead.
One would easily blow an ordinary sized individual
clear out of DeWitt County.[39]

And John Taylor, who was the intended victim of the Tumlinson
ambush, received mention by Pidge as well. He was back in
McNelly's camp, along with Lodwick "Hun" Tuggle[40] and Martin
V. King. John Taylor, "when on foot, reminds one strongly of
an old sundried bucket about to fall to pieces; when on horseback his powers of endurance are almost incredible."[41]

As Pidge observed in his letter written August 4, men did not
wear their pistols openly, but rather, "They have a cute way
to carry their six-shooters around here without breaking the
law." How? "Every man carries his coat tied behind his saddle, and in its folds is a peace preserver of the Smith & Wesson
persuasion, ready at all times to demonstrate to any officious
individual that his views on certain questions are not sound, and
his argumentative position untenable unless he is behind a tree."
Further, Pidge went on in typical mock-serious fashion, various
reports from Clinton were exaggerated, as "the citizens seem
to be anxious for peace and quietness, and some are ready to
fight for both at any time." Pidge found the Clinton jail conditions were worse than the Travis County jail, "for stench, filth
and general nastiness." Ten prisoners were confined in the jail,
one "very unjustly," as he had attempted to kill his mother-
in-law, "which is, or ought to be, justifiable homicide."[42] The
letters from Pidge, discussing the social conditions in DeWitt
County and in particular animosities between the feuding parties, brought additional statewide attention to the violence.

Pidge was keenly aware that the troubles would not be easily
settled. He was highly literate, and seeing the conflict first-hand
brought back to him his early years when he was in Virginia,

where he became acquainted with many of the great literary works of English poets and novelists. In fact, he paraphrased lines from Samuel Taylor Coleridge's epic *The Rime of the Ancient Mariner*:

> It was an ancient farmer man,
>   And he stoppeth one of three:
> "By thy Colt's improved and Henry gun
>   I pray thee tell to me
> If you belong to the Sutton gang
>   Or the Taylor companie?"

If the readers of the *Statesman* were not familiar with the work of Samuel Taylor Coleridge, they could at least appreciate the literary license of Pidge Robinson. Thanks to his contributions to the Austin *Statesman*, we have today reports of the actions of the feudists from the viewpoint of an observer who was not related to members of either feuding group. No other Texas feud had a writer like Pidge.

William Taylor's trial at Indianola for the Slaughter killing began on Wednesday, September 23, 1874. After opening arguments, Adj. Gen. William Steele addressed the court as to why there were armed men stationed in the court yard. Enough officials as well as private citizens had pointed out to the governor the possibility of an attempt either to release the prisoner by his friends or to lynch him by his enemies. Therefore his orders were to guard the prisoner "safely from both friends or foes, and see that the majesty of the law was upheld." Judge T. C. Barden then thanked the general and the governor and "expressed his gratification at the determination to see justice done, and directed the Sheriff to call upon the soldiers, if they were needed."[44] The next day the cases were called of the *State vs. James Taylor and William Taylor*. Attorney William H. Crain announced the State ready for trial in regard to prisoner William

William H. Crain, whose life was saved by Bill Taylor. *Courtesy Texas State Library and Archives Commission.*

Taylor, but asked that papers be sent to every county in Texas for the arrest of James Taylor. Taylor's defense counsel, made up of Colonel Slater of Victoria, Colonel Jockey of DeWitt County, and General Woodward of Calhoun County, then made an application for continuance.

Their reasons consisted of not having had adequate time to prepare his defense and the absence of witnesses Neill Bowen, Mannen Clements, and Thomas Caffall, all of Gonzales County. By their testimony Taylor would "prove he did not wound, injure, assault or in any manner harm William Sutton, with the killing of whom he is charged" and "that he was not present at the time and place at which said Sutton was killed [and] for those reasons a continuance was requested until the next term of court." Taylor was granted a continuance.[45] The steamboat *Morgan* was readied to transport Taylor back to Galveston jail on the twenty-fifth of September. From the court house to the wharf the guards were escorted by the Indianola brass band and a large group of citizens. Attorney Crain took the opportunity to address the guards, complimenting them on their conduct and their effectiveness in preventing any disturbances. At 3:00 p.m. the *Morgan* left Indianola to deliver Taylor back to Galveston jail.[46]

John M. Taylor was scheduled to be a defense witness for Bill Taylor. With the trial delayed he had nothing to do but return home to Yorktown, or else to McNelly's camp. On the twenty-fifth, Corporal L. P. Ellis and other men of McNelly's command, guarding the witness, were met by members of the Tumlinson party, ex-city marshal Brown and several others, as they were preparing to leave Indianola. The Rangers were ready, and perhaps eager, to fight. McNelly reported the incident to his superior: "Some of the Tumlinson party (headed by Rube Brown) threaten[ed] to kill Taylor & was only prevented from douing [*sic*] So by my guards drawing their pistols & threatening to Shoot anyone that attempted to come into the caboose car that my men occupied by my order." Brown later apologized to McNelly for his behavior, explaining that he and the others were drunk at the time. Perhaps McNelly forced them to apologize; nevertheless, McNelly admitted: "but I constantly fear a reancontre [*sic*] under just some like circumstances."[47]

Due to the delay in the trial the plans of others were disrupted. Pidge noted this in a letter, stating that John Taylor, Bill Taylor's uncle, had left the camp where he had been staying for some time and returned to his home. Ironically he lived not far from Capt. Joe Tumlinson, "one of the earliest settlers of the country." Then, Joe Tumlinson "has just sent to camp for a guard to keep the Taylors off. A guard is now at Taylor's to keep the Tomlinsons [*sic*] off. [Martin V.] King wants one to keep the Suttons off, and we have to mount one in camp to keep them all off." Young Pidge could find humor in any situation.[48]

Towards the end of 1874 a quietude did fall on the feuding families, most likely because McNelly's men were continually on the scout, making themselves highly visible. The weather helped at times; Pidge commented on the heavy rains, which caused the Guadalupe to overflow its banks. "Things seem to have taken a more quiet turn down here of late, though it may be the slumbering of the volcano before the eruption. The Guadalupe river is the only thing that has been on a rise lately, and has interfered somewhat with the usual pastime of night riding in this vicinity; it has been higher than ever known, ..." Between Clinton and Cuero there was "a perfect sea" forcing people to visit the town in boats, as Pidge described the situation.[49] McNelly informed Adjutant General Steele of the changed atmosphere: "Everything seems very quiet at present. I continue to send out 'scouts' in squads of four or five (four or five squads at a time) instructed to ride in a particular course ... and to approach towns and country stores in an unexpected manner as possible." McNelly found that the system did "a great deal of good and disperses congregations of these parties that usually meet at 'grog shops' to have difficulties or concoct devilment." Most of the men who had not welcomed McNelly's troops were "under indictment in some part of the State" and scattered when they heard of McNelly's men approaching.[50]

Another possible reason for events taking "a more quiet turn" was that McNelly placed certain Rangers in the homes of members of the feuding parties. Although McNelly did not report this detail to his superiors, Private William L. Rudd later told of it to a San Antonio *Express* reporter, Mrs. G. C. Mayfield. Her article was later reprinted in the popular twentieth-century

Frontier Times periodical. Ranger Rudd recalled that he was first quartered in the home of Captain Tumlinson, "the head of the Sutton party," and also was responsible for "making friends" in the home of Senator Pridgen, "who was just as strong a member of the Taylor party!" Unfortunately no further details of this effort of McNelly have been preserved.[51]

Not surprisingly, Pidge determined the feuding situation was not only among members of specific families who had wrongs to avenge. "This is also a family feud," he wrote, "and they are arrayed against each other in the opposing parties, from children of the same parents down to fourth cousins and step-neighbors-in-law, there are *a great* many strangers, too, among them."[52] The strangers were no doubt brought in as hired guns.

Pidge stressed to his readers, and perhaps to some of the feuding men as well, that he and the Rangers were there to act as neutrals and prevent violence. But young Pidge could not help but notice the fairer sex, writing that there were "a great many very handsome women and there are some Clinton belles whose beauty cannot be surpassed." The Rangers were treated very kindly, "by the members of both parties and what few neutrals there are left." All things considered, the Rangers were enjoying a very pleasant time, in spite of being "besieged by the henchmen of the opposing factions," but when this happened, they "put on a wise and knowing look, shake our heads and say, … 'let us have peace,' gentlemen of the Taylor party, keep yourselves calm and cool, friends of the Sutton band. …"[53] At least while the Rangers were there, the opposing forces were able, for the most part, to control their emotions, and their weapons.

Until the death of William E. Sutton, Joe Tumlinson had remained a secondary figure in the feud. With Sutton's death in early 1874, many considered it was now a feud between the Taylors and Capt. Joe Tumlinson's associates. Pidge came to know him as "Uncle Joe" and wrote that he had been "convicted, converted, baptized, and received into the church, and is considered by his friends to be sincere." Tumlinson's health was failing and he may have expected death was imminent. He was considered, Pidge wrote, a "soon one" by his friends and enemies. He impressed Pidge, who described him as "an old Indian fighter, and has a military head with no hair on it; ... [Tumlinson is] sixty-four years old and 'can ride a horse over any ground.'" Shortly after Pidge composed these lines Tumlinson did pass on, with his boots off, dying of natural causes on November 23, 1874.[54] Editor Rudolph Kleberg reported his demise, calling him a Texas veteran, a pioneer, and a man who was "fearless." He had been baptized only a few days prior to his passing, and met death "with the same calmness with which he had so often faced it in battle with the treacherous Indians and Mexicans." Tumlinson was buried with full Masonic honors, "mourned by his family and his many friends to whom his aged arm was still a strong protection."[55]

During the final months of 1874 it was apparent that McNelly would not be remaining in DeWitt County. Although the violence had decreased during his tenure there, the feud would continue; he had not caused the feuding parties to cease their grudges, only forced them to hold their hatreds in abeyance, creating a small degree of tranquility. In one sense McNelly failed in DeWitt County. He had not captured John Wesley Hardin nor James Creed Taylor, whom he considered were the leaders of the Taylor party, as they in fact were. The arrest of Bill Taylor was not accomplished by his Rangers. He did protect the court when in session, but none of the leading figures of the feud stood trial in DeWitt County. Governor Coke certainly realized these factors, and weighed them when making his decision as to keep McNelly in DeWitt County or send him elsewhere, to the Rio Grande frontier. During the winter McNelly spent some time in his home county of Washington, and some time meeting with his superiors in Austin. The company was left in DeWitt County during the winter months with Pidge

Robinson in charge. With merchants in Clinton expressing concern about payments for the company's supplies, rumors increased that the company would be disbanded. Such rumors reached the editors of the San Antonio *Express*, who expressed their dissatisfaction with the situation, criticizing Governor Coke, but not McNelly himself. The troops,

> organized with such a flourish at the beginning of Coke's reign, are to be withdrawn soon and disbanded. The Legislature gets the credit of doing it, because they failed to make the requisite appropriation to keep these troops in the field. During the winter there was little use for these troops on the frontier, and Coke used them as a kind of state police force to regulate some of his unruly partisans in DeWitt county and elsewhere.[56]

McNelly had been well received in the turmoil of the feud, at least by those citizens who wanted the violence to stop, and he would indeed be missed. Editor S. Lee Kyle of Hallettsville, Lavaca County, noted that he was due a "deserved compliment," not only to him as captain but also his officers and men, who had been on duty the last six months. Kyle kept himself well informed on the violence in neighboring DeWitt County. He knew McNelly, and no doubt knew the Kellys, or at least knew of that family's tragedy. "We knew Capt. McNally [*sic*] well as a gallant, enterprising and accomplished Confederate officer, while he served on the staff of the heroic [General Thomas] Green; and we know that no change of circumstances could make of him anything but a gallant soldier, and a most courteous and accomplished gentleman."[57]

Grave marker of Jim Taylor, killed with Arnold and Hendricks in 1875. Note crossed rifles at the top of the stone. *Courtesy Robert W. Shook.*

CHAPTER EIGHT

Bloody 1875

"A party of five men entered Ryan's saloon and killed
Reuben Brown ... a member of the Sutton party. His body
was riddled with balls. ... Marshal Brown was the man who
arrested Taylor for the murder of Sutton."
—New York Times, NOVEMBER 19, 1875

In spite of McNelly's good work in DeWitt County, he received criticism from some, and surprisingly from Sen. B. J. Pridgen. The senator had written to Governor Coke asking for Rangers to protect him and his family. The governor turned the note over to McNelly who responded on March 3, 1875, reminding the senator that there had been a guard at his house "continuous since last Aug. (1874) and of such strength as your family asked for." McNelly indicated the guard would remain there and felt satisfied the senator's family would be safe. In the same letter he indicated his surprise—but not anger—in learning of the senator's letter published in the *Pittsburg Dispatch* newspaper claiming that "parties had sought protection in my camp" but had not received it, and indicating that McNelly had been "very remiss" in performing his duty. McNelly pointed out that Pridgen certainly knew that charge was false and expected it to be corrected in the same newspaper.[1]

In spite of unwarranted criticism, McNelly felt confident about the situation in DeWitt County. His continuous Ranger patrols had obviously proved effective in reducing the violence between the two feuding groups, mainly because of his presence. Obtaining funds from the legislature to keep the company in the field had never been easy, and during the early months of 1875 the possibility of McNelly's company being drastically reduced in numbers or disbanded altogether was ever present. On March 4 McNelly wrote and complained to Adjutant General Steele that it was becoming more and more difficult for Clinton merchants to accept warrants for the company's necessary supplies due to uncertainty about how long the company would remain in DeWitt County. But he was able to conclude his letter with an optimistic "All quiet."[2]

Steele responded and ordered McNelly to buy only what was absolutely necessary for immediate use. If no appropriation came from the legislature to keep the company in the field, it would have to be disbanded. On the seventeenth the order arrived: he was to return the company to where it was first organized (Washington County) and muster out the men. But before this was done another order arrived: the legislature had at the last minute allocated sufficient funds to keep the company intact. But now it was ordered to go elsewhere: he could not remain in the feud country. On Good Friday, raiders from south of the Rio Grande had attacked the little community of Nuecestown, only a few miles from Corpus Christi. Nueces County residents then formed into mobs, intending to protect their lives and property at any cost. Due to the increasing troubles on the Rio Grande border and McNelly's effectiveness in DeWitt County, the Washington County militia company was sent to the border. South Texas ranchers could rejoice at McNelly's arrival, but what would happen in DeWitt County in his absence?

Feudist Bill Taylor still was in custody in the Galveston County jail, waiting for yet another chance to gain his freedom through a verdict of not guilty or even to escape. As the Galveston jail was one of the more secure jails in the state, his chances for escape were slim indeed. John Wesley Hardin, who had broken his brother-in-law out of the Gonzales jail, was unable to do so, as he had left Texas. But on the other hand, perhaps Taylor felt he could beat this charge. After all, previous court cases had been in his favor: he had been charged with carrying a pistol several times, but that amounted to nothing of great import. He had stood trial twice for theft of a steer and found not guilty.[3] Perhaps with good attorneys he could stand trial on this charge and be found not guilty as well. After all, Sutton and Slaughter were both armed, so a good case could be made for "self defense." But at his first trial for the killing of Sutton, he was found guilty. The verdict resulted in a sentence of ten years in the penitentiary. He still had to stand trial for the killing of Slaughter, so instead of going to Huntsville prison he was returned to the secure jail in Galveston.[4]

While Bill Taylor was confined behind the bars of Galveston jail, other legal events were taking place within the city itself. Twenty-two prisoners and thirty witnesses from DeWitt County and the surrounding area arrived for the trial of men "styled as kuklux." They were charged with "depriving the citizens of that section of country from the peaceful enjoyment of their rights and liberties." More specifically, they were charged with the murder of Senator Pridgen's former slave, Abram Bryant. This was a remarkable action: the killing of a former slave, in a formerly Rebel state, arousing such indignation leading to such a charge, that the rights and liberties of good citizens had been disturbed. No doubt the genesis of this action came from Senator Pridgen. The brutal murder of his servant became an excuse for him to combat his enemies (Sutton followers) in a court room setting, rather than attempting to destroy them through ambush or gunfight. Legal action was easier to control. Those charged had no connection to the Ku Klux Klan; the *News* was merely utilizing such terminology for publicity.

Galveston's *News* explained that the "movement" that resulted in their arrest and appearance "had its birth in the enmity long existing between the Sutton and Taylor-Pridgen parties."

A summary of the feud, amounting to a very brief feud history, followed in the columns of the *News,* which placed its origins back in the fall of 1868 when Charley Taylor "stole a number of cattle" from the widow Thomas. It was then that William Sutton "determined to avenge her wrongs" and pursued Taylor, with the result being the death of Taylor in Bastrop. Back in Clinton, Bill Sutton and Buck Taylor confronted each other, the gunfight ending with the death of Taylor and Dick Chisholm. The newspaper described other events including the killing of Major Thompson, the killing of Hays Taylor, and the killing of the Kelly brothers by Sutton, Meador, and White. The Kellys had "fired into a circus a few miles south of Cuero." This killing, still according to the *News* reporter, "gave a new phase to the whole affair" and resulted in continued defiance of the law, threats, and attempts at assassination between members of the two parties. The Sutton party and the Taylor-Pridgen party were the two contending forces. With the wounding of Sutton, the killing of Helm, Cox, and Christman, and the killing of Wiley Pridgen the last day of 1873, a compromise was agreed upon. But then William Sutton was killed.

What the *News* did not report in this early but brief history of the feud was that those named in the indictment had wanted to kill Bolivar J. Pridgen. Not finding where Pridgen was, they allegedly captured a former Pridgen slave, Abram Bryant, and murdered him when he would not reveal where the senator was. The twenty-two indicted as Ku Klux, men all allied with the Sutton side, were identified as Joseph Sitterle, Addison Kilgore, John J. Meador, W. C. Wallace, Joseph DeMoss, Buck Powers, John Powers, Peter Tumlinson, W. W. Peavy, Zan Peavy, Andrew Jordan, William Cox, Andrew Newman, W. P. Meador, William Pettit, Gus Tumlinson, Addison Patterson, Charley Lips, James Mason, Jeff White, J. W. Ferguson, and John Tumlinson. The *News* not only identified the men but also indicated where they resided.[5]

Returned to Indianola for trial, Bill Taylor no doubt pondered what he would do if found guilty of the murder of Slaughter. If he somehow escaped confinement it would be wise to leave the state. John Wesley Hardin had left Texas, and apparently few people even knew where he was. No one came to break Taylor out, but he was fortunate, as on September 15, 1875, during his trial, a hurricane struck the city of Indianola, then the most important port along the Gulf. As water continued to rise, Calhoun County Sheriff Fred L. Busch became concerned for the prisoners' safety, finally bringing them to the court house, to be guarded by deputies. However, as the storm continued, and the threatening waters endangered everyone's lives, the concerns for guarding the prisoners diminished. Both Taylor and another prisoner, Joe Blackburn, on trial for stage rob-bery and murder, their chains off, became heroes and saved numerous men and women from drowning. When the storm subsided two days later on the seventeenth, the two disarmed Sheriff Busch, took his horse, and escaped riding double. A mile from town they met freedman Guy Michot and took his horse, giving him ten dollars for the steed. Taylor told Michot to tell the sheriff they appreciated his kindnesses and that the horses and weapons would be returned, which they were.[6]

Another version of Taylor's good fortune relates how District Attorney William H. Crain himself took three prisoners from their cell, as the jailor refused to release them, fearing they would escape. Crain and the prisoners headed for the court house, but the wind blew Crain's hat off. Bill Taylor, in appreciation for some favor, gave his own to the attorney, saying, as he laughed: "Bill Crain will never prosecute me."[7] Yet another version, less plausible, has Crain himself falling into the treacherous waters and Taylor saving his life.[8] Another account, provided by John Fitzhenry, a policeman of many years experience, wrote that Taylor was released from jail, "and, with courage characteristic of these men, … dashed to the rescue of the drowning and saved dozens of lives."[9] Some hundred people were on the court house hill when the waters began to subside. Although no one can say with certainty how many people Bill Taylor and Joe Blackburn rescued, apparently a good number were in fact saved by the former prisoners. Fugitive Bill Taylor's prophecy at least came true as Crain never prosecuted him again.

After galloping away from Indianola and the people he had saved, fugitive Taylor chose to even the score with Rube Brown for the inconvenience of his arrest and incarceration. In some manner he sent word to Brown that he was marked for death, although when or how is unknown. Victor M. Rose considered Reuben H. Brown the head of the anti-Taylor party after the death of Sutton. He does not say why he determined Brown was the leader rather than Capt. Joe Tumlinson; possibly Tumlinson's health had prevented him from taking the leadership reins. Some writers have considered the feud itself more of a continuing conflict between the Taylors and the Tumlinsons, preferring to call it the "Taylor-Tumlinson Feud" rather than the more common term, "Taylor-Sutton Feud" or "Sutton-Taylor Feud."[10] Given that Rose was contemporary to the violence and knew many of the actual feudists, we will accept his determination that Reuben H. Brown was now the leader of the faction warring against the Taylors. Did Taylor make any attempt to kill Brown that was not recorded? Probably.

The Taylors did catch up with the former Cuero city marshal early on the morning of Thursday, November 18, 1875. Of course reports of the killing were not all in agreement, but what was agreed upon was that Brown was in one of the saloons of Cuero, either the Merchant's Exchange or A. G. Ryan's Saloon, dealing monte or simply playing cards, when five men entered the saloon, leveled their guns at him and blasted away. Brown was riddled with balls, an expected result with five men shooting at him. Their aim was good enough to ensure the death of Brown, but a black man—Thomas Freeman—and another were both seriously wounded.

Confusion reigned supreme in that saloon. Brown was a bloody corpse; Thomas Freeman was dying. He too would be a corpse within a few hours. The third shooting victim apparently survived his wounds. No one immediately came forth to identify the shootists, if they were even recognized. Probably the confusion was so great and the gun-smoke so thick that no one could say for sure who was involved. A report datelined Indianola stated that Brown was sitting at a table playing cards when a man walked in, "took a drink at the bar, took a look at Brown and walked out, when immediately five persons came in and commenced firing at Brown. They then dragged him outside and shot him again."[11] By this time the feud was becoming a national topic. Dispatches from Galveston reached New Orleans where they were telegraphed to New York, describing the killing as a "terrible tragedy" at Cuero. The *New York Times* stated that Freeman received two shots and was instantly killed while another was wounded in the face. Surprisingly no more than Freeman and the other unidentified man were wounded in the shooting, as "the saloon was crowded with men, both black and white."[12] The I.O.O.F. DeWitt Lodge of Cuero took charge of Brown's funeral. His remains were interred in the family cemetery some seven miles south of Clinton.[13]

Who were the assassins? In spite of the contemporary reports that five men were responsible for the shooting, Jack Hays Day wrote that only three men entered the saloon where Brown was dealing monte for a group of blacks. Day, who may have been aware of the action or even present, if not one of the assassins, indicated that most likely it was Jim Taylor who led the affray, as he had asked that he alone "be permitted to do the shooting when only one of the [Sutton] gang was to be killed." Day recalled his request as "Keep the dogs off and I'll do the rest."[14] Certainly Jim Taylor was one of the assassins; Bill Taylor was probably another, who after all had spent a year in jail thanks to Rube Brown, and he had warned Brown he would kill him. Two other men whose names now appear in the feud chronicles may have been shooting as well: A. R. Hendricks, whose origins are unknown, and Mason "Winchester Smith" Arnold, formerly of Lavaca County. The trio of Jim Taylor, A. R. Hendricks, and Mason Arnold had not acted together before, as far as known, but these three were to die together, and a later report, describing their deaths, indicated that "rumor" had it that it was Mason Arnold who had fired the first shot at the former city marshal.[15]

Mason Arnold was from Lavaca County, born circa 1848, the son of William and Ellen Arnold.[16] Like many other young Southern men, he had his own difficulties with Reconstruction government that may have been the reason he joined the Taylor party in DeWitt County. Arnold was accused of stabbing one H. M. Steinberger in Giddings, Lee County, on February 15, 1873, giving him a serious but not fatal wound.[17] Six weeks later Pvt. A. L. Roy of the State Police was on his trail, but doubted if he would catch up with him as Arnold was believed to be on the cattle trail to Kansas.[18] Private Roy may have had to give up the hunt as the police force was disbanded on April 22 of that year.

Hendricks remains a mystery figure in the history of the feud. He had served in the Confederate Army, having enlisted on August 14, 1862, at Greenville, Texas, in Company A, 2nd Texas Infantry, for the duration of the war. Taken prisoner, he was paroled on July 7, 1863, at Vicksburg. He did not return to his unit and was considered a deserter.[19] Following war's end his actions remain unknown for nearly a decade. He probably was in the Travis-Lee-Washington counties area when the call came for men to join the Ranger company, as on July 25, 1874, he enlisted with the rank of sergeant in McNelly's Washington County Volunteer Militia Company. On March 31, 1875, he was honorably discharged from McNelly's command, apparently having done nothing to warrant any special mention in McNelly's reports. During his eight months of Ranger service, Hendricks had to have learned about the various victims of the feud's violence. With such knowledge it would be unusual if he

Mason "Winchester Smith" Arnold, killed with Jim Taylor and A. R. Hendricks in 1875. *Courtesy Mary Ann Thornton.*

did not develop some opinions and feelings about the violence in general and the participants in particular, and may have actually met and developed a friendship with some. It is known that some Rangers were stationed in the homes of various feudists, thus it is probable that Hendricks may have lost his ability to remain neutral in dealing with those involved in the feud. What is certain is that he met and married one of the widows of the feud. On September 23, 1875, six months after his discharge, former McNelly Ranger A. R. Hendricks married Elizabeth Jane

Kelly, the widow of William B. Kelly, who had been killed back in August of 1870 with his brother Henry by a posse under the command of William E. Sutton. The nuptials took place in Fayette County.[20] Born Elizabeth Jane Day in 1836, she had first married Joseph W. Bennett who died mysteriously on July 9, 1862.[21] Her second husband, George W. Rivers, a musician in Company D, 5th Texas Cavalry, disappeared sometime after parole from a Union hospital.[22] She then married William B. Kelly but marital bliss eluded her when William was killed with his brother by members of the Helm-Sutton party.

If Taylor, Hendricks, and Arnold as well as others were involved in the killing of R. H. Brown, they did not have long to enjoy their "victory." With cousin Bill Taylor on the run and John Wesley Hardin hiding out in Florida with a reward of $4,000 for his arrest and confinement, Jim Taylor was now perhaps the most wanted man in Texas. As family members were well known by the authorities, he had few places to hide. That is perhaps why he believed with the right attorney he could possibly stand trial and come clear, and he contacted T. T. Teel, a very successful defense attorney. According to Jack Hays Day, Judge Teel, "one of the best criminal lawyers in the state of that day," had offered to defend Taylor free of charge. Teel had an impressive record in the court rooms; no doubt Jim Taylor believed Teel could clear his name.[23]

Jim Taylor, with Arnold and Hendricks and perhaps two or three others, appeared openly in town on the twenty-sixth of December, 1875. If Taylor met with Attorney T. T. Teel, the contemporary sources did not mention it. Others were well aware of their presence, however, and someone began the rumor that they intended to burn the court house down to destroy any papers that could be used against them. The men stabled their horses in Martin V. King's livery and were seen on the streets, well-armed, but apparently at ease.

What Jim Taylor was not aware of was the fact that his enemies were at work planning to capture or kill him, if not for the reward then at least for vengeance. Richard B. "Dick" Hudson, a strong supporter of the Suttons, acting as deputy under Sheriff Weisiger, gathered a half-dozen friends and prepared for war. The next day, the twenty-seventh, on the streets of Clinton the battle commenced: Taylor, Hendricks, Arnold, and two others —possibly Tom King, son of blacksmith Martin V. King, and "Hun" Tuggle or Ed Davis—against the Hudson posse. No one can determine which group fired the first shots, but Jim Taylor and his group were badly outnumbered. Realizing their situation, the group attempted to get to their horses in the King livery stable, but too late discovered it was locked, leaving them with no means to escape other than on foot. They had been betrayed.

The battle lasted but a few minutes. Running from the locked livery stable into a grove of trees Jim Taylor and perhaps Arnold and Hendricks received life-threatening wounds. Christopher Taylor "Kit" Hunter gave good aim with his Winchester, his shot breaking Taylor's arm. Hunter lost his hat from a shot fired by Taylor. Once wounded, and surrounded by enemies, Taylor, Hendricks, and Arnold could expect no mercy. Hudson and his party would finish them off quickly. Another shot from Kit Hunter did end the life of Jim Taylor. The bodies of Jim, the head of the Taylor party, Mason "Winchester Smith" Arnold, and A. R. Hendricks were gathered up and turned over to their friends and family for burial.

Various accounts written by contemporaries of the feud have recorded their version of the significant gun battle which ought to have ended the shooting phase of the Sutton-Taylor Feud. As to be expected, those sympathetic to the Taylors provide a version quite different from those sympathetic to the Suttons. Jack Hays Day, who believed Taylor was in Clinton that day to meet with Attorney Teel, wrote of the betrayal of Jim Taylor by Martin King. Taylor believed King was a friend and unsuspecting any treachery "was led into ambush by this Judas, about half a mile from King's house." Caught "unaware in a grove of big trees, Jim was shot to the ground. Mortally wounded he tried to fight back, but his assailants dodged behind the tree trunks, and he didn't have a chance." Before receiving the death wound he was shot in the right arm and both legs. Taylor and Arnold were both killed, and Hendricks wounded as well. On the road back to King's house someone finished off the wounded Hendricks. Day identifies one other of Taylor's party as Hun Tuggle, who, now in Jim Taylor's hour of need, chose to stay with Martin King and his life was spared. Relatives came and removed their bodies and buried them in the "old Taylor cemetery on the Guadalupe River."[24]

Lewis S. Delony, long-time DeWitt County resident and sympathetic to the Suttons, gave a different version of why Jim Taylor and several associates were in Clinton that day, in opposition to Day's statement that Jim Taylor believed Teel could clear his name.[25] According to Delony, who was raised in DeWitt County during the time of the feud, Jim Taylor, "with about forty armed men" rode into Clinton and "took possession of the town," making their headquarters at John Wofford's store diagonally across the street from the store where Delony clerked. Martin V. King owned a blacksmith shop and livery stable, and that is where the Taylor group placed their horses.[26] Delony points out that King's son Tom and an adopted son, Ed Davis, "were both with the Taylor gang, at that time." Sheriff Weisiger, fearing that the Taylors intended to burn the court house down to destroy any indictments against them, managed to gather a group of dependable citizens to arm themselves. Those guarding the court house, as Delony identified them, were Captain William Friend, a lawyer; Sterling F. Grimes, district attorney; Judge Henry Clay Pleasants, district judge; Sam C. Lackey, a lawyer; John and Jim Wofford, whose store the Taylors had taken possession of; Judge Kilgore, a druggist; Jim and Clate Summers and several others as well as himself.

Delony claims that they guarded the court house all day, but does not explain what the Taylors were doing during this period. Supposedly Sheriff Weisiger sent a black man to Cuero to ask "Captain" Hudson to gather a posse and bring help at once to Clinton. According to Delony, the Taylors "captured the negro, and took him across the bridge and hung him to a tree." Without hearing from Hudson, Sheriff Weisiger sent another young man, Charles Page, whose father had been killed by the Taylors, to carry another note to Hudson asking for help. Page did make it through the lines.[27] Impatient at the delays, Weisiger then went to Martin King, owner of the livery stable, and made a deal with him that if he would lock up the horses of the Taylors, then when the posse came they would not fire on his two sons: Tom King and Ed Davis. The deal was made.[28]

The posse, which probably intended to shoot to kill rather than actually arrest the trio, was composed mainly of feud veterans. As identified by Delony, the posse consisted of Dick Hudson, Curly Wallace, Bill Meador, Kit Hunter, Buck McCrabb, John McCrabb, Frank Cox, Bill Cox, Jake Ryan, and brothers Joe and Ed Sitterle. Hudson was the man in charge, who explained to him (Delony) that if the Taylors showed fight then King and Davis were not to be shot as King's father had agreed to lock up their horses. As Delony and Hudson finalized their plan, the Taylors were "running down the street, toward the livery stable, where their horses were." Then the posse dismounted and started running after them. Delony explains that Taylor, Hendricks, Arnold, King, and Davis all ran through an orchard and then entered an old log house. All five ran into it, but then ran out immediately, no reason given. As Jim Taylor exited the house, Christopher T. "Kit" Hunter raised his Winchester. Taylor dropped down on one knee and took aim at Hunter; both men fired at the same time. Hunter staggered and his hat flew off with a bullet hole in it. Hunter's aim was better, as his shot hit Taylor's right arm, breaking it, causing him to drop his Winchester. He picked it up with his other hand. Within moments Taylor, Hendricks and Arnold all had received multiple wounds, and they were dead on the field. This is the dramatic description of the gunfight on the streets of Clinton between Taylor, Hendricks, Arnold, and the posse under the leadership of Dick Hudson, as recorded by Lewis Delony.[29]

Delony's account of Jim Taylor having with him a gang of forty men is not believable, and his account is the only one that provides that number. Most likely there were but five men: Taylor, Hendricks, Arnold, King, and Davis. Possibly Hun Tuggle was present as well but apparently took no part in the fight.

An account that first appeared in the *Cuero Star* provides additional details, although unfortunately portions of the copy are missing. It began with the curious statement, "for the first time in the history of the unfortunate Taylor-Sutton feud," followed by the details of a "regular fight" between the two parties. Perhaps because there was no ambush, it was in open daylight with the two groups shooting at each other, "face to face," this report did not receive further coverage. The facts as near as could be determined were that Jim Taylor and "several of his party" were in Clinton. This fact was "very singular indeed," according to the paper, which said that Clintonites wondered what object Taylor had "by thus exposing himself to the public." About 5:00 p.m. ten members of the Sutton party arrived and inquired as to Taylor's whereabouts. When told he was at King's, they started in that direction. Jim Taylor was disabled early in the fight and he "fell back with his force" which consisted of two men, i.e., Hendricks and Arnold. They fell back to a cluster of live oaks in the Odom field where "they rallied once more and fired volley after volley towards the Sutton party." With a flare for the dramatic the reporter added that the Sutton party charged and "in a brief time their antagonists ... remained dead on the field. ..."[30]

A report from one identified as a "reliable source" provides perhaps a more objective report of the triple killing. It was sent to the *Galveston Daily News* and appeared in their January 1, 1876, issue, and was reprinted in the *San Antonio Daily Express* of January 7, with minor changes. Reliable Source's last comment—"The writer hopes this affair will be the last of the kind arising out of these old feuds"—appeared in the *News* but was omitted by the *Express*. It is printed here in full so as to contrast a report made days if not hours after the smoke had cleared, with the recollections of Delony and Jack Hays Day, recalled more than a half century later.

> Since Sunday night [December 26] Jim Taylor, with two or three men, have been in and about Clinton, walking through the streets with two six-shooters on each; and, as our sheriff was at home and remained there, no arrest was made. The party had, in conversation with Martin King, sent Dick Hudson word that they would come and kill him unless he left the county within 24 hours.
>
> Dick could not exactly see the point, and together with six or seven of the Sutton boys, went to Clinton Monday, Dec. 27th, to offer his services to the Sheriff. As they reached there and dismounted, the Taylors (five men) at once got their guns, and commenced firing and retreating through a field, the Sutton party after them, and after hard running and much shooting, Jim Taylor, Winchester Smith [Mace Arnold], (the man who is now recognized as having given Rup [*sic*, Rube] Brown the first shot when he was killed,) and Hendricks (one of Capt. McNelly's command, who married into the Taylor family) were killed. Mark [*sic*] King and young Toggles [*sic*, Tuggle] threw up their hands and surrendered, and were, therefore, not hurt.[31]

By being the man "who married into the Taylor family," A. R. Hendricks added one more sorrow in the life of his widow. Elizabeth Jane Day, now faced with the task of burying her fourth husband, certainly realized how dearly the feud had cost her.[32]

An additional account which deserves mention is that of Daniel Fore Chisholm. In spite of the errors, his account is somewhat similar to the contemporary accounts, although the conversation he added certainly was not recorded by anyone at the time. Not surprisingly he makes the Sutton party out to be "ruthless assassins" who, after the shooting stopped, "rode in a wide circle around Jim Taylor and Mace Arnold, until they were sure they were both dead. Then they rode up to them and one of the gang used a double-barreled shot-gun loaded with buckshot and shot one side of Mace Arnold's face and head off." Just as strange, Chisholm, "remembered" that Hendricks was still alive and asked Bill Meador if he could go see his wife for the last time. Meador volunteered the use of his own horse. But before Hendricks got very far, "the rest of the gang" met him. Dick Hudson asked of the group who would "finish Hendricks off" and Kit Hunter volunteered. He "put his gun against Hendricks' ear, and pulled the trigger." Chisholm states that the other two members of the Taylor party who escaped were Mart King and Hun Tuggle, with no mention of Davis.[33]

The posse that ended the lives of Taylor, Arnold, and Hendricks did face challenges as the Grand Jury brought charges against them. Indictments were found against each in the death of the three men. The Grand Jury met on April 3, 1876, and "upon their oaths" found that R. B. Hudson, J. F. McCrabb, William Cox, Jeff White, Henry White, A. Chamblin,[34] W. C. Wallace, John Meador, William Meador, and Christopher Taylor Hunter "with force and arms, unlawfully, feloniously and with their express malice aforethought ... with certain guns and pistols ... did discharge and shoot off ... leaden bullets ... of which [mortal wounds] they died." Jim Taylor's mortal wound was from a bullet "of the depth of four inches and of the breadth of half an inch" on the right side of his head. The mortal wounds of Arnold and Hendricks were no doubt similar. Witnesses called were J. J. Cooke, W. R. Friend, W. V. King, J. R. Hamilton, J. A. Wimbish, John Wofford, William Williamson, R. T. Kleberg,

View of the Taylor-Bennett Cemetery, south of Cuero. From left: replacement board marking grave of Mason Arnold, since replaced with granite stone; original marker for James C. Taylor; tall stone marks the grave of feud victim Pitkin B. Taylor and his wife Susan. Author's Collection.

S. C. Lackey, A. L. Lowrance, H. Tuggle, Eno. Speer, James Blair, and J. T. Gillett.[35]

Apparently the charges against several of these men were dismissed, as on the twenty-eighth of June 1877 only Hudson, Daniel J. White,[36] Henry J. White,[37] Hunter,[38] and Wallace stood trial in Cuero. Examining witnesses and hearing arguments of counsel occupied two days. The jury needed not more than ten minutes before returning with a verdict of not guilty. The same men, under indictment for the killing of Arnold and Hendricks, did not need to go to trial as the district attorney removed the indictment from the docket.[39] In sum, the men who were charged with the triple killing suffered no penalty for their deed. The fact that R. B. Hudson was a deputy sheriff no doubt gave them all the legal authority they needed for their actions.

Augustus W. "Gus" Pridgen, killed during the feud. *Courtesy Robert W. Shook.*

CHAPTER NINE

Last Killings

*"Augustus Washington Pridgen was brutally murdered
on Irish Creek in DeWitt county Texas by Some
of the members of the Sutton party on 2ⁿᵈ day of Feby 1876.
He was a harmless good man and with his death began the
downfall of the Sutton party."*
—FROM A PRIDGEN FAMILY BIBLE

The triple killing of the Taylor men—Jim Taylor, Mace Arnold, and A. R. Hendricks—perhaps caused many people of DeWitt County to breathe a sigh of relief. The leaders of both factions were now dead; many of their followers were either dead or had left the country. In spite of Bill Sutton and Jim Taylor now resting in their graves, all did not yet become peaceful in DeWitt County. A few more killings occurred in the Centennial Year, followed by a lengthy series of legal maneuvers. Only then did the violence in South Texas as a result of the Sutton-Taylor Feud end.

January may have been a peaceful month as 1876 began, as apparently the feudists avoided each other or were unable to find their victims. But with the month of February the killings began anew. Alfred Cone was killed on the first of February. Five men, tentatively identified as Joseph Allen, Alfred Day (but possibly his brother Jack Hays Day), two of the Callison men and one other, entered the community of Rancho in Gonzales County, some twenty-five miles southwest of the county seat, and looted the general store of S. Frank & Company. They then galloped off, firing their Winchesters indiscriminately. They were then joined by John Sharp (possibly a brother of the James Sharp killed by a Sutton posse in Bastrop in 1867), and rode to the house of Alfred Cone, where he was shot down. Sharp and Cone had had a difficulty back in 1874, and Sharp was only now taking his revenge. No further details of the earlier Cone-Sharp troubles are known. A man named Patterson who was working with Cone was allowed to escape and report the news to various citizens as well as relatives of Cone, who then informed the sheriff.[1]

Another killing that remains shrouded in mystery is the death of Augustus Washington "Gus" Pridgen, "in humanly murdered near Burns Station in DeWitt County" according to a Pridgen family Bible. The Pridgens were among the most vocal of the anti-Sutton followers, mainly due to Senator Pridgen's active efforts to prosecute Sutton, Helm, and others for the killings of the Kelly brothers. On February 2, the day following the killing of Alfred Cone in Gonzales County, Gus Pridgen was shot down by a hidden assassin. The Grand Jury ultimately indicted Calloway Maddox, but as late as 1886 he remained a fugitive from Texas justice. His final fate is unknown. Without knowing if Maddox was indeed the assassin it is difficult to determine if Pridgen's death was directly feud-related or simply the result of a private quarrel. In some quarters, such as the *Express* of San Antonio, Pridgen was simply the "latest victim in the Taylor-Sutton feud, in West Texas … murdered last week near Cuero."[2]

Young Joseph Allen, involved in the killing of Alfred Cone, also proved to be a fugitive from Texas justice. On the night of February 27, a Sunday, Henderson County Deputy Sheriff J. E. Goethry accompanied by a man named Deathredge from the same county, called on DeWitt County Sheriff William J. Weisiger for assistance in arresting Joseph Allen,[3] accused of a

Henderson County killing. Weisiger deputized Joseph N. Agee to take a posse and with Deputy Goethry and Deathredge make the arrest. By Monday morning, the twenty-eighth, the posse had reached the Allen house and surrounded it, suspecting the young man was there. The senior Allen denied his son was present, but the posse insisted on searching the house nevertheless. Inside, Deputy Agee observed a man-sized box and lifted the lid to investigate. Young Allen jumped out with a pistol in each hand and shooting. Agee was extremely lucky that day, as a bullet only grazed his head and then passed through his hat; another bullet wounded his right leg. Now the firing became general. Joseph Allen managed to run out of the house but was met with a deputy who filled him with buckshot. One posse member, J. E. Lampley, was not so lucky: the wounds he received caused his death.[4] In all the firing no one could say whose bullet wounded fugitive Allen. With one posse member dead and another wounded, the lawmen withdrew. Initial reports indicated that the Allens would not permit their son Joseph to be arrested, as "the Taylor party are guarding him and will certainly resist any attempt to execute the process against him."[5]

On March 3 Sheriff Weisiger summoned a large posse to accompany him to the Allen place to again attempt the arrest and determine who had shot and killed Deputy Lampley. The night was exceedingly dark and a drizzling rain was falling. The posse halted a few hundred yards from Allen's house where they rested until daylight. At the house County Judge O. M. Threlkeld, who accompanied the posse, thoroughly examined the dwelling and determined that posse members had unintentionally killed Lampley and wounded Allen; Allen had not killed Lampley. The posse nevertheless then arrested "old man Allen" and another son, probably Claiborn who was old enough to handle a gun. Because Weisiger had a posse of over sixty men, resistance would have meant certain death. With the two Allens in their custody, the posse then headed to the house of Mannen Clements, believing that the severely wounded Joseph Allen was hiding there.[6]

Mannen and his three brothers—Gip, Jim, and Joe—all sided with the Taylors; in fact they had signed one of the peace treaties back in 1873. The posse, with both father and son Claiborn in custody, arrived at Clements' house, described as "a small fortress or block-house pierced by numerous port-holes on each side." There young Joseph Allen was found, but in "such feeble condition that he could not be moved." The lawmen suspected he would be dead in a few days and therefore he was allowed to remain. While pondering their next move, Sheriff Weisiger and his men observed a group of men advancing on the house, all well mounted and armed, "evidently intent on mischief." Weisiger "promptly formed his men for attack" and bravely rode out to meet them and demanded to know their business. The group, seeing the sheriff was not going to be intimidated by their numbers, "put spurs to their horses and fled." Bill Taylor was recognized as one of the members of this group. Some members of Weisiger's group wanted to pursue them, but the sheriff considered that would be an unwise move, fearing an ambush—which would have been unlikely due to the superiority of the posse's strength of numbers—and "because the posse had been on horseback nearly twenty-four hours without food for themselves or horses, and had accomplished their object." They at least had determined the whereabouts of young Allen, and figured he would be dead soon anyway.[7] It is unclear why Allen had sought refuge from Henderson County authorities in far-off DeWitt—nearly three hundred miles southwest of his home county—unless it was simply a matter of seeking refuge at his father's home.

Based on Patterson's report as a witness to the killing of Alfred Cone, on Friday, March 12, Gonzales County Sheriff Alonzo T. Bass[8] gathered a posse and rode to the small community of

Rancho intending to arrest John Sharp and two men named Callison. They did not succeed in finding Sharp or the Callisons, but their show of strength "had a good effect on the lawbreakers of that section, as several known bad characters have left and others promised to leave immediately." Sheriff Bass did arrest William Phillips and William Dodd, the former indicted for a Karnes County murder and the latter for larceny in Wilson County. Citizens of Rancho and nearby Leesville "have organized companies determined to rid the country of these desperadoes," reported the Gonzales *Inquirer*.[9] No doubt some members of the newly formed companies had learned how to deal with suspected lawbreakers from Jack Helm and his State Policemen.

The action also made news in DeWitt County, and according to one report the sheriffs of Gonzales and Karnes counties—Bass and John M. Yeary—met "by appointment" at the Clements settlement, where DeWitt, Gonzales, and Karnes counties join, intending to arrest certain "refugees from justice who have made that place their headquarters." After surrounding a "dense thicket" they found the men they were looking for and arrested eight of them, two of them named Clements, though first names were withheld. The DeWitt County correspondent confidently reported that the sheriffs of DeWitt, Victoria, Goliad, Bee, Live Oak, Karnes, and Gonzales counties were going to have a "called meeting" to make "some arrangements" to more effectually enforce the law and arrest criminals.[10] The message, although unwritten and unreported, apparently was that mob law of the old Helm-Bell variety was now out of fashion and law officers intended not only to capture fugitives but deliver them to jail alive to await a just trial.

Not surprisingly, San Antonio's *Daily Express* commented on the activities of lawmen in the Gonzales, Karnes, and DeWitt counties area, reporting that the gathering point of various "desperadoes and murderers" appeared to be the house of Mannen Clements. Without citing a source, the *Express* continued by

pointing out that Clements and his three brothers were "said
to be kinsmen of the notorious John Wesley Hardin, and members of the murderous Taylor gang. ..." In spite of the cooperation of neighboring sheriffs the *Express* feared more action
was needed and now called for re-enacting the old State Police
law, "and want Captain McNelly sent back to execute it. [The
people] are awaking from their lethargy, overcoming their fear
of the desperadoes, and are determined to break up the gang and
redeem their country."[11] In spite of Gonzales County Sheriff
Bass scouring the country with posses numbering on one occasion eighty-four men, on another one hundred fifteen, he had
made few arrests. Perhaps the editor intended to call for the
presence of McNelly and his militia company that had been
stationed in DeWitt County back in 1874, rather than calling
for the vigilante actions of Jack Helm.

   Galveston's *News* found the events of Gonzales and DeWitt
counties especially newsworthy. One reporter provided a lengthy
report from Gonzales town, describing not only the cattle industry but also the various problems law officers encountered in
dealing with lawbreakers. The unidentified reporter spoke of
how "the entire face of the earth seemed to be covered with cattle," which proved to be eleven droves belonging to Captain
Richard King of Santa Gertrudis, numbering 30,000 head. After
this introductory paragraph he continued with news of the Taylors
and the citizens. Of the actions of those sheriffs seeking Allen,
the reporter stated that "the Taylor-Sutton feud of DeWitt county
had nothing directly to do with the late reported excitement in
this county," although several of the young men "are said to
belong to the Taylor party." The reporter had learned that two
months earlier, lawlessness "had become rampant on the boun-
dary line of DeWitt, Karnes and Gonzales counties," caused by
a dozen or more young men, among them "a young man named
Day, another Allen, two Callison boys and a man named Sharp."
Their bad conduct amounted to shooting up parties in their

James Clements, cousin of John Wesley Hardin and feudist. *Courtesy Mrs. Ray Caffall.*

neighborhood, shooting out the lights "and other similar acts." The only serious action of these young men, at least in the reporter's view, was the revenge killing of Alfred Cone, referred to above.[12]

Two different aspects of the reporting in 1876 are remarkable. One was the observation that there was indeed a "disposition on the part of the good citizens" to break up the identified type of lawlessness, i.e., the reckless shooting up of homes or communities, not to mention revenge killings; and, second, that if the elected sheriffs could or would not perform their duties then it was time to recall Captain McNelly and his state troops, although some may have preferred to have the old State Police Force recalled, of which McNelly was a captain, as was Jack Helm. Now, by early 1876, the Clements brothers were receiving considerable "bad press," and indeed the notorious John Wesley Hardin was their cousin. They had been supporters of the Taylor faction. It was said that "these desperate characters and the Taylors" made their headquarters at the Clements settlement, and the Clements brothers "are said to belong to the Taylor gang." The locations of the Clements family homes cannot be accurately pinpointed today, but the reporter found it was "appropriate" as "the brush on the creeks afford complete security from the sight of a posse, who are compelled to travel in Indian file." The reporter's final comments were encouraging to the law-abiding readers: "Every possible effort will continue to be made to break up lawlessness" although "little hope is entertained of success" unless Governor Coke sent "another command down there like McNelly's."[13]

It was clear that the public's attitude was in favor of just enforcement of the law, not mob violence; the public remembered the quality of McNelly—that no prisoners in his custody were murdered "attempting to escape"—and that his constant patrolling prevented much bloodshed. They also appreciated that he did not turn over prisoners to lynch mobs.

Captain McNelly's efforts in fighting raiders had attracted the attention of the nation's capital and he visited Washington, D.C.

to testify before a congressional committee on the troubles on the Rio Grande frontier.[14] He had left his men in charge of T. C. "Pidge" Robinson, a most capable lieutenant. Following his Washington testimony he visited Cuero in early March. On his brief visit he "found the town of Cuero in such a disturbed condition that I deemed it necessary (at the urgent solicitation) of a number of prominent citizens to remain over for a couple of days so that in case of any serious disturbance I might be of some service to the State if not to the local officers." McNelly learned of the Henderson County deputy sheriff's efforts to arrest Allen, that Allen was "said to be one of the 'Taylor' party" and had summoned a posse of eight or ten of what he termed "Suttons Party" to aid him in making the arrest. McNelly discovered that no one but a member of the Sutton Party could be found to arrest a Taylor, nor any but members of the Taylor Party could be found to arrest a Sutton. So "as might have been expected there was a fight and the deputy sheriff of DeWitt County was killed [and] Young Allen & another man was badly wounded & the Henderson county officer & party left in 'double quick' time without waiting to see whether their friends or the party they went to arrest was killed or not. ..."

McNelly learned also that a few days after this embarrassing incident some forty or fifty men "of the Gonzales county wing of [the] Taylor party" arrived at Allen's house and moved him over to Gonzales County. Not being satisfied with recovering one of their wounded, these men then sent word to the Sutton party "that if they wanted a fight to come up and try it." Not surprisingly, the Sutton party "wanted a fight," organized, and went to Gonzales County. "[A]s I came through," McNelly wrote, "they were ready to start so I waited until they returned," they having found Allen dying. They left him alone then, as they told McNelly "they had no ammunition to waste on half dead men when they were in the Taylor's jurisdiction." McNelly's superiors were more concerned about the situation on the border, with cattle thieves from Mexico raiding Texas cattle herds, and he had to return to the Rio Grande frontier.[15]

Although some considered the actions of the Clements brothers, the Cone killing, and other violent acts as having no connection to the Taylor-Sutton difficulties, they must be considered part of the dying embers of the feud, which had flared highest a few years earlier, especially during 1874. The fact that McNelly himself considered the Joseph Allen pursuit and violent reaction, resulting in at least one death and several wounded, as feud-related, places the action squarely amidst the acts of the feudists. And this was not all. One more tragedy did take place which must be considered among the final bloody acts: the raid on the home of Dr. Philip H. Brassell, the night of September 19, 1876.[16]

The Brassells were from Georgia, and this may be where the idea that the feud originated in the Carolinas and Georgia came from, since two of the Brassell family became victims. Both Dr. and Mrs. Mary Ann Brassell were natives of Fayette County, Georgia, born there 1827 and 1829, respectively. Their son George was born there September 15, 1854; the younger children were also born in Georgia. In Georgia Dr. Brassell served as a member of the Constitutional Convention of 1866 and the Georgia Legislature in 1868, 1869, and 1870. The family, perhaps hoping the climate of Texas would improve the doctor's health, moved to Texas in 1870, settling near Shiloh, a small community near Yorktown. Their choice of a residence placed them in the center of the feuding families. The 1870 census reveals there were two Brassell families. Household numbers twelve and fourteen contained a total of twenty-four people, all born in Georgia except the black domestic servant and her two children and a sixty-nine-year-old male born in New York. In 1870 P. H. Brassell is identified as forty-three and a "Doctor of Medicine." He claimed only $600 worth of real estate and no personal estate. His wife Mary Ann was keeping house, and they then had seven children: George F., occupation "Field Hand," Nancy, Theodore, Sylvanus, Martha Jane, Leonard, and Jeff Davis. All but George were listed simply as being "at home." Two households later, enumerator Willis Fawcett visited the family of John W. Brassell, whose occupation is recorded as "Grocer." He had no real estate but personal estate valued at $1000. His wife of course kept house; son James W. was also by profession a "Doctor of Medicine" while son T. W. was identified as a grocer.[17] The two families thus provided medical assistance as well as groceries to the communities of Clinton and Cuero and perhaps the surrounding area. Why Dr. Brassell and son George were murdered has never been determined conclusively, although there are valid speculations.

It was a night of terror and heartbreak for the Brassell family. The parents must have been exhausted, both emotionally and physically, as on the previous day, September 18, Dr. Brassell had made a disposition of his property, gave money to his wife to defray burial expenses, and picked out the burial site where he would be laid to rest. As a doctor, suffering from the "white death"—tuberculosis—he certainly knew he had only a very short time left to live.[18]

That night the family had retired for the evening but the house was disturbed about ten o'clock by someone hollering "Hello!" At first Mrs. Brassell thought it was the voice of a neighbor but later realized it was not. Whoever it was, the family was now awake, the dogs being disturbed as well. Dr. Brassell told her to get a lamp, as did the man from the outside. She promptly lit two lamps. Then the same mysterious voice said, "Surround the house, boys."[19] Sons Theodore and Sylvanus, who had been sleeping outside on the gallery, were taken out in the yard and guarded. Then a man whom the others referred to as "Mr. Sheriff" entered the house. "Don't be alarmed," he told the family, "we are after someone, but we have no idea if he is here; we won't hurt a hair on your head." Then a voice from the outside instructed them to "all come out here, you women folks; put on your clothes and come out of that house." The voice then said, "Old man, get up and come out of there; come out, old man." Dr. Brassell and son George then went outside, George without hat, shoes or coat.[20]

The man referred to as "Mr. Sheriff" then searched the house, after which George, Theodore, and Sylvanus were allowed to go back in and put on their clothes. Mrs. Brassell, certainly concerned with the house being searched, asked George who the men were. "Bill Meador, Jake Ryan and Joe Sitterlie [*sic*, Sitterle] are some of them; I know them all" was his reply. Mrs. Brassell did not recognize any of the men—she numbered them about eight or ten—but at first was not afraid because she believed her men had done nothing and they would not be harmed. She must have felt some anxiety when her sickly husband, taken from his bed, and sons George, Theodore, and Sylvanus, were all led away into the dark. The men then asked how best to get out of the yard, and George told them the same way they had entered. Dr. Brassell said, "Here is the gate; don't tear down the fence." They then asked the way to a Mr. Ainsworth's and it was pointed out to them.[21]

The four Brassell men at that point were, as they believed themselves to be, under arrest. Mary Brassell watched as the men were led away, thinking there were seven, or possibly eight or ten in all under "Mr. Sheriff." She took no particular notice of the men, knowing that her people had done nothing to be killed for. Ten minutes or so later she heard shooting. She went outside and yelled not to shoot anymore, then went back into the house and lay down. Her younger children were afraid that their father had been killed, but she "reckoned not." The clock was striking eleven as the shots echoed away.[22] What she did not know then was that her husband and George had both been shot to death while the other two boys escaped, running and hiding in the brush. Theodore had escaped and reached Mr. Ainsworth's house, informing him that the doctor and his brothers had been shot. Ainsworth and a Mr. Humphries then went to the Brassells' home where Mary Ann learned she was now a widow.

Mrs. Brassell proved to be a brave, strong woman, and now started to look for her men. She found the body of her husband some 250 yards from the house. It took another two hours or more to find the body of her son George, only thirty-five yards from the body of her husband. Of course she had to be wondering who would do such a thing. Her daughter Nancy thought there were more like fifteen or twenty in the party who raided their home. She was positive one of them was Jake Ryan. She had been asleep when voices roused her and she saw a face at the window. The man had raised the window; she told him to put it down, and as it was a starlight night "she recognized him distinctly." Nancy did not recognize the man who entered the house, but George then came in and said it was Bill Meador. He was "scared and trembling, and he was excited." Shortly afterwards she heard a scream, and thought it was brother Sylvanus, and then shooting. It was then that she and Mrs. Brassell both ran out of the house towards the sound of the shooting, and her mother called out to the dark not to shoot anymore. Later they found the bodies.[23]

Sylvanus later testified that after the barking of the dogs had awakened him he roused brother Theodore; then the two were taken outside while one of the men stated they wanted to search the house, looking for Bill Humphries. Sylvanus recognized six men whom he identified as William Cox, Jake Ryan, Joe Sitterle, Bill Meador, Dave Augustine, and James Hester. These men formed a group around him; hence he was able to recognize their faces as they were not wearing masks. They told him to show them the way to the Ainsworths' place. Two of the men walked while the others rode. After about 150 yards they stopped so the others could get their horses. When all the men were mounted, someone asked the boys which one was the youngest. Dr. Brassell answered Sylvanus was, and then George—who must have realized what was about to happen—answered: "If you are going to kill one, kill us all." The men said nothing but commenced shooting. Sylvanus, before running, saw Meador shoot his brother George "full in the face." He swore it was Dave Augustine who "shot my father." Theodore escaped to Mr. Ainsworth's place, running and ducking the shots fired after him. He later realized he had known some of these men who were now shooting after him: he had known William Cox some three or four years, in fact had gone to school with him; he had known Ryan and Sitterle about a year.[24]

Theodore's later testimony was substantially the same. He recalled that George told the men at one point that he was not going to go any farther, that "if they would take him to court they could find nothing against him." Here Bill Meador answered him, that he "hadn't been doing nothing but robbing his neighbors" and then shot him while Dave Augustine shot his father. Now both brothers ran, Sylvanus reaching the Ainsworths' while Theodore, after getting far enough, climbed a tree and hid in the darkness. Theodore testified that he recognized Meador, Augustine, James Hester, and Joe Sitterle.[25]

It is known that James W. Brassell, who considered himself a doctor of medicine at least in 1870, was indicted on April 11, 1876, in DeWitt County, the charge "Threat to take human life." His name is listed in the Adjutant General's published list of fugitives as late as 1878, which described him as a physician, provides a physical description of him and points out that he was "of gentlemanly appearance and address." Unfortunately there is no indication of whose life he had threatened to take.[26] Jack Hays Day believed that Dr. Brassell was killed because he had earlier defeated David Augustine in a school board election, Brassell considering Augustine unfit for the position. Because of this, Augustine "bargained with the Sutton gang to have him slain." Day, writing years later, considered Dr. Brassell "a highly respected citizen, very influential, and one of the top ranking Masons of the state." This could very well be true; the implication, however, that members of "the Sutton gang" would commit acts which amounted to murder for hire does not ring true.[27]

A more plausible theory is that the killings were a mistake on the part of the killers. Historian C. L. Douglas, in preparing his study of Texas feuds, interviewed Robert Pleasants, the son of Judge Henry Clay Pleasants, and from that interview and a study of the legal papers dealing with the subsequent trial and appeal, believed that one of the men accused of being among the killing group had a writ for the arrest of Theodore Brassell and William Humphries, issued upon the instance of a man named Hardin who claimed the two had threatened to take his life. What may have begun as an attempt to arrest Theodore Brassell, somehow "through some unexplainable misunderstanding" developed into the double killing.[28] Unfortunately there is no further identification of the mysterious Hardin. John Wesley Hardin was a fugitive in Florida at this time; no doubt someone else was using his name as an alias.

The double murder shocked South Texas. Many wondered why a doctor, a respected member of the community and "a good and peaceful citizen," would be the object of an assassination. Some considered son George to be of less than sterling quality, even to the point of one reporter writing that George "did not bear a good name in the community and his death is not regretted."[29]

Whether George Brassell's reputation was tarnished or not was irrelevant; the community was stunned at the murder of the doctor. N. A. Jennings, a young Philadelphian who had only recently joined McNelly's company and served during this period, later wrote that it was "a despicable murder" and was "committed by members of the Sutton party. They went at midnight to the residence of Dr. Brazell [*sic*], an educated, refined old gentleman, dragged him from a sick bed in the presence of his wife and daughter, and murdered him in cold blood. At the same time, they killed his son."[30] Some may have believed the mob only intended to kill George, but the doctor recognized them and as dead men tell no tales he too had to be killed.

After listening to the testimony "of a large number of witnesses [both] for the State and the defense" Justice C. C. Howerton placed the men under bond. The bonds were of a light amount as the parties reportedly had alibis "clearly established, and that they court for themselves a thorough investigation." The testimony was "merely circumstantial." Five men were initially placed under appearance bonds to "await the action of the next grand jury": they were Meador, Augustine, Ryan, Cox, and Hester. Meador's bond was a mere $100, while the others' were higher, $250.[31]

Although in some cases the citizens of DeWitt County certainly feared to bring an indictment against lawbreakers, in this case the Grand Jury, meeting on December 20, indicted seven men. Two indictments were returned, the first charging William D. Meador, Nicholas J. "Jake" Ryan, Dave Augustine, James Hester, Charles H. Heissig, Joe Sitterle, and William Cox, jointly with the murder of Dr. Philip Brassell. The second indictment charged the same men with the murder of George Brassell.[32]

Ironically, on that same twentieth of December, minister S. L. Bradley joined in holy matrimony Joseph F. Sitterle and Miss Melissa O. Cox, the daughter of the slain James W. Cox of a few years before, and the sister of William W. Cox. The marriage was performed with J.A. McCrabb and John Andrews as witnesses.[33] A month earlier, on November 22, the same minister had married William D. Meador and Miss Amanda Augustine in the presence of Bob Thomas and J. J. Sumners.[34] These two marriages became common knowledge of course, uniting the Sitterle, Cox, Meador, and Augustine families together. It would prove to be advantageous to the Rangers who were now called back to DeWitt County following the Brassell murders.

Dr. P. H. Brassell and his son George were buried in the Upper Yorktown Cemetery (then called Friar Cemetery) on the twenty-first by the Masonic fraternity.[35] While the public wondered about the slayings, and the murderers perhaps pondered their actions, another killing connected to the Sutton-Taylor hatreds occurred. Few details have been learned, but in early October Martin V. King was shot to death. He earlier had betrayed Jim Taylor and his friends by locking his stable doors in Clinton, preventing them access to their horses when a group of Sutton followers attacked. Jack Hays Day recalled that King was killed "in a drunken gambling spree in Clinton" but provided no details.[36] Reports reaching Victoria indicated that King and two men named Davis were playing cards in a Clinton saloon. A "difficulty" arose during the progress of the game, resulting in gunfire. King was shot and killed; "Doly" Davis was slightly wounded.[37] At the time King was working as the jailor in Clinton. Sergeant Lawrence B. Wright, a member of McNelly's command then stationed at Oakville, learned of the killing and informed Adjutant General Steele. "Martin King of Clinton," he wrote, "one of the best citizens of the county, was killed in Clinton on last Sunday night [October 2]. The murderer, a worthless vagabond, was arrested and lodged in jail. King was unarmed, and it is said that the murder was altogether unprovoked."[38] There is no indication of whether the Davis boys were sympathetic to the Taylors or not, but it would not be surprising if they took this opportunity to avenge the death of Jim Taylor. William W. Davis had signed the treaty of peace back in January of 1874, as did victim Martin King, but was he the man identified as "Doly" Davis? Or possibly it was nothing more than a drunken argument over a game of cards.

Judge Henry Clay Pleasants had called for help from the governor, and by December Rangers had arrived to guarantee a peaceful district court session. Help came in the form of

Judge Henry Clay Pleasants. Only with the presence of Texas Rangers was he able to hold court in DeWitt County. *Courtesy the Western History Collections, University of Oklahoma.*

Captain McNelly's replacement, a healthy Jesse Leigh "Lee" Hall, a man trained by McNelly in effective leadership.[39] On December 10, Lieutenant Hall wrote a lengthy letter to Adjutant General Steele from Clinton. He had but six men with him, the others of his detachment having been sent to Goliad, but expected the rest of his command to be back in Clinton soon. Hall believed he had "force enough to quell any trouble that may arise" but if any of the accused murderers were convicted in the upcoming District Court, he anticipated trouble, due to "great danger in case of conviction of any of the numerous murderers or an attempt at a rescue." Hall would have his men busy since they would have had to serve whatever papers the court might need, as "the Shff [sheriff] cannot be trusted to execute any writs whenever the Sutton party are interested, and that party or its members are defnts [defendants] in nearly all the cases of felony on the docket there being thirty one murder cases alone and each defnt has some friend who will assist him. ..."

Hall perhaps inadvertently explained why the feud had lasted as long as it had, complaining that "one half of this County is so mixed up in deeds of blood that they cannot afford for any member of the brotherhood to be sent to the penitentiary or prison for fear they may divulge some of their dark secrets. ..." Hall estimated he might need eight or ten additional men by the eighteenth, as that was the day the criminal docket was "taken up." Hall also explained why the situation was so difficult for peace-loving citizens, as the people of DeWitt County "are completely terrorized and trampled upon by the assassins and cut throats who got their hand in at shedding blood during the Taylor & Sutton troubles, then joined Vigilance Associations and now kill off the witnesses and intimidate the juries by threats of violence till it is impossible to convict one of them, and the great trouble is there is no telling when the end will come."[40]

Hall had kept himself busy since arriving in Clinton by gathering the witnesses in the Brassell case. It was not easy, as all

Texas Ranger Jesse Leigh "Lee" Hall as he appeared when City Marshal of Sherman, Texas. From *Scribner's Magazine*, 1873.

but three women had left the country, and even they had been notified that if they came before the Grand Jury they would be killed and their houses burned.[41] Hall had some of the witnesses in his camp to protect them from assassination; further, he was in communication with other witnesses who had fled the country. Hall believed that he could get their testimony by assuring them a guard. In case Steele thought he might be overreacting, Hall assured him that Dr. Brassell and his son had been "among the most respectable people. ... [He] was a man noted for his learning and general Christian deportment, a member of the Georgia legislature at the time his family moved to this State some years ago, and highly esteemed by every one who knew him." As to why he and his son were killed, Hall wrote that "no one seems to have the remotest idea for what reason or that there was any cause for its being done."[42]

Hall was sufficiently in the know that with warrants he could arrest the seven indicted men. Knowing that a wedding dance was planned, he presumed that all would be there, and could be captured together. The date had been set for Friday night, December 22. There are various versions of the arrest of the indicted men. Ranger N. A. Jennings, who was in the service during this time, left a dramatic account of the arrest, as did Ranger George P. Durham. Jennings explains that shortly before this Hall had met with Judge Henry Clay Pleasants, whose district took in DeWitt County. The "old Judge," according to Jennings, assured Hall that if he (Hall) did his part, then he would "see that the courts deal justice. Together, we can bring order out of chaos."[43] Durham does not mention this but did write that the Rangers gave Judge Pleasants an escort everywhere he went, day and night. One or two Rangers even stayed in his home. "When he came down the street it looked like a parade. We naturally had orders to kill at the flick of a hostile eyebrow," wrote Durham.[44] Unfortunately Hall only identified the men arrested in his monthly report, not the men who were guarding the judge, or which Rangers he had with him making the arrest. Both Jennings and Durham left detailed accounts of conversation that could not have been recorded by either. Even the number of Rangers with Hall is open to debate: Jennings gave the number as seventeen, including Hall[45]; Durham states that a dozen accompanied Hall to make the arrest.[46] Hall's monthly report merely provides the names of the seven men arrested on December 22, and that they were delivered to the jail in Clinton.[47]

There were no dramatics in Hall's brief report. Years later Hall was interviewed by famed artist Frederic Remington. Remington, in writing up this interview, recalled that Hall,

> by secret-service men, discovered the perpetrators, and also that they were to be gathered at a wedding on a certain night. He surrounded the house and demanded their surrender, at the same time saying that he did not want to kill the women and children. Word returned that they would kill him and all his Rangers. Hall told them to allow their women and children to depart, which was done; then, springing on the gallery of the house, he shouted, "Now, gentlemen, you can go to killing Rangers; but if you don't surrender, the Rangers will go to killing you." This was too frank a willingness for midnight assassins, and they gave up.[48]

Hall erred in at least two aspects: he did not use "secret-service men" and the arrest was not made at a wedding, but at the wedding dance two nights later. However, his threat to kill the wanted men if they resisted rings true. Violent resistance would have resulted in gunplay and several if not all of them would have been killed. McNelly's men never resisted a fight.

In stark contrast to this reporting of the wedding dance with Rangers interrupting the festivities, men being arrested, and the potential for gunplay, was the report of the wedding itself. Due to the paucity of extant newspaper files we are fortunate to have the report that appeared in the *Victoria Advocate* from a correspondent who identified himself only as "C.," a pseudonym representing Clinton or Cuero. "Of course our county [DeWitt] cannot have so many gallant young men and beautiful young ladies, without an occasional wedding," C. wrote. The most recent was that between Joseph Sitterle, "formerly of your city, and Miss Cox of Clinton. They were married on last Wednesday [December 20] at the residence of Mr. John Andrews,[49] and although your reporter had not on the wedding garment for this occasion, yet he learns that it was a gay affair in every respect."[50]

Fred Duderstadt, a good friend of John Wesley Hardin and feudist. *Courtesy Mrs. Francis Hartmann.*

CHAPTER TEN

Prisoners and Trials

"I am a prisoner and must stand trial. ... I want to stand trial. I am sick and tired of fleeing . ... [A]ll I ask is that a mob be not permitted to murder me."
—JOHN WESLEY HARDIN, INTERVIEW IN THE AUSTIN *Daily Democratic Statesman*, AUGUST 29, 1877

In the nineteenth century the average newspaper had relatively free rein as to what to print. Inaccuracies and half-truths could be printed as fact, and the correspondents who simply signed their names as "Justice" or "Pidge" or "Citizen" could fearlessly write what they believed or pleased with no sense of obligation to double check their so-called facts. The popular *Statesman* of Austin accepted a correspondent's report in which accused Bill Meador was named. Someone convinced the editor that Meador was innocent and the *Statesman* printed a retraction, rare in nineteenth-century journalism, saying it had done "injustice to Bill Meadow [*sic*] and others. They are not murderers, but only charged with the crime. It has not been proven, and they have not been executed." The correspondent further claimed that not only were there "five representative devils of Cuero" in the Travis County jail, but "there were fifty more who should be there." The *Statesman* had to admit this was all a "gross wrong" to the people of Cuero, as the town was now "as law-abiding a place as any in Texas." Further, as

243

if to be done with the entire matter, the *Statesman* declared
that the "Sutton-Taylor feud, of which so much has been said,
and which has been the cause of many of these false impressions
affecting Cuero, is at an end." The Suttons still remained, while
"the other parties to the strife have left the country. The Suttons
are an honest, law-abiding people. They were the first to attack
the desperadoes and robbers, West. [*sic*] Hardin and the rest,
who once frequented the country. This is all ended," concluded
the editor, and he was "well pleased to announce the fact."[1] No
doubt Meador and the others charged with the murder of the
Brassell men were pleased to read this in the popular *Statesman*.

Ironically, on the same page and in the same column, a letter from R. B. Hudson explained how the one party came to
be called "the Suttons," but surprisingly condemned some of
McNelly's men at the same time. Hudson, a former state policeman who had endured the troubles from their inception, agreed
with the *Statesman* that the Taylor-Sutton feud had now subsided. That it had ended was true, he said, and he quickly pointed
out that the "Suttons are all here yet, sir." The Suttons, according to Hudson, were never anything but "honest working men
against a band of thieves, who overrun the country and murdered whom they pleased." Hudson further explained why the
one group took the name of the Suttons: "because Bill Sutton
was the first man to resist the thieves in this county." According
to Hudson, the leaders of the thieves were John Wesley Hardin
and Jim Taylor. Following the killing of Bill Sutton in 1874,
Hardin and Taylor "gathered two large herds of cattle under
the muzzle of the Winchester and six-shooter." Then Hudson
spoke of the herd "captured in Hamilton county, and Jim
Taylor and West. Hardin killed Deputy Sheriff Webb. ... They
then returned to this county, [where] Jim Taylor and two of
his associates were killed." Then Hardin "and others" left the
country to renew their "thefts and murder" and, according to
Hudson, "we have not been troubled with outlaws since." R. B.
Hudson no doubt believed what he wrote to the editors of the

Statesman. But then he concluded with a most amazing state-ment that places every other statement he made in doubt. Hudson added, "we are [under] no obligation to anyone but the good citizens of the so-called Sutton party for getting rid of [the outlaws]; *but indebted to Capt. L. H. McNelly's company for many recruits to the thieving party*" (emphasis added).[2]

Hudson may have thought of himself as a leading citizen of the community, having been born in Texas in about 1830, and by 1870 a successful farmer claiming $1500 worth of real estate and $1000 of personal estate.[3] He also served on occasion as a deputy sheriff. It had been back on December 27, 1875, that Jim Taylor threatened him, giving him but twenty-four hours to leave the country, or else he would be killed. Instead of running, Hudson chose to face his adversary and gathered about him Sheriff William Weisiger, W. C. "Curry" Wallace, Bill Meador, Christopher Taylor "Kit" Hunter, Buck and John McCrabb, Frank and Bill Cox, Jake Ryan, Joe and Ed Sitterle, and perhaps others. These were the men who Hudson, acting as a deputy sheriff under Weisiger, brought with him to Clinton. Several had signed one or both of the earlier treaties of peace, and they were now ready to engage in combat.[4] Jim Taylor, Hendricks, and Arnold were all killed. On June 28, 1877, the following men were placed on trial for the killing of Jim Taylor: Hudson, D. J. White, H. J. White, C. T. Hunter and W. C. Wallace. Why the others who were involved were not also charged and tried is unknown. After two days of testi-mony the jury retired, and within ten minutes returned with the verdict of not guilty. They were also indicted for the kill-ings of Hendricks and Arnold, but since they were acting under the command of Sheriff Weisiger—a legally constituted body—the district attorney moved to strike the indictment from the record, which was done.[5]

The year of 1877 was important for those whose main con-cern was the establishment of law and order. The major fugi-tive from Texas justice, John Wesley Hardin, would be finally captured, not by a single Texas county sheriff but by a group of lawmen, which included Dallas detective John Duncan; Texas Ranger John B. Armstrong, who had been "trained" under Captain L. H. McNelly; two Florida lawmen—William Henry Hutchinson and his deputy A.J. Perdue—and a railroad official, William Dudley Chipley. In addition there were some twenty other men deputized for backup. The arrest took place in far-off Pensacola, Florida, on the twenty-third of August 1877.

Armstrong and Duncan placed Hardin in the Travis County jail where he was kept until his trial in Comanche for the murder of Deputy Sheriff Charles M. Webb. In custody Hardin explained to a *Statesman* reporter how the killing happened. According to Hardin, he was at the back door of Jack Wright's bar-room, and Webb was there as well, talking with someone. Hardin spoke to Webb, and as Webb turned to face Hardin,

> he pulled his pistol and commenced firing on me. When he pulled his pistol I started to argue with him upon the question of the difference between us. He did not hesitate, but fired, when I jumped to one side [being wounded]. Bud Dixon and Jim Taylor, my friends, being present, and seeing that Webb had the drop upon me, commenced to defend me with their pistols. Webb got in his second shot when he was down upon his knees. The boys still fired, and during all this time I fired not one single time, seeing that Webb was already equally matched.[6]

This was Hardin's version of the affair in 1877; if Jim Taylor or the Dixon brothers who were already dead had been there, a different explanation might have been offered to the *Statesman* reporter. At his trial Hardin was found guilty of second degree murder and sentenced to a term of twenty-five years in the penitentiary at Huntsville. He was ultimately pardoned in 1894 due to the efforts of many friends and influential Texans.

While incarcerated in the Travis County jail, waiting his trial and ultimately the appeal, Hardin shared space with Bill Taylor, still incarcerated for his involvement in the killing of Sutton and Slaughter back in 1874. Three members of Sutton's followers were also there, charged with the Brassell killings. These individuals were all confined temporarily due to the security of the Austin jail, as many county jails were still considered insecure. Editorialized the *Statesman*: "Bill Taylor, ... breathes hard and is nervous to the last degree, with three of the Sutton gang, here in the Travis county jail. ... Wesley Hardin, ... the most reckless murderer ever known in Texas, was committed to our jail yesterday. He has killed, so the story goes, twenty-five or thirty white men besides Mexicans and negroes."[7] Hardin recalled in later years that while in the Travis County jail he met "some noted men." He recalled Bill Taylor, George Gladden, John Ringo, cousin Mannen Clements, and brother-in-law Brown Bowen among others.[8] At the time the jail consisted of a large room filled with iron cages. A reporter visited the jail and with the jailor viewed the scene. "It was a hot day in July. ... The room was dark and not very well aired. The men were stripped to the waist and the perspiration was dripping from their bodies. The cages were of solid ironbars, the floor was sheeted with iron. ... From one to three occupants were in a cage."[9]

Law and order was changing; no longer were prisoners routinely shot or hung, with the excuse that they were trying to escape. The celebrated fugitives were being incarcerated instead, both Hardin and Bill Longley behind bars. Ironically, in May of that year 1877, Jane Hardin's uncle, Joshua Bowen, had written to her, advising her to tell her brother Brown to "look out and it mite [sic] be better for him to move his Range for awhile. ..." Hardin had heard that one of the Taylors had been killed, but didn't know which one. Joshua responded: "James Tayler was killed by the Suttin Party [.] Billy Tayler was recaptured a few days Scince [sic] and is in Austin Jail[.]" Further, the Clements boys had all moved on—except Joe—and perhaps the best news of all was that "The Sutton Outfit is nearly Broken up They have got 5 in Austin Jail and two under Bond for killing two of Brazzels [*sic*][.] Every thing has changed here. ..."[10]

Certainly, things had changed. If both Bowen and Hardin had heeded the news from Uncle Joshua Bowen neither may have been captured.

The year would be devoted to battles in the court room for numerous former feudists, besides Bill Taylor, Wes Hardin, and those who had killed Jim Taylor, Hendricks, and Arnold. As late as October, Bill Taylor was transported down to Indianola for a new trial. He was in charge of the noted Ranger John B. Armstrong and a detachment of six men. While Taylor was on the road to Indianola, Brown Bowen was standing his trial, indicted for the killing of Thomas Haldeman back in 1872. On October 18, 1877, Bowen was found guilty of murder in the first degree and sentenced to pay the supreme penalty. The end came on May 17, 1878, Bowen protesting to the very end that John Wesley Hardin was the real killer. On the gallows, Rev. Eli Y. Seale read his *ante-mortem* statement, which not only provided his excuse for his waywardness but provided additional commentary on the times. Bowen stated he had lost his mother at an early age and with his father gone to Florida he was left to care for his sisters.

> The country was divided into parties who were killing each other. What was I, a poor, unguided boy, with no mother to guide his erring way, to do! For self-protection I had to stay with my friends. These friends showed me no bad example, but at the same time were looked on not as the best of citizens, and of course the world included me in that number.

Bowen admits he was influenced by "bad company" but then identifies men who took the law into their own hands.

I recollect in my early days having been with my father. When near Helena we came to a place where a man was taken out and hung by a mob for stealing a yearling. His name was Lewis. With what horror did I, a boy, look at such a crime! J. Tomlinson [*sic*], A. Strickland and J. Strickland came after my father to help take that man out of jail and hang him. My father would not go. Oh, what a curse these mobs have been to Texas ever since, and what a bad effect it has had upon me and many others![11]

No doubt this was old "Captain Joe" who led the mob; but the Strickland name does not appear elsewhere in the literature of the feud.

On the gallows Bowen explained why young Thomas Haldeman was killed, that Hardin killed Haldeman "for the only reason that he was afraid of him being a spy" for Joe Tumlinson, Jack Helm, and W. W. Davis.[12] Hardin "told me himself these men had sent [Haldeman] to watch him." Although the jury convicted Bowen of the killing, there is still considerable doubt that he was the actual trigger man, due to one of the witnesses later explaining that he testified against Bowen through fear of Hardin.[13]

Later that year Ranger Armstrong again had the Brassell prisoners in his care. He and his detachment arrived in Cuero to incarcerate them in the new DeWitt County jail. The jail, according to the Cuero *Bulletin*, "will probably be completed for the occupation of prisoners within a month, as the contractors have now sufficient stone to finish the structure."[14]

On Sunday, the sixteenth of December 1877, Lieutenants Lee Hall and Armstrong arrived from Austin with seven well-guarded prisoners. Judge H. C. Pleasants had made it clear he would not attempt to try the prisoners without a strong guard of State Troopers.[15] The case was called for Tuesday the eighteenth,

and at two o'clock in the afternoon the seven were ushered into
the courtroom: Dave Augustine, William Meador, Jake Ryan,
James Hester, William Cox, Joseph Sitterle, and Charles H.
Heissig. The latter two had been out on bail. Both the state and
the defense announced ready for trial. J. H. Browne of Helena,
County Attorney Sterling F. Grimes of Cuero, and William H.
Burges of Seguin represented the state. Rudolph Kleberg of
Cuero, Captain J. W. Stayton of Victoria, and Lane and Payne
of Goliad were there for the defense. The prisoners were allowed
a severance to be tried in the following order: Augustine and
Hester; Sitterle, Ryan and Cox; Heissig and Meador. Due to
many witnesses being absent the court adjourned to ten o'clock
the next day. Commented the reporter, "This is one of the most
important trials that has ever taken place in this district, and
has attracted a good deal of attention throughout the State.
Judging by the legal talent engaged on both sides, it will be a
fight among giants."[16]

The fight was indeed a fight among giants, and it lasted until
the turn of the century. At the December term of District Court
in DeWitt County, on December 24, the jury was impaneled
for the trial of Augustine and Hester. Four days were occupied
in selecting the jury. The State "fought the defense step by step,
and exhausted challenges ... , while the defense only challenged
nine in all." The State had eighteen witnesses and the defense
between fifty and sixty summoned.[17] Perhaps not surprisingly
on December 29, 1877, Augustine and Hester were acquitted
of murdering George Brassell. On the same day the charge of
murder against Charles H. Heissig was dismissed, and also on
the same day the venue against the others—William D. Meador,
Jake Ryan, Joe Sitterle, and William Cox—was changed. The
reason for the change of venue was that Pleasants was "satisfied that there exists in this county influences resulting from
the terrorism prevailing among the good people of the county
which will prevent a trial alike fair and impartial to the accused

and the State." Hence the venue was changed to the County of Bexar, to take place in San Antonio.[18]

The quartet presented objections to the change of venue: Judge Pleasants had no authority to change the venue upon his own motion; the section allowing this was unconstitutional; and the court of Bexar was not the closest county to that of DeWitt. The objections were overruled.[19]

Then Cox, Ryan, and Sitterle severed their case from William D. Meador. They were jointly tried and each was convicted of the charge of murder in the first degree on April 17, 1878. They appealed the conviction on questions of constitutionality. The legal explanation filled many pages in the cases argued and adjudged before the Texas Court of Appeals. A technicality freed the trio, in that the Constitution provided that "all prosecutions shall be carried on in the name and by the authority of 'The State of Texas,' and conclude 'against the peace and dignity of the State.'" However, the indictment both in the copy and in the transcript and in the original concluded, "against the peace and dignity of the *statute*" instead of "against the peace and dignity of the State." This was a serious error for the prosecution's case. The result was—at least for Cox, Ryan, and Sitterle—good fortune, as the final decision was that because "illegal and inadmissible evidence was allowed to go to the jury, over objections of defendants, and because the indictment is fatally defective [i.e., the word *statute*], the judgment of the court below is reversed and the cause remanded." Following this turn of events the defendants were granted bail. They chose to leave not only DeWitt County, but in fact chose to leave the state, settling farther west in New Mexico Territory where their fortunes improved. They settled out their lives in the area of Las Cruces.[20] Jack Hays Day summed up the actions resulting in the trio's good fortune, but with his anger almost spilling over onto the page. "Three were tried and condemned to death [but] the lawyers found a flaw in the indictment and the cases were thrown out of court. They were set free. Separating, they fled before the grand jury met to re-indict them."[21]

Charles Heissig did not flee and paid the ultimate price by becoming yet another victim of the feud. Carl Heinrich Heissig was his given name, but when he and his wife came to America from Prussia in the early 1850s he Americanized it to Charles. They arrived at the port of Indianola on June 12, 1853, and later moved to the Upper Yorktown area where Heissig operated a combination freight stop with a restaurant, bar, and dance hall. Family lore records he "unwittingly became a witness to the brutal murder" of the Brassells. His testimony has not been recorded so it is impossible to determine what he saw or claimed to not have seen, but someone believed he needed to be silenced. During the evening of May 15, 1880, Charles Heissig was shot to death in front of his home and business. No one was ever identified as the killer, but rumor had it that he knew something and his testimony could be injurious, hence his murder.[22]

Dave Augustine suffered the most of the men who were charged with the Brassell murders. Less than forty years old when charged with participating in the killings, Augustine swore that he was at home with his wife and children that night in September. In October 1898 he wrote the governor, Joseph Draper Sayers, asking for a pardon, with numerous petitions and hundreds of names affixed thereto. He stated that he was then a resident of Crockett County, that he was an old man, "infirm and broken in body and mind" and no doubt could not live much longer. He claimed to have never done anything wrong before the charge brought against him, that after the charge he had spent a total of seven years lying in jail waiting for a trial, and had never asked for a continuance. The case had been changed to Guadalupe County and dismissed for want of evidence by the district attorney. It was then changed to Coleman County. Convict William Templeton was pardoned from prison for the purpose of obtaining other indictments against him. He was then tried in Gonzales County but endured two mistrials. In Hays County the trial was declared a mistrial and continued. He was convicted then. At one time owning cattle and sheep on a ranch valued at $100,000, he now had little of value. Those who signed his request for pardon included John H. Power, Sheriff Thomas Stell of DeWitt County, County Judge C.O. Sumners, Texas pioneer George Lord, several Pridgens, including B. J. himself, as well as his son Oscar who also had served as a Texas Ranger, and W.W. Peavy among many others. Governor Sayers took pity on the old man and pardoned Dave Augustine. Although claiming to be infirm and broken in body and mind Augustine survived until January 20, 1912. He died in Tom Green County.[23]

Charles S. Bell outlived his partner Jack Helm by a half-dozen years, passing away at the Soldiers' Home in Dayton, Ohio, on February 18, 1879. A lengthy obituary in the *New York Times* reviewed his life, telling of escapades during the Civil War as well as his actions following the war's end, including his writing "a series of romantic adventures relating to his own experiences" for the *New York Ledger*, and then editing a "small sheet devoted to brokers' interests and finance" on Wall Street. When his health began to deteriorate, Bell went to Arkansas hoping the climate would be beneficial, but not finding any improvement there he returned to Ohio to die. He was described as one of "those heroic spirits, who, amid the clash of contending arms in a great war, help to make the history of a nation." There was no mention of his activities in Texas that resulted in his becoming a fugitive after Reconstruction ended. He entered the Soldiers' Home on the seventeenth and died on the following day, the cause of death given as consumption.[24]

Wyatt Anderson also chose to leave the feud troubles in Texas behind, relocating to Animas, New Mexico. His daughter Mary had married William P. "Buck" Taylor, who was shot and killed along with Dick Chisholm by members of the Sutton party.[25]

Of the other major feudists, the fate of Bill Taylor remains a mystery. Having escaped from the Indianola jail due to the destructive hurricane, he was later located in Coleman County in West Texas. Lt. B. S. Foster's company of Rangers was there scouting for fugitives from justice. Judge J. R. Fleming learned of his presence and issued a bench warrant for Taylor's arrest. A Ranger scout arrested Taylor on April 15, 1877. L. C. Williamson, Coleman County clerk, telegraphed the good news to Adjutant General Steele in Austin.[26] Judge Fleming wrote Major John B. Jones, head of the Frontier Battalion, commending Lieutenant Foster for the "promptness" in "sustaining the Civil authorities ... and in the execution of the Bench warrant issued by me for the arrest" of Taylor.[27]

Other serious charges were brought against Bill Taylor as well. In June 1880 he was in the DeWitt County jail when the census was taken, one of eleven prisoners under the care of jailer Louis Doross or DeMoss.[28] It is unclear why he was in jail now, but perhaps it had to do with a charge having no connection with the feud. A nineteen-year-old mulatto woman—Martha Brown—brought the charge of rape against him and several others before County Attorney Rudolph Kleberg on January 9, 1880. Taylor, Orlando C. Hanks, Mark Davis, and Joe Bennett were the men charged. Taylor stood his trial on June 28, 1882, nearly eighteen months after the alleged rape, was found not guilty and was discharged. One of the jury members was DeWitt County Sheriff Thomas M. Stell. Ironies abound with this incident in Taylor's life: Orlando Hanks, who later became a member of the famous "Wild Bunch" of outlaws of the American northwest at the turn of the nineteenth century, was the stepson of James W. Cox, a victim of an ambush planned by John Wesley Hardin. Mark Davis was probably an adopted son of Martin V. King, involved in the killing of Jim Taylor, Hendricks, and Arnold. Joe Bennett was the son of Elizabeth Bennett-Rivers-Kelly-Hendricks.[29] Bill Taylor ultimately came clear of the charge of killing Gabriel W. Slaughter, although he spent considerable time in jail in the process. Who received the $500 reward for his capture is unclear, but as late as November 1877 Attorney John D. Stephens of Comanche inquired about the reward to Gov. R. B. Hubbard. Hubbard's reply was that the amount had been paid in 1876, but with no indication as to who received it.[30]

What finally happened to Bill Taylor? The evidence is not conclusive, but unlike cousin Jim, he did leave Texas. An affidavit prepared and signed in 1916 by W. W. Taylor (son of "Buck" Taylor), and Thomas J. Bailey (who had married Buck's sister Elizabeth) stated that Bill Taylor "was killed in Oklahoma in the year 1895 and had never married. ..."[31] If indeed the Bill Taylor who died in Oklahoma in 1895 was feudist Bill Taylor (the name is fairly common), then he wisely chose to leave the feuding country. He thus proved wiser than many of his friends who lost their lives feuding with their neighbors.

Creed Taylor. His last photograph, taken by G. B. Snow in San Antonio,
April 21, 1905. *Courtesy the Robert G. McCubbin Collection.*

CHAPTER ELEVEN

With the Smoke Cleared

"[The] Sutton-Taylor feud, of which so much has been said,
and which has been the cause of many of these false
impressions affecting Cuero, is at an end."
—*Austin Daily Democratic Statesman*, MAY 5, 1877

After the pardon of David Augustine, perhaps the citizens of DeWitt County felt it was safe to say that the Sutton-Taylor Feud was finally over. The Brassells had been long buried; their accused slayers had endured their trials at no doubt great expense. Some participants had sold out and moved elsewhere. No one could be considered a winner in the conflict, although the men who did the actual fighting and survived may have considered themselves the victors. There were certainly plenty of graves in South Texas—marked and unmarked—to enumerate the losers. Some no doubt felt law and order was victorious; others may have felt just as strongly that mob law was an acceptable means of dealing with suspected desperadoes.

It had been thirty long years of feuding, and certainly Texans were exhausted with the terrors they had endured. Not only had the state experienced the savagery of Unionists and pro-Southern men fighting within the state's boundaries, but it then endured the conflict of Reconstruction, which was in many respects a continuation of the declared war. Perhaps the tendency for men to fight their own personal battles was a natural continuation of the nation's internecine struggles and the inevitable result of their learned military experience.

The State of Texas was the ground for many feudists who fought against their neighbors. As we have seen, the characteristics of feuding in the nineteenth century were not unique to the Lone Star State, as several famous vendettas occurred in neighboring New Mexico and Arizona territories. In those two territories, the Lincoln County War from which arose the iconic Billy the Kid remains the best known; the Graham-Tewksbury Feud, on the other hand, produced no such romantic figure. Also known as the Tonto Basin War, or the Pleasant Valley War, the latter conflict remains less known among the general public no doubt because the troubles did not produce such an iconic figure.

Within the boundaries of Texas the early feud between the Regulators and the Moderators of East Texas cost many lives and was ended only when President Sam Houston appealed to the leaders of both factions to end their hostilities, which they did. Following the Civil War, feuds were more frequent. In Mason County men chose sides following basically ethnic lines. In Lampasas County the Horrell brothers and their allies fought against Pink Higgins and his followers. In far-off El Paso County feuding arose between Anglos and Hispanics over the right to control the precious commodity of salt.

DeWitt County was the heart of the Sutton-Taylor Feud, although numerous killings occurred beyond the county lines. For instance, in 1867, two sons of Creed Taylor, brothers Hays and Doboy, experienced a difficulty with Maj. John Thompson in Mason County, many miles from DeWitt County, resulting in the deaths of Thompson and a sergeant. Some killings began in DeWitt County, but bled into neighborhing counties. Charles Taylor and James Sharp were suspected of theft in DeWitt County. A DeWitt County posse under the leadership of Sheriff James F.

Blair and William E. Sutton pursued the pair. Sutton's portion of the posse caught up with Taylor and Sharp. Taylor was shot down in Bastrop County; Sharp was captured. In neighboring Caldwell County prisoner Sharp was shot down, the posse leaving his body for someone else to bury.

Months later William E. Sutton was again involved in a killing: now Buck Taylor and his companion Dick Chisholm were shot down in Clinton following an argument. Sutton now had been involved in two confrontations that resulted in four men dead. In each situation Sutton had companions acting with him. These men, seeing how Sutton accomplished his mission of eradicating individuals he perceived as thieves, naturally followed him. William E. Sutton now became the leader of all those individuals who believed the rigors of the law were unnecessary. Vigilantism became the norm for dealing with accused desperadoes, personal enemies, or anyone considered an outlaw by the occupying military forces. Others who developed a reputation for brutal vigilantism included Joseph Tumlinson and Jack Helm. This trio, Sutton, Tumlinson and Helm, became a ruthless triumvirate who waged their personal war against the Taylor family and its allies.

Part of the uniqueness of the hatreds and violence between those who followed William E. Sutton and those who were either sympathetic to the Taylor cause, or were related to them and banded with them through loyalty, is the length of the conflict as well as the cost in lives. The conflict lasted longer than some declared wars between countries, and longer than nearly all other feuds of Texas or other states or territories. The difficulties the Taylors experienced in Mason and Bastrop counties, resulting in a total of five men dead, mark the beginning of the shooting phase of the feud.

The double killings of the Brassells in late 1876 essentially marked the end of the shooting phase of the Sutton-Taylor Feud. The key leaders of both factions were dead, but a few followers still believed the vigilante method was best. The mysterious deaths of Martin V. King and Charles Heissig followed. Due to the leadership abilities of Texas Ranger J. L. Hall and Judge Henry Clay Pleasants, disagreements entered into the justice system without violence.

Then the battles began in the court rooms, where attorneys could argue verbally about the law. The families of the murdered Brassells, Heissig, and M. V. King no doubt believed that justice had not been served, as the accused murderers of the Brassells finally went free. The streets of Cuero and Clinton and the highways and trails of DeWitt County were much safer, however, thanks to the work of Hall and Pleasants.

The Sutton-Taylor Feud finally ended with the pardon of Dave Augustine in 1899, although even as late as the early twenty-first century hard feelings still exist. Some descendants of the feuding men and women are suspicious of those inquiring about the feud. Others refuse to even discuss the matter. The conflict, at least openly, had lasted over three decades, thus justifying Dr. Sonnichsen, the late doyen of Texas feud history, to give the title "Thirty Years A-Feuding" to his chapter on the feud.

If the Sutton-Taylor Feud was not the costliest in human lives, it certainly claimed a sizeable number. No one can say with certainty how many men were killed in the skirmishes, ambushes, and gun battles. (See appendix 6.) Occasionally the body of a man was found along some road or fence line, his identity perhaps undeterminable, his slayer unknown. One example will suffice: "The body of a dead man was found near Mr. Neil Bowen's fence on the Sandies, Gonzales county, a week ago. He was a stranger, and looked to be about eighteen—or twenty years of age." This simple statement from the *Daily Democratic Statesman* of Austin, September 4, 1877, leaves many questions unanswered. Was he a victim of the feud? Was he "imported" to commit murder for the remnants of the

Taylor or Sutton faction? Was the young man killed because of feud hatreds or did death come as a result of some private desire for revenge? Since Neill Bowen's son and son-in-law were both involved in killing Sutton followers, one cannot help but suspect this killing near his fence had some connection to the feud. One might suspect Brown Bowen's or John Wesley Hardin's possible involvement, but they were both prisoners in the Travis County jail at the time. Men could cover great distances even on horseback; with revenge a priority distances could seem shorter. There was no way of learning the answers to these questions unless someone finally confessed to the killing. The Brassell killings provide an excellent example of this phenomenon of men killed for no apparent reason: some in 1876 believed they were victims of the feud's hatred, while other contemporaries claimed their deaths had nothing to do with the feud. Only because the family survivors could identify the men who killed their father and brother was some degree of justice finally achieved. Even though it cannot be determined exactly why those men killed the doctor and his son, evidence is clearly sufficient to place their murders among the final tragic acts of the feud.

The wrongs committed on both sides certainly fit the classic example of the blood feud. Hatreds lasting over generations, illegal violent acts committed by both sides, the feud carried on although the original "cause" may have been forgotten. It was difficult in the 1860s and '70s to pinpoint a single cause for what became known in its day as the Sutton-Taylor Feud. In spite of the murkiness of the sparks that ignited the flames of the feud, the shooting of Charles Taylor and James Sharp in Bastrop and Caldwell counties, respectively, was a significant event. As leader of the posse, William E. Sutton was considered responsible for the deaths of these two men. If that was not the direct cause of the feud then certainly the killing of William P. "Buck" Taylor and Richard T. "Dick" Chisholm in

Clinton on Christmas Eve was. Here again, William E. Sutton was directly involved. He may not have been the only man shooting but he was considered responsible for the deaths of two more men, another Taylor and his relative. If any among the Taylor family members was keeping score at this point—Christmas, 1868—it was four Taylors lost, two Taylors fugitives from justice, and no revenge yet taken. Cousins Hays and Doboy Taylor had their own problems with the military, which forced them into the same violence of the feud, although their initial killing was not a primary cause for the other Taylors to become feudists.

During the turmoil following the Civil War the bedrock holding society together was in shambles. If there was a perceived wrong, such as an insult, a suspected theft, a challenge, one could not simply rush to a justice of the peace or a local officer of the court to make a complaint. The tradition of upholding family honor would have prevented that even if the court was physically present, and in many instances the court was miles away. With the Sutton-Taylor Feud, it was a *perceived wrong* that caused William E. Sutton to join a posse in pursuit of stolen animals. Acting upon this, members of the posse killed two men, effectively utilizing vigilante action rather than turning their prisoners over to the court system. This double killing later resulted in hard words between several "Sutton men" and another Taylor and his companion, resulting in the deaths of the latter pair. Whether he intended to become a leader in the difficulties that followed, or merely by force of personality accepted the leadership, he became the leader of the vigilantes, and his followers were called "the Suttons." William E. Sutton now became the substitute for a strong legal system: to many his actions then and in the following years, until his early death in 1874, amounted to being the titular head of a vigilante organization.

In response, the Taylor family, or clan, perceived Sutton as waging war against them for no legitimate reason, believed forceful retaliation was the only solution, and felt obliged to defend themselves with violence. Their backgrounds would not have permitted any other means. A Taylor's blood had been spilled; the honor of the family's name demanded vengeance. That the Sutton-Taylor Feud was a classic example of the blood feud is shown with a casual perusal of the victims: William E. Sutton, Gabriel W. Slaughter, James W. Cox, Jake Christman, Jack Helm—all were friends who lost their lives in the feud. On the other side Charles Taylor, Pitkin B. Taylor, Jim Taylor, A. R. Hendricks, and Mace Arnold: they were all family or friends fighting the Suttons. In all there were at least eighty victims, men who died by gunshots or a rope around their neck in a large area of the state ranging from Calhoun County and San Patricio County, to Bastrop and Mason counties.

The feud was of two generations: numerous fathers and sons fought their perceived enemies. Pitkin Barnes Taylor was shot down by hidden assassins; his son carried on the feud and was shot down in 1875 with two companions. A brother of Pitkin Taylor, Creed Taylor, served time in a military jail for the violent actions of his sons against the military. His only known "crime" was that Hays and Doboy were his sons and of course, as a father, he sheltered them.

A characteristic of most feuds is that numerous families become involved. Many are forced to choose a side due to whom they marry. Although it is an exaggeration to say that every man in DeWitt County had to choose sides, many did feel an *obligation* to; some may have actually been threatened if they did not. That obligation came from their personal friendship, their marriage or simply a blood tie. But many who chose to avoid direct involvement did not feel it safe to remain and left the area. The best example is that of James Sutton, brother of William E. Sutton. Instead of remaining in the DeWitt County area to fight alongside his brother, he moved away and lived in peace through the remainder of his long life. No one can definitely answer the question of why he made that choice.

The period following the Civil War was chaotic in many areas of the state, even though the number of battles fought on Texas soil was relatively small. Although many of the younger men in the area of DeWitt, Gonzales, and Karnes counties may have been ignorant of much of the social dishevelment, they were certainly aware that the *ante bellum* society had been radically altered. Uniformed men of the North now were stationed in the Southern towns. Those who sympathized with the Rebel cause were treated as outlaws in many cases. Former soldiers were often destitute when they returned to their homes.

After the South's defeat, Texas became part of the Fifth Military District. Elections were overseen by troops. Former slaves were now citizens; they could sit on juries whereas those who had fought for the South could not. Opportunistic men from the North invaded the South intending to enrich themselves at the expense of the defeated Texans. Resentment of the new social order became the rule. From the social turmoil the most noted reactionaries who gained notoriety included John Wesley Hardin, William P. Longley, and Ben Thompson. Hardin, who could have continued his desperate life as a lone gunman, chose to ally himself with the Taylors. He was not related to them, but his cousins the Clements brothers were fighting on their side. He believed the Taylors had been wronged.

With the entrance of John Wesley Hardin among the ranks of the Taylors, the tactics changed. Hardin added significant aggression to the Taylor actions. Ambushes resulted in several deaths among the Sutton leadership, which resulted in the two sides signing a peace treaty. A short period of relative calm did follow, but then there was another killing. When citizens directly involved themselves in another attempt to end the hostilities, a second treaty was signed, which lasted nearly three months before William E. Sutton and companion Gabriel Webster

Slaughter were shot down. By now the violence between the Suttons and the Taylors attracted statewide attention.

The face of the feud changed again with John Wesley Hardin's killing of a deputy sheriff in Comanche County, resulting in the lynching of six of Hardin's friends and relatives, and the shooting death of two others. Hardin became a fugitive and left the state for three years of relative obscurity. The lynching in Comanche and Clinton attracted the attention of the governor, who sent Capt. L. H. McNelly and a force of Texas Rangers (technically his Washington County Volunteer Militia Company) to the troubled area of DeWitt County. The presence of the Rangers resulted in six months of relative peace, but after McNelly's forced departure to the Rio Grande frontier the troubles began anew. More killings followed, notably that of Cuero City Marshal Brown, and later in 1875 Jim Taylor and two companions were shot down on the streets of Clinton.

The deaths of William E. Sutton and his arch enemy James C. Taylor should have ended the Sutton-Taylor Feud, but a few more killings followed, most notably the double killing of Dr. Brassell and his son. Again the Texas Rangers, now under the leadership of Lt. Jesse L. Hall, were sent to DeWitt County. The arrest of seven followers of Sutton for the brutal Brassell killings ended the shooting phase of the feud. Now the court battles followed. In spite of strong evidence of who the Brassell killers were, only one was sentenced to prison, and he received a pardon before entering prison walls. Dave Augustine received a pardon in 1899, twenty-three years after the killing of the Brassells, and thirty-two years after the first blood was shed back in Mason during the argument between two Taylors and two men of the military. William E. Sutton had been dead since 1874, but due to his personality and leadership abilities, those who believed in his cause were termed "the Suttons" even after his death. No single Taylor gave his name to the feud.

The essential points of the Sutton-Taylor Feud were the double killing of Buck Taylor and Dick Chisholm; the vigilante activity of Jack Helm and Charles S. Bell; the entrance of John Wesley Hardin into the ranks of the Taylors, which revealed the increased aggression of the Taylors behind Hardin's leadership; the double killing of Sutton and Slaughter in 1874; the entrance of McNelly and his squad of Texas Rangers; the triple killing of Jim Taylor and his two companions; and finally the double murder of Dr. Brassell and his son, which shocked the community and resulted in the Texas Rangers again being called in, although now under a different commander. Following the arrest of the alleged murderers the animosity between the Taylors and the Sutton followers may have continued, but it now was confined within the legal system.

Captain McNelly was undoubtedly correct in his assessment of the character of the feudists and the reasons the violence continued. He arrived in DeWitt County in August 1874, and in his monthly report to Adjutant General Steele he noted: "The leaders are men long accustomed to doing as they please regardless of consequences and have never experienced restraint upon their movements until now."[1] In other words, even with a county sheriff, deputies, and several judges living in Clinton itself, enough men acted as a law unto themselves that many men paid the ultimate price. Finally, in 1877, with Rangers holding their Winchesters at the ready beside him, Judge Henry Clay Pleasants was able to hold court without fear of immediate reprisal. It was a significant lesson to the court system and citizens who wanted to live peaceably in their community. The law was to be considered the supreme arbiter of all differences between men; there was such majesty to the law that no matter how much vigilante activity might occur, eventually it would persevere.

Fortunately for the good citizens of DeWitt County, and perhaps those who still resided in Clinton, as the twentieth century approached, men could look back on early decades and reminisce. It may not have been the "good old days" but at least one reporter harkened back and contributed this item printed in the Cuero newspaper:

> A few years ago when the Sutton and Taylor parties paid their respects to our little burg, things could happen on very short notice. But time has brought a great change. Things never "happen" now and seldom "come to pass" as some of our "bachelor boys" could tell you when they are disposed to divulge secrets.[2]

Only two decades before, Jim Taylor, A. R. Hendricks, and Mace Arnold lost their lives on the Clinton streets; no doubt some of the "bachelor boys," or even some of the gray haired men, could relate how the event had "come to pass."

Children of Feudists. From left: Jeff Butler III; Pitkin B. Taylor II, son of Jim and "Mollie" Taylor; and Frank Butler. The Butlers were sons by her second husband. *Courtesy E. J. Thormaehlen.*

EPILOGUE

All Is Forgiven

"The joy shared by Taylor, Tumlinson and Sutton descendants on that day touched many hearts, and will radiate to touch many others. ..."
—MARJORIE BURNETT HYATT, *Gonzales Daily Inquirer,*
JULY 26, 1988

lthough Jim Taylor's two friends who died with him received little recognition, a special event occurred in 1988, which provided some degree of fame. On July 10 of that year, at the Taylor-Bennett Cemetery just south of Cuero on Highway 87, the graves of A. R. Hendricks and Mason "Winchester Smith" Arnold were marked with new granite headstones. Sympathizers had originally marked their final resting places with plain wooden boards, long since worn away and discarded.[1] What could have been a private little ceremony became a special event with over 125 people representing the various sides in the conflict and considerable media coverage as well.

Both Hendricks and Arnold had been killed along with James Creed Taylor on the streets of long-disappeared Clinton on December 27, 1875, by a group of Sutton's followers. Jim Taylor's gravestone, apparently installed shortly after his death, still stands proudly not far from the final resting place of Arnold and Hendricks.

269

Marjorie Burnett Hyatt of Smiley, Gonzales County, had researched the genealogy of many of the feud's participants. It was through her efforts that headstones for Arnold and Hendricks were provided and set by Joe and Carol Solansky of Gonzales. The Freund Funeral Home of Cuero provided a tent at the cemetery to shade the visitors from the blazing July sun. Television coverage was provided by KVCT-TV of Victoria with David and Cynthia Salm filming. Signatures in the guest book showed interested people had come from thirty-two towns in three states.

Ms. Hyatt's efforts at bringing these people together did not happen by chance. She had long researched the feudists and their families, strictly from the point of view of a genealogist. In so doing she came in contact with many descendants. Perhaps not so remarkable is that there were descendants gathered in that cemetery whose ancestors over a century earlier may have been deadly enemies. Although at the time there were no known descendants of Arnold or Hendricks, there were descendants of Jim Taylor, William E. Sutton, and Joseph Tumlinson present that day, among others whose names loomed large during the feud.

Several authors presented the Cuero Public Library with various historical works: the late Karon Mac Smith of Nixon, on whose land Jack Helm is buried; Rick Miller of Harker Heights, Texas, whose book on Jack Duncan details the biography of the Dallas detective involved in the capture of feudist John Wesley Hardin; Patsy Goebel of Cuero, whose inventories of the numerous DeWitt County cemeteries continue to be an invaluable tool for historians and genealogists; Donaly E. Brice of Lockhart, a research specialist at the Texas State Archives, as well as this author, then a resident of Wisconsin, donated a copy of their work dealing with Texas history.

Everyone was pleased with the number of guests in attendance, many of whom gathered following the ceremony for lunch and refreshments at the Longhorn Ranch Restaurant not far from the cemetery.

The new stones bore the following inscriptions:

Mason Arnold
Alias Winchester Smith
Born 1847–Killed Dec. 27, 1875
At Clinton, Tx.

and:

A. R. Hendricks
Killed at Clinton, Tx
Dec. 27, 1875
Husband of Elizabeth Day Bennett Rivers Kelly

In spite of the summer heat, no tempers flared, no loud re-marks were made, but there were plenty of handshakes and smiles. There were many who were strangers to one another, and many who were distantly related but had not seen each other for some time. All found it a most pleasant and reward-ing time.

Ms. Hyatt pointed out that the guests "expressed apprecia-tion for being brought together for this special occasion. It was a heart-warming experience for me, for several reasons." As she had organized the entire event, seeing "those stones installed was a real reward. Some have said, 'There are still bad feelings about the feud.' The joy shared by descendants of the Taylors, the Tumlinsons and William Sutton on that day touched many hearts, and will radiate to touch many others as the events of the day are related to others."[2]

David Salm, who filmed the entire event for Victoria's KVCT-TV, signed off his segment by mentioning the five men killed in the feud that are buried in that cemetery and con-cluded: "because of the events of this day, the hatchet is also buried here."[3]

Although the figurative hatchet may have been buried in the Taylor-Bennett Cemetery in 1988, four years later the popular History Channel television series produced a program which could have brought the old feelings of animosity to life again. Entitled *Vendettas: Sutton vs. Taylor* with narration by well-known media commentator Roger Mudd, it described the Sutton-Taylor Feud as "one of the longest running gun battles" and the "bloodiest [feud] in Texas history."

Mudd interviewed several well-known individuals in the historic museum in Cuero: Patsy Goebel, responsible for the three-volume DeWitt County cemetery inventory books; highly acclaimed illustrator and historian Jack Jackson, who grew up in the feud country; Bena Taylor Kirkscey, a Taylor descendant and long-time editor of the *Taylor Family News*; Leon Metz, popular chronicler of Old West gunfighters and author of biographies of John Wesley Hardin; and Robert Sutton, a great-grandnephew of William E. Sutton.

One viewpoint asserted by *Vendettas* is that the feud began on Christmas Eve, 1868, with the killing of William P. "Buck" Taylor and his cousin Dick Chisholm by William E. Sutton and his friends. To underscore the fact that historians often disagree, another view presented was that it had begun two years prior, with defeated Confederates returning home from the eastern battlefields, then being subjected to Union occupation troops and freedmen. The late historian-artist Jack Jackson stated it was "a powder keg with a rapidly burning fuse" which exploded with the Christmas Eve killings. The reason Taylor was killed according to Jackson was that he was "a second generation [cattle] rustler." In fact the theme of the program insists that the Taylors were indeed rustlers, or at least managed to acquire more than their fair share of mavericks off the range.

Only a few incidents of the feud could be highlighted in the limited time available, but the major players were Jack Helm, described as a "hard, tough mean individual" by Leon Metz; John Wesley Hardin, a dangerous killer; Jim Taylor, son of Pitkin whose death is described and re-enacted; and Joe Tumlinson. After the killing of Helm by Hardin and Taylor, Bill Sutton became the leader. The History Channel production suggests that Tumlinson, who should have been on the Taylor side due to having married a Taylor, perhaps fought alongside Sutton because he knew who would be the likely winner in the struggle.

Just as it was impossible to explain fully the causes of the conflict in the limited time offered, it is impossible to explain today—nearly a century and a half after the events—within the pages of a single volume. In addition no one can say with absolute certainty why these individuals living in the same general area fought so hard against each other. There were many others who returned home from the war to find their lives totally in disarray, their homes gone, and the state filled with occupation troops. Most managed to avoid conflict with their neighbors. There was but one Sutton involved, but he had many friends, men who were willing to risk their lives for him and with him. When he was killed, Gabe Slaughter was at his side, whose only "hostile act" was perhaps being his friend and being with him when the Taylors caught up with Sutton. And for that Slaughter died.

The Taylors were a large family. Many of the young men were perhaps hot-headed, but so were many other young men who avoided feuding with anyone. The young men were descended from Texas pioneers who had fought Mexicans and Indians before being forced to choose between the Union and the newly created Confederacy. If indeed the Taylors increased their cattle herds at the expense of mavericks and cattle belonging to others, so did many another rancher. In fact some of the most respected cattle kings were not immune from taking another man's calf. In that sense the Taylors were no different from many of their contemporaries. But they paid a high price; they were singled out as if to make an example of for others. As Bena Taylor Kirkscey stated during the filming of *Sutton vs. Taylor*: "I really don't think there's anyway to understand why the Taylors apparently were singled out for the ruthless treatment they were given. It's a question that's been pondered by the generations since then. I don't think there's ever been an answer to it. We don't know why."[4]

Feudists and Related Individuals

The following does not identify all the individuals mentioned in this work. It is merely a clarifying listing of individuals and their relationship to others which otherwise may be uncertain. It is thus intended to be only an aid to appreciating the relationships among those individuals.

Anderson, Alexander Hamilton "Ham" (1849–1874), shot to death near Comanche in the aftermath of the Charles Webb killing.

Anderson, Richmond (1848–?), son of Walter "Watt" and Lou Bailey Anderson. Signed the 1874 treaty of peace.

Arnold, Mason "Winchester Smith" (1848–1875), killed with James C. Taylor and A. R. Hendricks in Clinton.

Augustine, David (1838–1912), was found guilty of Brassell killings; pardoned before reaching prison.

Barekman, Alexander Henry (1842–1874), shot to death near Comanche in the aftermath of the Charles Webb killing.

Beck, James P. (?–?), signed bond for Sheriff Jack Helm.

Bell, Charles S. (1843/44–1879), leader with Jack Helm of vigilante group against the Taylors; later himself a fugitive from Texas justice.

Bell, James C. (?–1869), killed by Helm vigilante party; no relation to Charles S. Bell.

Bell, William (?–1869), killed by Helm and vigilante party; no relation to Charles S. Bell; relation to James C. Bell is uncertain.

Blair, James Francis (1826–1901), Sheriff of DeWitt County, 1866–1869. Deputized William E. Sutton.

Bockius, James Monroe "Doc" (1831–1909), narrowly escaped from a lynch mob in Clinton in 1874; had worked for John Wesley Hardin as cattleman. Married widow of George C. Tennille; later post master of Sedan, Gonzales County.

Boston Jr., Hugh (1854–?), signed 1874 treaty of peace; Sutton sympathizer.

Bowen, Joshua Robert "Brown" (1849–1878), found guilty of murder of Thomas Haldeman; legally hanged in Gonzales.

Bowen, Neill (1829–1889), father of Joshua Robert "Brown" and Jane Bowen; became father-in-law of John Wesley Hardin.

Brassell, George (1854–1876), slain with his father by Sutton sympathizers.

Brassell, Mary Ann (1829–1883), wife of Dr. Philip H. Brassell.

Brassell, Nancy (1856–?), daughter of Dr. Philip H. Brassell.

Brassell, Dr. Philip H. (1827–1876), native of Georgia, murdered by Sutton sympathizers.

Brassell, Sylvanus S. (1861–?), son of Dr. Philip H. Brassell; escaped death night of raid on the Brassell home.

Brassell, Theodore C. (1858–1927), son of Dr. Philip H. Brassell; escaped death during the night of the raid on the Brassell home.

Brown, Reuben H. (1851–1875), son of P. T. and Miriam K. Brown; City Marshal of Cuero; killed by Taylor sympathizers.

Bryant, Abram (1809–1874), former slave of Senator B. J. Pridgen; murdered by Sutton sympathizers.

Buchanan, William Francis "Billy" (1846–1874), attempted to betray Taylors into ambush; killed possibly by B. J. Pridgen.

Chisholm, Richard H. (1793–1855), married Hardinia Taylor; father of Richard T., Glenn T., Bradford A. and Mary Ann Chisholm.

Chisholm, Richard "Dick" (1849–1869), killed with "Buck" Taylor by William E. Sutton and party in Clinton.

Choate, Crockett (1842–1869), killed by Helm and vigilante group.

Choate, John (1818–1869), cousin of Crockett Choate; killed by Helm and vigilante group.

Christman, John W.S. "Jake" (1837–1873), Sutton sympathizer; killed with James A. Cox in Taylor ambush.

Clark, Jeff (?–?), companion of Hays and Doboy Taylor when Littleton and Stannard were ambushed and killed.

Clements, Emanuel "Mannen" (1845–1887), cousin of John Wesley Hardin.

Clements, James (1843–1897), cousin of John Wesley Hardin; married Anne C. Tennille, daughter of George C. Tennille.

Clements, John Gibson "Gip" (1851–1929), cousin of John Wesley Hardin; married Elizabeth C. Evans.

Clements, Joseph Hardin (1849–1927), cousin of John Wesley Hardin; married Amanda S. Tennille, daughter of George C. Tennille.

Cook, James (?–?), companion of Hays and Doboy Taylor when Littleton and Stannard were ambushed and killed.

Cox, James W. (1827–1873), DeWitt County farmer and associate of Sutton; killed in ambush by Taylors.

Cox, John Frank (1853–?), son of feud victim James W. Cox.

Cox, William W. (1855–?), son of James W. Cox.

Davis, W. W. (?–?), Gonzales County cattleman; sympathizer of the Sutton party.

Day, Alfred C. (1855–?), son of Susan Day; brother of Jackson Hays Day; in Huntsville State Prison in 1880.

Day, Elizabeth Jane Bennett-Rivers-Kelly-Hendricks (1836–1887), of her four husbands, two were killed during the feud.

Day, Jackson Hays (1856–1948), witness to killing of Buck Taylor and Dick Chisholm; wrote memoir, *The Sutton Taylor Feud*.

Dees, Martha Ann (1846–1929), married James Sutton.

Delony, Lewis S. (1857–1948), witness to the killing of Buck Taylor and Dick Chisholm; wrote memoir, *40 Years a Peace Officer*.

Dowlearn, Patrick Hays "Bud" (1854–1924), Taylor sympathizer; may have been part of ambush party killing Cox and Christman.

French, Horace (1849–?), friend of William E. Sutton; witnessed Sutton's marriage; survived ambush by Taylors.

Fulcrod, — (?–1869), killed by Helm and vigilante group.

Glover, Edward J. (1840–1874?), son of Hinesberry and Emily S. Martin Glover; associate of the Taylors.

Goens, John (?–?), one of men who killed Wiley W. Pridgen according to Jack Hays Day.

Goodbread, Nancy (circa 1815–1867), first wife of Creed Taylor; mother of John Hays and Phillip Goodbread "Doboy" Taylor.

Haldeman, David (1809–1895), father of John T. and Thomas J. Haldeman.

Haldeman, John T. (1846–1918), brother of Thomas J. Haldeman.

Haldeman, Thomas J. (1848–1872), killed by Joshua Robert "Brown" Bowen.

Hardin, John Wesley (1853–1895), younger brother of Joseph G. Hardin, cousin of the four Clements brothers active in the feud; captured in Florida in 1877.

Hardin, Joseph G. (1851–1874), lynched by mob in Comanche in aftermath of Charles Webb killing.

Heissig, Carl (Charles) Heinrich (1822–1880), witness to the killings of the Brassells; killed May 15, 1880, by unknown party.

Helm, John Jackson Marshall "Jack" (1840–1873), DeWitt County sheriff; vigilante leader against Taylors; killed by Hardin and Taylor.

Hendricks, A. R. (?–1875), a McNelly Ranger; then joined Taylors; killed with Jim Taylor and Mason Arnold in Clinton.

Hudson, Richard B. (1821–after 1890?), signed bond for Jack Helm; daughter Rebecca married W. C. "Curry" Wallace, Sutton sympathizer.

Humphries, Mary Elizabeth (1854–1951), witness to the killing of Buck Taylor and Dick Chisholm; wrote memoir, "The First One Hundred Years."

Hunter, Christopher Taylor "Kit" (1856–1923), cousin of William E. Sutton; part of posse that killed Taylor, Hendricks, and Arnold.

Jacobs, Andrew J. (?–1869), Sheriff of Goliad County; killed allegedly by the Peace brothers.

Jones, Ausby Rutland (1823–1869), killed by Jack Helm and vigilante group.

Kellison, George (?–?), companion of Hays and Doboy Taylor; with them when Hays was killed in 1869.

Kelly, Amanda Jane (1848–1933), wife of Henry Kelly.

Kelly, Delilah (1818–1882), mother of the two Kelly brothers killed in the feud.

Kelly, Eugene A. (1850–1924), arrested by Sutton party in 1870; brother of Henry and William Kelly.

Kelly, Henry P. (1848–1870), killed by Sutton party along with brother William Kelly.

Kelly, Mary Elizabeth "Mollie" (1855–1924), married James C. "Jim" Taylor.

Kelly, Tobe (William T.?) (1856–?), son of William and Margaret Ann Clark Kelly; witnessed the killing of Buck Taylor and Dick Chisholm.

Kelly, Wiley (1844–1929), arrested by Sutton posse; later tried and acquitted.

Kelly, William B. (1846–1870), killed by Sutton posse along with brother Henry Kelly.

King, Martin V. (1835–1876), killed probably by Taylor sympathizers to avenge death of James C. "Jim" Taylor.

Kirkman, Sam (?–1869), killed by Helm and vigilante group.

Littleton, Captain John (1825–1868), veteran of Cortina War and Civil War; killed in ambush by Taylors.

Lunsford, James W. (1819–1869), killed by Jack Helm and vigilante group.

McCarty, Andrew (?–1869), killed by Jack Helm and vigilante group.

McCrabb, John Frederick "Buck" (1846–1909), friend of William E. Sutton; part of posse that killed Taylor, Arnold, and Hendricks.

McDonald, Laura Eudora (1853–1930), wife of William E. Sutton.

McDougall, John (?–1867), army sergeant killed with Major Thompson by Hays and Doboy Taylor in Mason.

Mason, James (?–?), one of men who killed Wiley W. Pridgen, according to Jackson Hays Day.

Meador, John J. (1846–?), part of posse that killed the two Kelly brothers; signed 1874 treaty of peace.

Meador, William D. (1850–?), signed 1874 treaty of peace; married Amanda Augustine in 1876.

Morris, William B. "Dave" (1822–1869), father-in-law of Martin Luther Taylor; killed with him by Helm vigilante group.

Newman, Elizabeth (1819–1906), second wife of Joseph Tumlinson.

Nichols, Lazarus (1825–1882), signed both treaties of peace.

Nichols, Morgan Oliver "Mack" (1851–1897), son of Lazarus Nichols; signed treaty of peace.

Olive, Ira (?–1869), alias Wills, killed by Helm and his vigilante group.

Patterson, Robert Andrew "Addison" (1843–1877?), with Sutton when ambushed but survived.

Peace, Christopher (1850–?), accused of killing Goliad County Sheriff Andrew J. Jacobs; brother of Madison Peace.

Peace, Madison "Matt" (1843–?) accused of killing Goliad County Sheriff Andrew J. Jacobs.

Pell, Fred (?–?), companion of Hays and Doboy Taylor when Captain Littleton and Stannard were killed.

Poole, Tobias (?–1869), killed by Helm vigilante group.

Pridgen, Augustus Washington "Gus" (1838–1876), son of Henry and W. E. Pridgen; cousin of Bolivar Jackson Pridgen; Taylor associate.

Pridgen, Bolivar Jackson (1829–1903), strong supporter of the Taylors; allegedly killed Billy Buchanan.

Pridgen, Oscar F. (1854–1944), son of Senator B. J. Pridgen; married Mary A. Lowe on November 22, 1876, married by W. H. H. Biggs in Cuero.

Pridgen, Wiley Washington (1841–1873), son of W. W. and Mary Baker Pridgen; brother of Senator B. J. Pridgen; killed Neill Brown in 1867.

Pulliam, Thomas (?–?), part of the Sutton posse in the Bastrop County affair in which Charles Taylor and James Sharp were killed.

Pursell, Reuben C. (1842–1869), killed by Helm and vigilante group.

Ragland, Henry (1842/43–?), private in State Police, signed 1873 treaty of peace.

Ragland, W. J. (possibly James W.) (?–?), signed 1874 treaty of peace.

Robinson, T. C. "Pidge" (1847–1876), served as lieutenant under Capt. L. H. McNelly from 1874–1876; killed in Virginia while on leave from McNelly's company.

Rowland, Buck (?–?), companion of Hays and Doboy Taylor when Captain Littleton and Stannard were killed.

Ryan, Nicholas Jacob "Jake" (1855–after 1910), part of group charged with murder of the Brassells.

Samples, Alexander H. (?–?), part of the Sutton posse in Bastrop County affair in which Charles Taylor and James Sharp were killed.

Sharp, James (?–1868), killed near Lockhart, Caldwell County, by Sutton posse.

Simmons, C. C. (1842–?), State Policeman; part of posse that killed the Kelly brothers.

Sitterle, Ed (1855–?), brother of Joseph; member of posse that killed Taylor, Arnold, and Hendricks in 1875.

Sitterle, Joseph (1853–?), son of Stephen and Madaleine Sitterle; signed 1874 treaty of peace as Sutton sympathizer.

Skidmore, F. O. (1849–1915), seriously wounded in 1869 when the Choates were killed by Helm and vigilante group; died in Mexico.

Slaughter, Gabriel Webster (1851–1874), friend of William E. Sutton and killed with him by Bill Taylor in Indianola.

Spencer, Lavinia Amanda (1855–1903), second wife of Creed Taylor.

Spencer, Randolph W. (1846–1870), son of Elijah and Carroll W. Spencer; with Hays and Doboy Taylor in Mason when Thompson and McDougall were killed.

Spencer, William Addison (1840–1922), married Caroline H. Taylor in 1866; brother of Randolph W. Spencer.

Stannard, William (?–1868), friend of Capt. John Littleton; killed with him in an ambush by Taylor party.

Stapp, James (?–1869), killed by Helm and vigilante group.

Sumners, Joseph Clayton (1850–?), with Sutton when Buck Taylor and Dick Chisholm were killed in Clinton.

Sutton, James (1844–1919), brother of William E. Sutton; took no part in the feud.

Sutton, William E. (1846–1874), leader of the Sutton faction until his death at hands of James C. Taylor.

Taylor, Alfred P. (1845–?), son of Rufus P. and Elizabeth Lowe Taylor. Part of the Sutton posse in the Bastrop County affair in which Charles Taylor and James Sharp were killed.

Taylor, Amanda Jane, see Amanda Jane Kelly.

Taylor, Charles (?–1868), killed by Sutton posse in Bastrop, Bastrop County.

Taylor, Creed (1820–1906), son of Josiah Taylor Sr.; married Nancy Goodbread and then Lavinia Spencer.

Taylor, Hardinia (1812–1853), married Richard Chisholm.

Taylor, Hephzibeth Luker (born circa 1790–1841), wife of Josiah Taylor Sr.

Taylor, James (1825–1852), son of Josiah Taylor Sr.; killed in California.

Taylor, Johanna (1815–1858), married to Joseph Tumlinson in 1832.

Taylor, John Hays (1842–1869), son of Creed Taylor killed in feud by C. S. Bell posse; buried on Creed Taylor's ranch in Wilson County.

Taylor, John Milam (1835–1906), brother of William P. "Buck" Taylor.

Taylor, Joseph (1833–1923), son of William Riley Taylor; signed for bond for Jack Helm.

Taylor, Josiah Jr. (circa 1821–1864), married Sarah Jane York.

Taylor, Josiah Sr. (born circa 1781–1830), patriarch of the Taylor clan; father of William Riley, Hardinia, Johanna, Creed, Josiah Jr., Pitkin B., Rufus P., James, and Mary Jane Taylor.

Taylor, Martin Luther (1845–1869), son of Rufus P. Taylor; married Sophronia Morris, daughter of W. B. "Dave" Morris; killed by vigilantes in McMullen County.

Taylor, Mary Jane (1830–1891), married Achilles Stapp.

Taylor, Phillip Goodbread "Doboy" (1845–1871), son of Creed Taylor, killed in Kerr County by Sim Holstein.

Taylor, Pitkin Barnes (1822–1873), father of Amanda Jane and James Creed Taylor.

Taylor, Rufus P. (1824–1854), son of Josiah Taylor Sr.; married Elizabeth Lowe.

Taylor, Rufus P. "Scrap" (1854–1874), lynched in Clinton by Sutton sympathizers.

Taylor, William P. "Buck" (1837–1868), son of William Riley and Elizabeth Tumlinson Taylor. Married Mary Anderson in 1866; accused of being in the party who allegedly killed Captain Henry J. Nolan in La Vernia, Wilson County; killed by William E. Sutton in Clinton.

Taylor, William Riley (1811–1850), son of Josiah Taylor Sr.; married Elizabeth Tumlinson in 1830.

Taylor William R. "Bill" (1855–1895?), cousin of James C. Taylor; killed Gabriel W. Slaughter in Indianola in 1874.

Templeton, William (1854–?), signed 1873 treaty of peace; was in Huntsville prison in 1880.

Tennille, George Culver Jr. (1825–1874), "advisor" to Taylor side of feudists; killed by Gonzales County sheriff's posse.

Thomas, Robert (?–?), part of the Sutton posse in the Bastrop County affair in which Charles Taylor and James Sharp were killed.

Thompson, Major John A. (?–1867), killed at Mason by Hays and Doboy Taylor and Randolph W. Spencer.

Tuggle, John Alfred "Kute" (1846–1874), signed 1873 treaty of peace; lynched by mob in Clinton.

Tuggle, Lodwick "Hun" (1848–?), signed 1873 treaty of peace.

Tumlinson, Ann Elizabeth (1842–1923), married Littleberry Wright.

Tumlinson, John Jackson Jr. "Peg Leg" (1848–1920), married Isabelle Cresap.

Tumlinson, Joseph "Captain Joe" (1811–1874), son of John J. and Elizabeth Plemmons Tumlinson; married, first, Johanna Taylor, second, Elizabeth Newman.

Tumlinson, Martha E. "Matt" (1849–?), married William W. Wells in 1867.

Tumlinson, Peter Creed (1855–1936), brother of Captain Joseph Tumlinson; signed 1873 treaty of peace.

Tuton, Oliver K. (1805–?), signed 1873 treaty of peace.

Wallace, W. C. "Curry" (?–?), Sutton sympathizer; married Rebecca Hudson, daughter of R. B. "Dick" Hudson.

West, T.C. (?–?), accused of involvement with the Buck Taylor party in alleged killing of Capt. Henry Nolan in La Vernia.

Wheaton, Henry (?–1869), killed by Helm and vigilante group.

White, Joseph P. "Doc" (?–?), friend of William E. Sutton; with him in Clinton when Buck Taylor and Dick Chisholm were killed; one of men who killed Wiley W. Pridgen, according to Jack Hays Day.

White, Daniel Jefferson "Jeff" (1851–?), brother of Doc White.

Wells, William W. (1841–?), friend of William E. Sutton, married a daughter of Captain Joe Tumlinson.

Westfall, Henry (?–1870?), companion of John Hays Taylor; wounded by C. S. Bell posse in 1869; reported killed in 1870.

Wills, James (?–1869), alias of Ira Olive; killed by Helm and vigilante group.

Wright, James (?–?), accused of involvement with the Buck Taylor party in alleged killing of Captain Henry Nolan in La Vernia.

Wright, L. B. (1830–1882), married Ann Elizabeth Tumlinson.

APPENDIX TWO

Children of the Feud

No doubt because of the number of families involved, the Sutton-Taylor Feud left perhaps more children growing to adulthood who never really knew their father than any other feud. The following provides an incomplete list of the children born either after their father was killed or only a short time before.

Child's Name	Father Killed	Child Born
— Longee	April 3, 1868 (Longee)	March–April 1868
William Walter Taylor	December 24, 1868 (William P. "Buck" Taylor)	June 2, 1868
Harriet Bell	July 2, 1869 (James C. Bell)	November 1869
Molly Taylor	November 23, 1869 (Martin L. Taylor)	February 3, 1870
Henry Peter Kelly Jr.	August 26, 1870 (Henry P. Kelly Sr.)	March 29, 1870
Wilhemena Kelly	August 26, 1870 (William B. Kelly)	1870
Willie Slaughter Sutton	March 11, 1874 (William E. Sutton)	August 24, 1874
James Cox	July 20–21, 1873 (James W. Cox)	After July 1873
William Henry Taylor	December 27, 1875 (James C. Taylor)	June 18, 1876

APPENDIX THREE

1873 Treaty of Peace

The following "Agreement" between Tumlinson and Nichols, et al., dated August 12, 1873, appears in Robert C. Sutton Jr.'s book *The Sutton-Taylor Feud*, and as far as known is the only source for its existence. The original was preserved in the family of Joseph Tumlinson, then handed down to E. A. "Dogie" Wright whose copy was used by Sutton for his book. The preamble is as follows:

Be it known by those persons whose names are hereto signed, that we severally recognize the fact that disputes and controversies of a nature likely to result in blood shed have existed between the undersigned. Those whose names are in the left column hereto [are] of one party, and those whose names are in the right column of the opposite party, and for the purpose of promoting peace and quiet and order in this community, we each for himself, here promise on honor, to abstain from all hostile acts, or demonstration calculated to create a breach of peace or to induce anyone to suppose that any violence is intended. And be it further more severally known promise on honor that we will not connect ourselves with any organization of any armed character contrary to the spirit and meaning of above agreement. And we further promise and agree that should we or either [sic] of us at anytime know of any organization being in existence for the purpose of doing violence to any man whose name is hereto signed, that we will as soon as is our power to give notice of such organization to the party so threatened. To which we hereto sign our names, this the 12th day of August, A.D. 1873.

Joseph Tumlinson [his mark]

A. F. Newman

C. C. Simmons

R. B. Busby

W. B. Belding

Wm. Lechie

Ed Power

P. C. Tumlinson

J. W. Amment [Avant?]

J. W. Ferguson

C. V. Busby

W. N. Templeton

H. Ragland

Wm. Peavy

R. Power

O. K. Tuton

H. H. Tuton

R. H. Brown

Jazinis [Lazarus] Nichols

Geo. C. Tennelle [Tennille]

E. J. Glover

M. Clements

A. J. Allen

J. W. Hardin

Gibson Clements [his mark]

John L. Reynolds

J. M. Taylor

P. H. Dowlearn

J. P. Beck

E. J. Heins

Jas. Clements

J. H. Clements

M. O. Nichols

E. A. Kelly

A. C. Day

Y. Hanks

J. S. Howard

J. W. Brassell

J. J. Coche

All signed in my presence
Signed, H. B. Boston
County Clerk, DeWitt County, Texas

Author Sutton explains that the original copy in his possession "was inadvertently destroyed years later by children at play." As far as Mr. Sutton knew, it appeared for the first time in print when his history of the feud was published in 1974. He was a grandnephew of William E. Sutton.

APPENDIX FOUR

Treaty of Peace

The following is the second known treaty of the feuding forces. This appeared in print on page one, column one of the *Cuero Weekly Star* of January 9, 1874. The printed treaty did not list the names in column format; the names on the left represent members of the Taylor group; the names on the right represent members of the Sutton group.

THE STATE OF TEXAS,
County of DeWitt,
    We, the undersigned, individually and collectively, do pledge our-selves, and solemnly swear to keep the peace between each other, and obey the laws of the country, now, henceforth and forever; fur-thermore, we pledge ourselves nevermore to engage in any organi-zation against any of the signers of this agreement.

Lazas [Lazarus] Nichols	*William Sutton*
A. J. Denmark	*D. J. Blair*
J. T. Bratton	*J. W. Ferguson*
C. H. Clement	*S. F. McCrabb [John F.?]*
W. W. Davis	*Ed. Powers*
Jas. Clements	*Jos. I. Sitterle*
R. R. Randle	*John Pettis*
O. F. Pridgen	*J. C. Johnston*
A. Tuygle [Tuggle]	*J. E. Smith*

B. J. Pridgen

J. Ludarstaett [sic, Duderstadt]

A. P. Allen

J. Howard

L. Tuggle

M. V. King

F. Duderstad [sic, Duderstadt]

R. Anderson

Geo. C. Tennille

J. H. Clements

Thos. Caffall

F. Hartken

W. E. Sanders

J. C. Taylor

R. Myers

J. Irwin

J. H. Day

G. W. Harris

M. Nichols

J. C. Taylor

R. P. Taylor

A. C. Day

A. G. Flowers

W. R. Taylor

J. J. Sanders

James Robinson

James Goodrick

W. O. Harrison

E. J. Hines

J. T. Robson

Jesus - - -

Marteano Garreo

J. W. Glover

J. Brown

John Andrews

W. M. Murphy

Sam H. Wofford

Walton Scurry

J. J. Meador

Buck Power

James Floyd

William Lackie

C. T. Hunter

W. R. Scurry

John H. Power

Addison Kilgore

H. Boston Jr.

Frank Cox

W. W. Peavy

Add. Patterson

W. T. Petit

Jno. J. Tumlinson

Ed. Parkinson

W. L. Mador [sic, Meador]

G. A. Peavy

John Gyns [Guynn?]

James Hasson

W. Templeton

W. C. Wallace

M. J. Ryan

John Hewcant

W. J. Ragland

Ed. Payton

Joe. DeMoss

J. G. Berry

D. W. Mason

J. A. McCrabb

G. W. Slaughter
George Mertz

All of which sworn to and subscribed before me, this the 3d day of
January, A.D. 1874.

O. K. Tuton,
J. P. DeWitt County

Treaty of Peace—
Galveston Daily News

he treaty of January 3, 1874, that appeared in the *Cuero Weekly Star* was later reprinted with variations in the *Galveston Daily News* of May 19, 1875, on the occasion of twenty-two citizens of DeWitt and other counties arriving there for preliminary motions in their trial for the murder of B. J. Pridgen's former slave, Abram Bryant. The number of names differs as well as spelling variations. It is presumed that the Galveston reporter had a copy of the Cuero newspaper, but chose not to include other names, suggested by unknown persons. Where there is a spelling question the choice of the Cuero reporter is given, as presumably he would know the proper spelling of those who lived in the area, whereas the Galveston reporter would not. Unfortunately the names were not presented in columns indicating which were Suttons and which were Taylors.

TREATY OF PEACE

THE STATE OF TEXAS,
County of Dewitt [sic],

We the undersigned, individually and collectively, do pledge ourselves and solemnly swear to keep the peace between each other and obey the laws of the county, now, henceforth and forever. Furthermore, we pledge ourselves never more to engage in any party organization against any of the signers of this agreement.

295

Lazarus Nichols, A. J. Denmark, J. T. Bratton, O. H. Clements, W. W. Davis, James Clements, R. A. Randle, O. F. Pridgen, A. Tuggle, B. J. Pridgen, R. Anderson, George C. Tennille, J. H. Clements, Thomas Caffall, F. Hartkoss, W. E. Ganden, J. M. Taylor, R. Myers, J. Irwin, William Sutton, J. M. Ferguson, F. F. McCrabb, Ed. Power, Joe F. Sitterle, John Pettit, J. C. Johnston, J. E. Smith, J. Brown, John Andrews, W. M. Murphy, Sam H. Wofford, Walton Scurry, John H. Power, Addison Kilgore, H. Boston, Jr., Frank Cox, W. W. Peavy, Add. Patterson, L. C. Day, G. W. Harris, M. Nichols, J. C. Taylor, R. P. Taylor, A. C. Day, A. G Flowers, W. R. Taylor, J. J. Sanders, James (his X) Robinson, James (mark X) Goodrick, M. O. Harrison, J. H. Hines, F. Robson, mark, Jesus Narteano (his X) Garsed, J. W. Glover, (mark X,) W. F. Petit, John J. Tumlinson, Ed. Parkinson, W. L. Meador, G. A. Peavy, John (his X) Guyns, James (mark X) Kassen, mark, W. Toureeton, W. C. Wallace, M. J. Ryan, John Newcourt, W. J. Ragland, Ed. Hayton, Joseph Demoss, J. G. Berry, J. W. Mason, J. A. McCrabb, G. W. Slaughter, George Merz, D. J. Blair.

All of which sworn to and subscribed before me, this the 3d day of January, A.D. 1874.

> O. R. Sutton [sic, O. K. Tuton]
> Justice of Peace No. 1,
> Dewitt County, Texas

It would be helpful to know who managed to have a copy of the treaty in Galveston in May of 1875, well over a year after the treaty was signed in Cuero. Did whoever it was have a copy of the Cuero newspaper on hand, or a copy of the treaty itself? If so why were there numerous discrepancies between the two lists of names? Logically the typesetter in Cuero would be somewhat familiar with the names of those who had signed there, or at least he could certainly ascertain the correct spelling if there was any question.

APPENDIX SIX

Victims of the Sutton-Taylor Feud

This list does not claim to be exhaustive, but does include known victims of the feud.

Year	Victim	Location of Death
1867	John A. Thompson	Mason County
	Sergeant McDougall	Mason County
1868	Longee (accidental)	Bastrop County
	Charles Taylor	Bastrop County
	James Sharp	Caldwell County
	John Littleton	Wilson County
	William Stannard	Wilson County
	William P. Taylor	DeWitt County
	Richard T. Chisholm	DeWitt County
	James C. Bell	DeWitt County
1869	Andrew J. Jacobs	Goliad County
	James S. Stapp	Goliad County
	Rutland Jones	Goliad County
	Tobias Poole	Goliad County
	James W. Lunsford	DeWitt County
	Half dozen unknown	DeWitt and Gonzales counties
	Charles Moore	DeWitt County
	George W. Blackburn	Goliad County
	Reuben C. Purcell	Goliad County

Year	Victim	Location of Death
	James Wills	Fayette County
	Henry Wheaton	Fayette County
	Sam Blackburn	San Patricio County
	Madison Peace	Goliad County
	Andrew McCarty	Goliad County
	William Bell	Goliad County
	John Choate	San Patricio County
	Crockett Choate	San Patricio County
	— Kuykendall	San Patricio County
	John Hays Taylor	Karnes County
	Henry G. Woods	DeWitt County
	William Faust	DeWitt County
	William Kerlick	DeWitt County
	Chris Kerlick Sr.	DeWitt County
	Martin L. Taylor	McMullen County
	William B. Morris	McMullen County
	Ira Olive, alias Wills	San Patricio County
1870	— Lunn	Matagorda County
	— Lunn	Matagorda County
	— Lunn	Matagorda County
	John B. M. Smith	Matagorda County
	Joseph Grimes	Matagorda County
	William Kelly	DeWitt County
	Henry Kelly	DeWitt County
	Henry Westfall	"near the Nueces River"
1871	Philip G. Taylor	Kerr County
1872	Thomas J. Haldeman	DeWitt County
	John B. Morgan	DeWitt County
1873	Pitkin B. Taylor	DeWitt County
	James W. Cox	DeWitt County
	John W. S. Christman	DeWitt County
	John J. M. Helm	Gonzales County
1874	William E. Sutton	Calhoun County

Year	Victim	Location of Death
	Gabriel W. Slaughter	Calhoun County
	Joseph G. Hardin	Comanche County
	William A. Dixon	Comanche County
	Thomas K. Dixon	Comanche County
	Alexander H. Anderson	Comanche County
	Alexander H. Barekman	Comanche County
	Charles M. Webb	Comanche County
	Rufus P. Taylor	DeWitt County
	Alfred Tuggle	DeWitt County
	James White	DeWitt County
	William F. Buchanan	DeWitt County
	George C. Tennille	Gonzales County
	Abram Pickens/Bryant	DeWitt County
	James G. McVea	DeWitt County
1875	Reuben H. Brown	DeWitt County
	James C. Taylor	DeWitt County
	A. R. Hendricks	DeWitt County
	Mason Arnold	DeWitt County
1876	Alfred Cone	Gonzales County
	Augustus W. Pridgen	DeWitt County
	J. E. Lampley	Gonzales County
	Dr. Philip H. Brassell	DeWitt County
	George Brassell	DeWitt County
	Martin V. King	DeWitt County
1878	Joshua Bowen	Gonzales County
1880	Charles H. Heissig	DeWitt County

Number of Victims by County

Bastrop County—2
Caldwell—1
Calhoun County—2
Comanche County—6
DeWitt County—34

Fayette County—2
Goliad County—9
Gonzales County—8
Karnes County—1
Kerr County—1
McMullen County—2
Mason County—2
Matagorda County—5
San Patricio County—5
Unknown County—1
Wilson County—2

A Southern Vendetta

The following "history" of the feud appeared in the October 27, 1874, issue of the *New York Times*, with no indication of the contributing correspondent, or if it had appeared in some other publication prior to the *Times*. One might guess that it was written by Napoleon A. Jennings, who years later wrote of his experiences as a Texas Ranger serving under Capt. L. H. McNelly in 1876. In his memoir, *A Texas Ranger*, first published in 1899, Jennings writes of first visiting Texas in September 1874, at the age of eighteen. As a young man he read some copies of the *Texas New Yorker*, which he described as "a paper published in the interests of some of the Southwestern railroads" which "inflamed" his mind "by the highly colored accounts of life in the Lone Star State." He read every word in those papers, and believed all that he read. He later learned that Col. J. Armory Knox, of *Texas Siftings* fame, was among those who contributed "the most lurid" articles for the *Texas New Yorker*.

Did Jennings write this "history" of the Sutton-Taylor Feud? Internal evidence is that he did, as these similar lines appear in his book published twenty-five years later:

> DeWitt County was notorious for a feud which for over a quarter of a century had existed there between the Taylor and Sutton factions. The Taylor-Sutton feud

301

began back in the '40s, in Georgia, removed to Texas
with the opposing families, and was flourishing at the
time of which I write, 1876. No vendetta of Corsica
was ever carried on with more bitterness than was this
feud in Texas. Scores of men had been murdered, nay,
hundreds, on both sides, and still the war was kept
up. Every man in the county had to choose sides in the
feud. ... Every man went armed to the teeth. Midnight
murders were of frequent occurrence. Waylaying on
the roads was considered the correct thing and shooting from ambush was taken as a matter of course.
(278)

The idea of the feud commencing years before it flared up
in Texas also appears in Dora Neill Raymond's biography of
Texas Ranger Capt. Lee Hall. Hall entered DeWitt County in
1876 shortly after the Brassell killings, but very likely heard
various stories about not only what had happened the night
of the double killing, but how it all began. Raymond relates
that Hall learned "the trouble started in the Carolinas, flour-
ished in Georgia in the forties, and was brought to Texas with
the household goods of the Taylors and the Suttons, who, oddly
enough, elected to settle in DeWitt as neighbors" (59).

In contrast however, McNelly Ranger George Durham, in
his memoir related to Clyde Wantland for his book *Taming the
Nueces Strip*, told how he became "well acquainted" with Jack
Hays Day and learned that the feud began in 1868 with the
killing of Buck Taylor and Dick Chisholm. Durham accepted
Day's belief that the idea the feud "was carried up from the
South, and went back before the Civil War" was nothing more
than a "lot of windy stories" (173).

As yet no evidence of a killing of a Sutton by a Taylor, or vice
versa, in one of the "cotton states" prior to the Texas troubles
has been found. Although no solid evidence supports the theory

that the feud started long before the 1867–1868 difficulties, there may be a grain of truth in it. If nothing else, the 1874 article in the *New York Times* is the first printed version claiming the feud originated in the Deep South prior to it being continued in Texas.

The following is the complete article from the October 27, 1874, issue of the *Times*.

A Southern Vendetta

It began a score of years ago, in one of the cotton States. The whisky which a man named TAYLOR had drank prompted him to bring the existence of an urbane person named SUTTON to an untimely end. A pistol-shot avenged a fancied insult, and the murderer was left unpunished. The machinery of law was rude in the rough section where the brawl had occurred, and the surviving male representatives of neither the SUTTON nor the TAYLOR families seemed to think it incumbent upon them to give the slayer up to the courts. A year or two after the murder, the TAYLOR family emigrated to Texas, evidently to avoid danger of future collision with the family of the murdered man. Soon afterward, the SUTTONS also went to Texas, and, as fate would have it, settled in an adjacent county, but each family lived in ignorance of the other's whereabouts until the close of the late war.

More than a decade had passed since the original "difficulty" between TAYLOR and SUTTON, and one might imagine that the animosity of the injured family would have been somewhat appeased by the flight of time. But a little circumstance, which once more brought the families into collision, resulted in a vendetta which has few parallels in any country, and certainly none in the United States. A young Taylor, finding his desire for adventure stronger than his prudence, made across the county line one day, and stole a horse. The theft was discovered, and he was pursued, and fell by the rifle of a SUTTON. This aroused all the angry memories of the past, and in a short time neither TAYLORS nor SUTTONS dared to leave their houses without being armed to the teeth. Open warfare was declared, and the citizens of the two counties in which the hostile families resided gradually took sides. It is said that as many as twelve hundred persons were at one time so much interested in the vendetta, and so committed to one or the other side of the quarrel, that, had there been a general fight, they would, without hesitation, have joined in it. If they met on country roads, or at taverns, or in the market places, the implacable feud was carried on with a more intense bitterness than that of the Montagues and Capulets; a corpse was the result of every meeting; ambushing was common; a dead TAYLOR lying in front of a clump of bushes, with his brains blown out, marked the vengeance of the SUTTONS; and a lynched SUTTON, taken suddenly from his horse by a gang of desperadoes, and hung to a tree, testified to the sleepless hate of the TAYLORS. At last so many people became embroiled in these occasional murders, which are said to have numbered fifty, that the condition of affairs in the two counties became intolerable. Business and agriculture were almost entirely suspended; the courts were blocked with the suits and counter-suits of the two principals in the vendetta, and both sides desperately determined to bring matters to a climax. So they took the field in warlike array.

At this juncture, it was discovered that the SUTTONS were more numerous than the TAYLORS, and that they also had a larger number of adherents. After some guerrilla warfare, the TAYLORS were surrounded, and, rather than become the victims of a wholesale massacre, they consented to adjourn to the county seat of the county in which they then were, and there enter into a solemn compact to cease the vendetta, and "call it square." The compact was made; the two counties were wild with excitement; travel was once more unobstructed, and some confident persons laid aside their arms.

But one month later, as a veteran SUTTON was seated with a companion on the deck of a steamer at Indianola, about to start for Galveston, a young TAYLOR shot them both dead. He was subsequently arrested at Galveston, and when, two months ago, he was sent to Indianola for trial, he was accompanied by two militia companies, who had been ordered to protect the majesty of the law against any further pursuance of the most remarkable vendetta of modern times. The murderer now lies in prison awaiting his sentence, and, meantime, the TAYLORS and SUTTONS are once more vigorously at war.

The practice of the vendetta in this country is slowly dying out, even on the border, but it dies hard. The family feud has so long been a precious legacy to many Southern and South-western poor whites that when it is no longer to be counted on they will feel as if robbed of a treasure. The courts are gradually assuming power to take and try the original offender, and sometimes to see that he meets the fate of his victim, only at the end of a rope legally placed about his neck. Prompt action of this kind is the only thing which will effectually annihilate the vendetta in States where every grown man in the back country carries deadly weapons. In a few years, the remote section of Texas, over which the TAYLORS and SUTTONS have tracked and fought each other for nearly ten years, actuated by a feud whose real origin many of the partisans had forgotten, will be as free from lawless violence as the quietest county in the New-England or Middle States. But perhaps that blessed time cannot arrive until the last TAYLOR and the last SUTTON have exchanged fatal shots, or until the State Government declares outlawed every one who makes an effort to perpetuate the disgraceful and barbarous battle. If both families would heroically resolve to meet once more at the county town where their late compact was made, and there each and all simultaneously poison themselves, they would gratify the rest of the world.

Endnotes

Chapter One

1. Sonnichsen. *I'll Die Before I'll Run: The Story of the Great Feuds of Texas* (New York: Harper & Brothers, 1951), 22. Hereafter cited as *I'll Die.*
2. Letter of Thomas M. Stell of Cuero to Mrs. J.A. Callaway, dated May 19, 1939. Copy of original letter donated to the Cuero Museum by Robert Giles in 1989. Letter reproduced in the *Taylor Family News* 5, no. 1 (February 1995): 1–2.
3. The names of the children are recorded on the official Texas Historic Grave Marker south of Cuero, DeWitt County. The name of Hardinia is also seen as Hardina in some documents, such as the Josiah Taylor Sr. "Family Group Sheet" printed in *Taylor Family News* 9, no. 2 (May, 1999): 7–8.
4. Eddie Day Truitt, *The Taylor Party* (Wortham, Tex.: privately printed, 1992), 99. Hereafter cited as Truitt, *Taylor Party.* Dovie Tschirhart Hall gives the date of Creed Taylor's birth as April 20, 1820, in *The New Handbook of Texas,* Vol. 6 (Austin: The Texas State Historical Association, 1996), 215. Hereafter cited as *New Handbook.*
5. Printed Program, "Dedication of Official Texas Historical Grave Markers for Josiah Taylor and Hephzibeth Taylor." This is dated Sunday, April 29, 1973, and shows the markers were unveiled by M. O. Bennett, a Josiah Taylor descendant. See also the Thomas Stell letter of May 19, 1939, to Mrs. J. A. Callaway reprinted in *The Taylor Family News* 5, no. 1 (February 1995): 1. And *San Antonio Daily Express,* June 28, 1905; letter in response to an article appearing in the *Express* of April 17, 1904. Edward A. Lukes, s.v. "Green DeWitt," in *New Handbook.*

6. Hall, s.v., "Creed Taylor," in *New Handbook*. Dovie Hall is the great-great-granddaughter of Creed Taylor. A. J. Sowell. *Early Settlers and Indian Fighters of Southwest Texas* (Austin: Ben C. Jones & Co., 1900; repr., Austin: State House Press, 1986), 807. Hereafter cited as Sowell.

7. Gonzales County Marriage Record, Volume A, 3. Their names appear as "Pattrick Dowlin" and "Hephebeth Taylor." Patrick Dowlearn was a neighbor of the Josiah Taylor family, their lands adjoining. The marriage bond is dated July 20, 1830, and is preserved in the archives of the Gonzales County courthouse annex. The one child of this union was Joshua Martin "Bud" Dowlearn, born about 1832. See "Hephzibeth Luker Taylor Dowlearn" by Bena Taylor Kirkscey in *Taylor Family News* 9, no. 3 (August 1999): 1–2. Rosalie Key Myers gives the date of their marriage as July 25, 1830, in *Dowlearn-Lowe*, 1. This is a 22-page pamphlet privately printed, 1992, no place.

8. Hall, s.v., "Creed Taylor," in *New Handbook;* Sowell, 808. And "Fought with Ben Milam" in *Texas Field and Sportsman* (no author cited; 1947?), 190. This is an article in the vertical file entitled "Creed Taylor," in the Center for American History Collections, Austin, Texas.

9. Sowell, 808–9. Sowell noted in his narrative that Creed had dictated his memoirs to him in 1900 when he was living on the James River in Kimble County. A brief sketch of Taylor is found in the *San Antonio Daily Express,* June 28, 1905, entitled "Last Word from Creed Taylor." This is basically a listing given by Creed of the highpoints of his life from birth until 1840, what he did and where he lived. Here he states he was born in Alabama in 1820.

10. Leta Horine and Lynn Taylor, "Creed Taylor: His Family and Descendants," *Taylor Family News* 8, no. 3 (August 1998): 2–3.

11. The exact date of Creed Taylor's death is elusive. Frederica Wyatt, in an e-mail to this author dated December 1, 2006, quoted his great-great-granddaughter, Dovie Hall, as relating that he died "two days after Christmas, 1906" which would mark the date as December 27. However, Dovie Hall, in her entry in the history of DeWitt County, gives the date as December 26, 1906. See *DeWitt County History,* 766. Charles M. Yates, in his "In Search of Creed Taylor" writes that Taylor died on December 26, 1906. See *Taylor Family News* 11, no. 1 (February 2001): 1.

12. The keynote speaker at the marker dedication was Robert S. B. Giles, "a descendant of both factions," who stated that Taylor's "will to survive in the struggle against man and nature remains a desirable challenge to those who survive him. He defended our political interests in the two great struggles with the Mexican Republic that brought nationhood and later, statehood to Texas." Giles' speech at the marker dedication appears in the *Newsletter* of the Kimble County Historical Survey Committee, Vol. 3, nos. 3–4 (May–June 1967), and in the June 29, 1967, issue of the *Junction Eagle*.

13. This marker, located on U.S. Highway 87 in the Cuero City Park, also mentions Josiah Taylor and James J. Tumlinson as "participants in the Battle of Salado Creek, Bexar County, 1842."

14. This marker is located on Farm-to-Market Road 1534, some nineteen miles east of Junction.

15. Truitt, *Taylor Party,* 99.

16. Gonzales County Marriage Record, Vol. A, License # 28, 10. The names appear as "Joseph Tumblinson" and "Joannah Taylor." Tumlinson's birthplace here is given as Illinois; Taylor's is given as Alabama.

17. Samuel H. Tumlinson, s.v.v., "John Jackson Tumlinson Sr.," "John Jackson Tumlinson Jr.," and "Joseph Tumlinson" in *New Handbook.* And Marjorie Burnett Hyatt, *Fuel for a Feud* 3rd. rev. ed. of *The Taylors, The Tumlinsons and the Feud* (Smiley, Tex.: privately printed, 1990) F-194. Hereafter cited as Hyatt, *Fuel.*

18. Gonzales County Marriage Record, Vol. A, License # 10, 4. Both Taylor and Tumlinson signed with their mark. The amount of their bond was also $10,000 "lawful money of the United Mexican States." William R. Taylor's birth date is from Truitt, *Taylor Party,* 99.

19. Article in *The Texian Advocate,* November 9, 1848, citing a description of the engagement prepared and signed by R. H. Chisholm and H. M. Pridgen dated October 20, 1848. This appears in an article "Last Indian Fight" in *Taylor Family News* 5, no. 4 (December 1995): 7–8; research by Ray Murtishaw. See also "Emily Henrietta Porter" by Bena Taylor Kirkscey in *Taylor Family News* 5, no. 2 (June 1995): 3–6, which contains additional information. See also s.v. "John York" by Ruby Farrar Pridgen in *New Handbook.*

20. Truitt, *Taylor Party,* 99.

21. Hyatt, *Feul,* F-178 and F-179.

22. Typed copy of license in Marriage Record Book A, License # 1, 1. Marriage performed by J. A. Miller, Minister of the Gospel.

23. Gonzales County Marriage Record, Vol. A, License #96, 29. Their marriage was performed by Edmond Bellinger, Chief Justice, Gonzales County.

24. Family Group Sheet of Josiah Taylor Sr. in *Taylor Family News* 9, no. 2 (May 1999): 7. "Texas Ranger Service Records 1830–1846," reproduced in Truitt, *Taylor Party,* 106.

25. The *Stockton Journal* (Stockton, California), September 7, 1852, describes the death of Taylor. This item was discovered by Tim Farnham and is printed in full in the *Taylor Family News* 8, no. 1 (February 1998): 1.

26. James T. Johnson, "Hardships of a Cowboy's Life in the Early Days of Texas" in J. Marvin Hunter, compiler and editor, *The Trail Drivers of Texas* (Austin: University of Texas Press, 1986), 762.

27. Sonnichsen. *I'll Die,* 32.

28. DeWitt County census, enumerated August 7, 1860, by John R. Foster, 484. Daughter Lucy Charlotte McDonald was born February 9, 1844, and married Augustus Washington "Gus" Pridgen on March 12, 1868; sister Sarah Jane, born in 1850, married Joseph Alexander McCrabb on March 21, 1867. DeWitt County Marriage Records.

29. Additional family information and military service records provided by Mack C. Sutton to author.

30. James Sutton is buried in the Stockdale City Cemetery, Wilson County. The double headstone shows he was born October 10, 1844, and died May 28, 1919. On the same stone is the name of his life-long partner Martha Ann Dees, born March 2, 1846, and died September 23, 1929. Sutton also has a military marker indicating his service in Waller's Regiment, Texas Cavalry, C.S.A. Author's notes.

31. Laura's mother Leah died on December 10; her father John W. died days later on December 16, 1858. Interview with Cynthia Salm, great-great-granddaughter of William E. Sutton, February 19, 2007. Sutton Family Bible in Sutton Family Collection, Texas Ranger Hall of Fame and Museum, Waco. Widow's Application for Pension, #16896, applicant Mrs. Laura E. Sutton of

Victoria County. Sutton's marriage was performed on October 20, 1869, at the home of William J. McDonald, by Rev. J. T. Gillett. Among the witnesses were Horace French and Belle DeMoss. "Rite of Matrimony" in Sutton Family Collection. Victoria County, Marriage Record Vol. 1, 1838–1870. The DeWitt County census shows Sutton as a well-to-do farmer with $1200 worth of real estate and personal property valued at $500. Living with them were Cynthia McDonald, Bill's mother, and seven-year-old Mary, his sister; a thirteen-year-old Henry Clay from Mississippi; C. W. Shults and Mary Shults, both in their seventies, and one John O'Conner, a twenty-year-old laborer from Canada. DeWitt County census enumerated July 25, 1870, by Willis Fawcett. The family name is spelled in a great variety of ways, but I have used *Shults,* the spelling as it appears in the Sutton Family Bible.

32. These factors are clearly identified by Ann Patton Baenziger in "The Texas State Police During Reconstruction: A Reexamination" in *The Southwestern Historical Quarterly* 72, no. 4 (April 1969): 471. See also Carl H. Moneyhon, *Texas After the Civil War: The Struggle of Reconstruction* (College Station: Texas A&M University Press, 2004).

Chapter Two

1. "Communication from Governor Pease of Texas, Relative to the Troubles in that State." Prepared at Austin, February 8, and referred to the Committee on Reconstruction and ordered to be printed, May 11, 1868, 7. *House Miscellaneous Document No. 127,* 40th Congress, 2nd Session, U. S. House of Representatives, hereafter cited as Pease, 1868.

2. *Houston Daily Telegraph,* December 15, 1867, in an article headlined "Murderers at Large."

3. Randolph W. Spencer's brother William Addison Spencer had married Caroline H. Taylor, the daughter of Creed and Nancy Goodbread Taylor. "Spencers from North Carolina to Texas" in *Taylor Family News* 16, no. 1 (May 2006): 2–4.

4. Francis B. Heitman, *Historical Register and Dictionary of the United States Army,* Vol. 1 (Washington, D.C.: Government Printing Office, 1903), 956–57.

5. *Tri-Weekly Austin Republican,* November 23, 1867, reprinting an article from an undated *San Antonio Express.* Elsewhere in the same issue the *Republican* commented, "No one who

has a single feeling of humanity in his heart, can read this news without shuddering with horror and indignation. It looks as though there is a determination among rebel desperadoes in Texas to exceed the 'dark ages' in their acts of crime and barbarism." Initial reports which reached the press were in disagreement. One report indicated that Major Thompson was sitting in a room of the sutler's store when called upon to settle a disturbance between the Taylors and some drunken soldiers. Thompson ordered the arrest of the Taylors, but added that if the soldiers were to blame they would be punished. The Taylors resisted arrest. Thompson then armed himself with a six-shooter and, with the sergeant's assistance, attempted the arrest, the result being both were killed, "the ball entering the face of Major Thompson just below the eye and coming out through the opposite side of his neck. His wife was not present or a witness, ..." *Houston Daily Telegraph,* November 30, 1867.

6. Dr. John J. Hulse to Capt. Lewis G. Huntt, November 15, 1867, as found in the Company Letter Book, Vol. 93, Fort Mason, in National Archives, and quoted in Margaret Bierschwale, *A History of Mason County, Texas Through 1964*, edited by Julius E. DeVoss (Mason, Tex.: Mason County Historical Commission, 1998), 495–96.

7. Glenn James and Henri Rupe Capps, *The Life of Thomas W. Gamel*, annotated by Dave Johnson (Ozark, Mo.: Dogwood Printing, 2003), 8.

8. J. B. Polley, "The Taylor Boys Made Things Interesting," *Frontier Times* 9, no. 3 (December 1931): 113. Hereafter cited as Polley, "Taylor Boys." P. G. Taylor's nickname is spelled in various ways. Polley uses "Do'boy"; Victor M. Rose spells it "Doughboy," but spells the brother's name correctly as "Hays." See Victor M. Rose, *The Texas Vendetta; or, the Sutton-Taylor Feud* (New York: J. J. Little & Co., 1880; repr. Houston, Texas: The Frontier Press of Texas, 1956), 12. Hereafter cited as Rose, *Vendetta*. Marjorie Hyatt, in *Fuel for a Feud*, inexplicably identifies him as Phillip DuBois Taylor, which could logically explain the nickname of Doboy. However, since the reports all give his initials as P. G., his marriage license gives the initials as P. G., and his mother's maiden name was Goodbread, it is certain that his nickname came from his mother's maiden name.

9. Ass't. Adj. Gen. E. D. Townsend, of the War Department, Washington, D.C., to Brevet Major General R. C. Buchanan, 5th

Military District, New Orleans, July 9, 1868, National Archives, Record Group 393, Barry Crouch Collection.

10. Proclamation of Gov. E. M. Pease, October 28, 1868, offering rewards for the Taylors and Spencer, as well as for several others. Pease stipulated that the reward was "for the *arrest* and *delivery* of *Each* of the *Persons* so charged to the *Commanding Officer* of the *Post* at *Austin* or *San Antonio*, or if *Either* of them should be killed in *resisting an arrest* by lawful authority, then a *like Reward* upon the presentation of Satisfactory proof that *Either* of them was So Killed." The wording effectively guaranteed payment whether "dead or alive." Found in National Archives, Record Group 393, Barry Crouch Collection. Words in italics were underlined in original.

11. Rose, *Vendetta*, 13.

12. Capt. Creed Taylor's company of volunteers "called into the service of the Confederate States, in the Provisional army" was to serve from February 13, 1864, for a three-month period. Taylor's company consisted of a 1st Lieutenant, three sergeants, three corporals, and eighteen privates, including his son P. G. Taylor, then sixteen, and T. C. West, then eighteen. In addition, B. (Bradford) Chisholm was 3rd Sergeant; Thor. (Thornton) Chisholm was a private. Muster roll in Texas State Archives, folder 401-1301.

13. *Galveston Daily News*, December 3, 1867.

14. DeWitt County Marriage Record Book C, License # 548, 155. The Taylor-Anderson marriage was performed by DeWitt County Justice of the Peace E. M. Edwards, and witnessed by L. B. Wright and J. J. Brantley. Wright, later a DeWitt County justice, had married Ann Eliza Tumlinson, thus she probably witnessed the marriage as well. The child of the Taylor-Anderson union, born June 2, 1868, was named William Walter Taylor, the first names of his father and grandfather. At the age of twenty-one W. W. Taylor began ranching near his great-uncle, Creed Taylor, in Kimble County. He later served as Kimble County sheriff for a total of eleven years. In 1917 he was appointed a Texas Ranger by Gov. William P. Hobby. W. W. Taylor died February 22, 1945. In 1967 the Texas Historical Survey Commission and the Texas Law Enforcement's Youth Development Foundation placed an "outstanding law officer's historical marker" at his grave site in the Junction Cemetery, Kimble County. See Frederica Burt Wyatt, "William Walter Taylor," *Taylor Family News* 12, no. 2 (May 2002): 1–2.

15. Capt. George W. Smith, 35th Infantry, Commander of San Antonio Post, November 23, 1867, to Lt. Charles E. Morse, Assistant Adjutant General, 5th Military District of Texas, Barry Crouch Collection.

16. Report of Capt. Edward Miller to Lt. L. H. M. Taylor, Galveston. Monthly report prepared January 31, 1867 at Victoria, written on letterhead of "Office Sub-Assistant Commissions." In Barry Crouch Collection. Miller's work in other areas of the state is in Barry Crouch, *The Freedmen's Bureau and Black Texans* (Austin: University of Texas Press, 1992).

17. *Galveston Daily News*, November 12, 1868, reprinting an item from an undated *New Orleans Crescent*.

18. James M. Smallwood does not clarify the question of Captain Nolan's demise. In his study of the troubles in DeWitt and surrounding counties he writes how in September 1865 Captain Nolan allowed two of his soldiers to lag behind the rest of the squad and that both were killed by the Buck Taylor gang. Yet a few pages later he writes that in September Buck Taylor, Martin Taylor, and several others "ambushed a small squad of troopers, killing Captain Nolan and at least one enlisted man." *The Feud that Wasn't* (College Station: Texas A&M University Press, 2008), 6, 13.

19. As yet little contemporary documentation concerning this killing has been found. Taylor and several associates allegedly had assaulted a teacher of a freedmen's school in Victoria, and then in September 1865 killed two men of Captain Nolan's 18th New York Cavalry in Victoria County. James Smallwood, "Sutton-Taylor: A Feud?" *South Texas Studies* 3 (2005). The Taylors and Spencer were described as "the same gang who murdered the freedman at Lavernia [sic] a few months since, and who were allowed to go free from a too easy sense of justice on the part of our authorities. ..." Article in an undated *San Antonio Express* printed in the *Tri-Weekly Austin Republican*, November 23, 1867, and also the *Chicago Tribune* of December 6, 1867.

20. This was John Burch, the only Burch yet surfacing in the literature on the Taylor family. His name appears on a list of associates provided by Creed Taylor on June 8, 1867.

21. T. C. West served as a private in Capt. Creed Taylor's Company in early 1864, according to a roster of men stationed at Helena, Karnes County. Other men who served in the same unit and who

figured in the feud included A. H. Sample, 1st Lieutenant; Bradford Chisholm, 3rd Sergeant; Privates Thornton Chisholm, D. W. Fore, H. Tuggle, P. G. (Doboy) Taylor and West. Ford's Muster roll in the Texas State Archives.

22. George W. Smith, to Lt. Charles E. Morse at Austin, November 23, 1867, Barry Crouch Collection.

23. Ibid. Attachment A, secured with Smith's report to Morse.

24. Blair was elected sheriff June 25, 1866, and served until February 15, 1869. See Sammy Tise, *Texas County Sheriffs* (Hallettsville, Tex.: Privately printed, 1989), 157. Hereafter cited as Tise.

25. Ralph Calhoun to Robert C. Sutton Jr., March 1945, in Robert C. Sutton Jr., *The Sutton-Taylor Feud* (Quanah, Tex.: Nortex Press, 1974), 32–33.

26. *Galveston Daily News*, May 19, 1875, printing a brief history of the feud.

27. The names of the posse members with Sutton come from the Bastrop County Court Records and the *Daily State Journal* of Austin, August 6, 1871. This article is entitled "Crimes in Bastrop County," and was extracted from records of the Department of the Chief of Police. The listing shows crimes dating from October 1857 to July 10, 1871. A. H. Samples served as 1st Lieutenant in Capt. Creed Taylor's Volunteer Company. Bob Thomas is presumably the same Bob Thomas who was elected DeWitt County District Clerk on June 25, 1866. *Register of Elected and Appointed State and County Officials August 1866–1870*, Microfilm reel #3501, 254–55, "Election Returns" in Texas State Archives.

28. *Flake's Evening Bulletin*, April 1, 1868, reprinting an article, "Killing Affair" from the *Bastrop Advertiser* of March 28 of that year.

29. *Austin Daily Republican*, November 1, 1870. This statement appears in an editorial by editor Alfred H. Longley, reminding readers that Sutton stood charged with murder of Charles Taylor "and a German citizen, and the wounding of another German" in Bastrop, "a little over two years ago." Longley wrote that Sutton and the other posse members "plundered Taylor of his clothes and fine saddle, and would have killed Mr. Sharp, but for the interference of the citizens."

30. Special Officer Charles S. Bell to General J. J. Reynolds (?), June 5, 1869. This letter supports the family tradition that Charley Taylor had stolen a horse with a fancy saddle. Bell writes: "Charley Taylor was a murderer, and at the time of his death was riding a horse

he had stolen, and he resisted the execution of the writ which Sutton attempted to serve on him." Letter courtesy Rick Miller.

31. *Galveston Daily News*, April 2, 1868.

32. *Galveston Daily News*, April 2, 1868. Bastrop County citizen J. Schultz to Gov. E.M. Pease, written at Bastrop April 4, 1868. Longee was one of several husbands to die violently during the feud before their children knew them. Of the accidental death of Longee, Bell wrote in the June 5 letter: "It is true an innocent man was killed at the same time Taylor was, but it was an unavoidable accident, occurring while Sutton was performing his duty."

33. *Flake's Evening Bulletin*, April 1, 1868, reprinting an article from the *Bastrop Advertiser* of March 28, 1868.

34. *Galveston Daily News*, April 7, 1868.

35. C. S. Bell to General Reynolds, June 5, 1868, in which he advised, "[I]t might be well to direct the District Attorney of Bastrop Co. to enter a *nolle pros* [*sic: nolle prosequi*, a motion by prosecuting attorney to discontinue prosecution] in Sutton's case; the more so, as proceedings against men who kill desperadoes in attempting to arrest them, discourages the people from acting against them, and gives a *quasi* encouragement to bad men. Of course, a trial results in the acquittal of the accused in such cases, but the detention and costs of such proceedings are a matter of real moment to those so unfortunate as to incur them."

36. At the end of 1860 there were but 122 counties in the state; a decade later there were 129 counties. Dick Smith, s.v. "County Organization" in *New Handbook*.

37. *Report of Special Committee on Lawlessness and Violence in that State*. Printed in Senate Journal, 40th Congress, 2nd Session, Miscellaneous Document No. 109, 3. This report, dated June 30, 1868, and signed by E. J. Davis, President of the Convention, was also printed in booklet form and is preserved in the Texas State Archives.

38. Ibid., 5.

39. Frank L. Britton, *Report of the Adjutant General of the State of Texas, for the Year 1872* (Austin: James P. Newcomb and Company, 1873), 9. Although the report is for the year 1872, the figures concerning jails were true as of January 1, 1869, a mere six months following the publication of the report on lawlessness and violence.

40. Report of Hiram Clark, July 2, 1868, Barry Crouch Collection, in "Freedmen's Bureau/DeWitt Co."

41. Pease, 1868, 7. The report was prepared by Secretary of State W. C. Philips on February 8, 1868; date of publication was May 11, 1868.
42. Ibid., 8.
43. Ibid., 17.
44. *Flake's Evening Bulletin*, April 2, 1868.
45. Pease, 1868, 22; Robert W. Shook. "Bolivar J. Pridgen" in *Texas Bar Journal*, April 1965, 281.
46. Thomas W. Cutrer, s.v. "John Littleton," *New Handbook*; and Muster Roll of Capt. Creed Taylor, Texas State Archives.
47. Karon Mac Smith, *On the Watershed of Ecleto and the Clear Fork of Sandies* (Seguin, Tex.: Tommy Brown Printing, 1983; rev. ed. 1984), 142–43.
48. Hedwig Krell Didear, *Karnes County and Old Helena* (Austin: San Felipe Press, 1969), 68–69.
49. Polley, "Taylor Boys," 117. Polley's version of the deaths of Littleton and Stannard appears on 117–19.
50. John S. Mason, Major 35th Infantry, to Lt. C. E. Morse, Acting Assistant Adjutant General, Fifth Military District, Austin, December 11, 1868. Copy provided by T. Lindsay Baker, from the Baker Research Files.
51. Polley explains that the ambush site was a "pocket-like depression in the middle of which there was a seep, or wet-weather spring, known as Black Jack Spring." See "Taylor Boys," 118. *Nockenut*, as contemporary maps spelled the name, but later spelled *Nockernut*, no longer exists. Ed Bartholomew, writing in *Texas Ghosttown Encyclopedia* in 1982, commented that by 1890 the population was 80, but today was "Gone" (p. 74). Thomas Cutrer wrote the ambush took place "near Nockernut" (s.v., "John Littleton" in *New Handbook*). Claudia Hazlewood, s.v. "Nockernut, Texas" in *New Handbook*, described the community as having a population of *ten* in 1990. The late historian Karon Mac Smith, who lived much of her life in the immediate area, used the *Nockenut* spelling as she had learned it from others. Smith records that it was the belief among locals that both Littleton and Stannard were buried in the "local graveyard," which would be logical considering the proximity to where they met their deaths. "One Grave—Or Two?" in *On the Watershed of Ecleto and the Clear Fork of Sandies*, 142–43.
52. *Galveston Daily News*, December 25, 1868, reprinting an item from an undated *Goliad Guard*.

53. In Creed Taylor's company of volunteers was one "J. Clark," aged fourteen years, who presumably is the Jeff Clark of the ambushing party, now eighteen.

54. Deposition of William A. G. Lewis, sworn to and subscribed at Headquarters in Helena on September 9, 1869, before Capt. G. H. Cooper. Lewis's sworn statement dated September 9, begins: "Sometime about the middle of last November ..." an understandable error as he was recalling the event some time later and no doubt paid little attention to dates. It remains curious that the group of men who planned to ambush and kill Littleton and Stannard so easily accepted Lewis into their midst. Lewis, or his father, perhaps was sympathetic to the fugitives, and at least initially Lewis indicated he would keep silent. Original deposition in National Archives; copy provided by M. G. "Jerry" Spencer, Grapevine, Texas. Unfortunately William A. G. Lewis has not been found on any census and no further information is known about him or his family.

Chapter Three

1. Craig H. Roell, s.v., "Clinton, Texas." *New Handbook*. Frances Peyton, "Clinton" in *DeWitt County*, 85–86.

2. Betty Dooley Awbrey and Claude Dooley, *Why Stop? A Guide to Texas Historical Roadside Markers*, 4th ed. (Houston: Gulf Publishing Company, 1999), 126.

3. Joe Hugh Hutchins, "Richard H. Chisholm and Family" in *DeWitt County*, 339–40; Hyatt, *Fuel*, F-33, F-34.

4. Tobe Kelly was the son of William and Margaret Ann Clark Kelly, and was born about 1856. See Truitt, *Taylor Party*, 75.

5. Lewis S. Delony. *40 Years A Peace Officer: A True Story of Lawlessness and Adventure in the Early Days in Southwest Texas* (Abilene?: privately printed, 1937), 8. Hereafter cited as Delony. Delony was the son of Lewis Henry DeLony and Mrs. Sarah Ann Murphree, the widow of John Murphree. They were married on November 20, 1856, and Lewis S. was born on October 21, 1857. His grandfather Lewis Henry had fought in the Napoleonic Wars; his father had fought Indians under Captain John C. "Jack" Hays, and also was a Confederate veteran.

6. Curiously there were two of the siblings charged with the killing of Taylor, Hendricks, and Arnold in Clinton later in the feud: H. J. and D. J. (Henry Junius White and Daniel Jefferson White).

See *Galveston Daily News*, July 7, citing a report from Cuero dated June 30, 1877.

7. Sumners was the son of Tennesseean Abraham Sumners. In 1860 Abraham is listed as a farmer with $2000 in real estate and $11,150 in personal estate. Others in the household are twenty-three-year-old Mary C. from Kentucky, no relationship shown but possibly his second wife. Others ranging in age from fourteen to two years of age are William T., John J., Joseph C., Nancy E. and Mary C. DeWitt County census enumerated August 10, 1860, by John R. Foster, 499. A decade later "J. C. Summers," as written by enumerator Fawcett, is living in the household of Bingham White, farmer and stock raiser and his wife Eliza Ann. J. C. Summers now is shown to have been married in January to Mary V. Harrell, both twenty years of age. DeWitt County census enumerated August ---, 1870, by Willis Fawcett, 260. Their post office was Clinton. Sumners is the correct spelling as that is how the name is spelled on their headstones in Hillside Cemetery in Cuero. Kerr Bingham White was appointed sheriff of DeWitt County on January 10, 1848, elected on August 7, 1848, and served until August 15, 1850. See Tise, 157.

8. Tise, 157.

9. Weisiger had been appointed October 11, 1873, and then was elected December 2, 1873, and re-elected to four terms, concluding his shrievalty on November 16, 1881.

10. Mary Elizabeth Humphries Ainsworth, "The First One Hundred Years," copy in author's collection, 14. Typed copy provided to author by Patsy Goebel, Cuero, Texas. Ainsworth dictated her reminiscences to her son George O. Ainsworth in February 1951. They comprise sixty-eight pages of single spaced type. Mary Ainsworth, the fourth child of George Washington and Mary Jane Humphreys, was born in 1854 and died August 24, 1951. She is buried in Post, Texas. A copy was also donated to the DeWitt County Historical Museum.

11. Jack Hays Day, *The Sutton-Taylor Feud* (San Antonio: Sid Murray & Son, 1937), 11. Hereafter cited as Day, *Feud*.

12. Alexa Taylor Green's reminiscence is recorded in Hyatt, *Fuel*, 13. Green's father was William Walter Taylor, born June 2, 1868, only child of Buck Taylor.

13. Rose, *Vendetta*, 12–13.

14. Louise and Fuller Artrip, *Memoirs of Daniel Fore (Jim) Chisholm and the Chisholm Trail* (Privately printed by Artrip Publications, 1949), 36–37. D. F. Chisholm, one of the six children of Glenn Thornton and Jane P. "Jennie" Fore Chisholm, married Lula R. Denham and lived until October 1, 1954. His uncle, Bradford A. Chisholm, was the father of Richard T. Chisholm, born in 1849, and killed with Buck Taylor.

15. This is credited as a Taylor family motto by Victor M. Rose, in *Vendetta*, 10.

16. *San Antonio Express*, December 27, 1868.

17. Ibid., January 8, 1869.

18. *Galveston Daily News*, January 5, 1869.

19. *Houston Union*, January 6, 1869.

20. Rose, *Vendetta*, 13.

21. On the outside of the letter Reynolds, on December 29, noted that Bell had been employed by him in Arkansas in 1865 and "gave entire satisfaction." Copy of original courtesy Rick Miller.

22. David Pickering and Judy Falls, *Brush Men and Vigilantes: Civil War Dissent in Texas* (College Station: Texas A&M University Press, 2000).

23. DeWitt County census, enumerated July --, 1870, by Willis Fawcett, 240.

24. When John Jackson Marshall Helm (as his name appears) appeared in DeWitt County he courted Margaret Virginia Crawford; the couple were married on January 3, 1869, in Clinton. The marriage was witnessed by her father, James A. Crawford, and performed by Minister of the Gospel A. H. Walaker. Marriage Book C, License # 819, 290. She was the daughter of James A. and Rachel Crawford of Virginia and Tennessee. DeWitt County census, enumerated June —, 1860, by John R. Foster, 461. What happened to Mrs. Helm after Jack's death has not been determined.

25. Barry A. Crouch. Notes from unpublished study of the Texas State Police in Barry A. Crouch Collection, Victoria Regional History Center, Victoria College/University of Houston-Victoria Library. Hereafter cited as Crouch Collection.

26. Tise, 157.

27. Petition from Citizens of DeWitt and Lavaca Counties, undated, probably in mid-1867, in Crouch Collection. Fifty-six-year-old Virginia-born M. G. Jacobs was by 1870 a well-to-do stock raiser of DeWitt County, claiming $1600 in real estate

and $7000 in personal estate. His wife Mary A. was twenty-four, and they had four children. Mary A. Jacobs was from Florida; all the children were born in Texas. Their post office was Clinton. DeWitt County census, enumerated June --, 1870, by Willis Fawcett, 234.

28. Correspondence from J. J. Helm to Brig. Gen. James Oakes, written at Austin, July 15, 1867. Document and attached petition in Crouch Collection. General Griffin had taken command of the Military District of Texas in December 1866. He succumbed to yellow fever in Galveston on September 15, 1867, shortly after Helm's communication to his office.

29. *Victoria Advocate*, September 23, 1868. This particular issue is missing from the newspaper files, but is reprinted in Rose, *Vendetta*, 15–19.

30. These were the sons of Henry and Rachel Peace. The Georgia-born farmer was in Texas perhaps as early as 1842, as the 1860 census shows their six children, James M. (Madison?), Sarah, Christopher, Sidney, Caroline, and John H., all Texas born. The oldest was seventeen, suggesting a birth year of 1843. DeWitt County census, enumerated July 11, 1860, by John R. Foster, 479. Foster spelled their name "Pease."

31. Jenkins was appointed July 15, 1868. Tise, 207. *Galveston Daily News*, June 8, reporting news from an undated *Goliad Guard*, and June 23, reprinting "Texas News" from the *Gonzales Inquirer* of June 19, 1869.

32. Lt. William Thompson to Capt. Charles E. Morse, Secretary of Civil Affairs, HQ, 5th Military District, Austin, June 21, 1869, written from Helena. Copy in Barry Crouch Collection. There is no known blood relationship between the two Jacobs, sheriffs of adjoining counties.

33. "Doc" White was Joseph Priestly White, one of eight children born to Daniel Jefferson and Elizabeth McCullough White, according to Nantie P. Lee, grand-niece of D. J. White. "Captain James Knox White Family" in *The History of DeWitt County, Texas* (Dallas: Curtis Media Corporation, DeWitt County Historical Commission, 1991), F983, 815. Hereafter cited as *DeWitt County*.

34. Lt. William Thompson to Capt. Charles E. Morse, June 22, 1869.

35. DeWitt correspondence in *Flake's Daily Bulletin*, July 9, written from Clinton, July 4, 1869.

36. Goliad County Census, enumerated July 25, 1870, by Edward S. Roberts, 384. On the Nonpopulation Census schedule (also known as "Mortality Schedule") someone scrawled "Murder" over Roberts's notation that Bell had been killed by the Vigilance Committee. Widow Francis Bell was enumerated by Edward S. Roberts the year after James C. Bell's death, listed as head of household, age twenty-nine. Her six children ranged in ages from Mary, eleven years old, to eight-month-old Harriet, born in November 1869.

37. Nonpopulation Census Schedule for Goliad County, listing those persons who died during the year ending June 1, 1870, identified by Edward S. Roberts. Roberts identified seven Goliad County individuals "Shot by vigilance committee" in his report. Apparently it was common knowledge which individuals fell victim to the vigilance committee, rather than those who may have been murdered by others for other reasons.

38. This is a lengthy communication from Jack Helm, addressed to the "People of Texas" and probably appearing in a newspaper. It was then reprinted in Rose, *Vendetta*, 16. The particular issue of the newspaper has not been located.

39. Goliad County Census, enumerated July 13, 1870 by Edward S. Roberts, 363. In the Oak Hill Cemetery in Goliad is the marked grave for Ausby Rutland Jones, born January 17, 1823, and died July 21, 1869. This is perhaps the Jones killed by the Regulators.

40. Jakie L. Pruett and Everett B. Cole, *The History and Heritage of Goliad County* (Austin: Eakin Publications, 1983), 29. Researched and compiled by the Goliad County Historical Commission.

41. *Galveston Daily News*, July 24, reprinting an item from the *Lavaca Commercial* of Lavaca County of July 22, 1869.

42. Nonpopulation Census Schedule for DeWitt County, listing those persons who died during the year ending June 1, 1870, identified by Willis Fawcett. Lunsford was a native of North Carolina. DeWitt County census, enumerated June --, 1870, 298. Lynching today is generally considered to be death by hanging, although any type of punishment without a legal trial is a form of "lynch law" be it a rope, a bullet, or other form of punishment.

43. *Galveston Daily News*, August 1, 1869, reprinting an item written at Gonzales on July 23 to the editors of the *News*.

44. Nonpopulation Census Schedule for Goliad County, identified by Edward S. Roberts. Here he is identified as Reuben Pursell,

twenty-seven-years of age, married and a native of Kentucky. The stock raiser was "Shot by vigilance committee."

45. This list appears in *Taylor Family News* 4, no. 4 (November 1994), in article "Records from the National Archives" contributed by Ray Murtishaw.

46. This report from the *Goliad Guard* of August 7, 1869, was reprinted in both the *Galveston Daily News* of August 13 and *Flake's Daily Bulletin* of the same date.

47. Day, *Feud*, 11.

48. Ibid., 12.

49. *Galveston Daily News*, August 20, reprinting an item from the *San Antonio Daily Express* of August 13, 1869.

50. *Galveston Daily News*, August 24, reprinting the card from the *Victoria Advocate* of August 19, 1869. This also appears in Rose, *Vendetta*, 14–15 in slightly different form. Rose states that Helm issued "the following address" soon after taking the field, hence what was printed in the various newspapers may have been handwritten notes which would explain the difference between the "address" and the various printed versions.

51. *Flake's Daily Bulletin*, August 26, 1869. Could Editor Flake have been aware of Helm's activities in northeast Texas following the war's end? It would seem so.

52. For a treatment of Baker, with material on Bickerstaff and Lee, see *Cullen Montgomery Baker: Reconstruction Desperado* by Barry A. Crouch and Donaly E. Brice (Baton Rouge: Louisiana State University Press, 1997).

53. Rose, *Vendetta*, 16–18.

54. The inscriptions on the markers read as follows:

SACRED TO THE MEMORY
Of John Choate
Who was born
In the state of Louisiana
And was killed at his residence in
San Patricio Co. Texas
On the 3rd day of August A.D. 1869
A good man and true has gone to his rest.
He was an affectionate husband,
A good neighbor,
A warm friend and a zealous Mason.

The inscription on the grave of cousin Crockett was of equal praise for his qualities:

SACRED TO THE MEMORY
Of Crockett Choate
Who was born
In the State of Texas, A.D. 1842
And was killed
At the residence of his cousin in
San Patricio Co. Texas
On the 3rd day of August A.D. 1869

This tells of a grave by the dashing wave,
A fond friend's lip that did quiver,
Of an eye that's hid by a leaden lid,
And a voice now still forever.

From author's notes.

55. *Galveston Daily News*, August 20, 1869, reprinting an item from an undated *Gonzales Inquirer*.

56. Rose, *Vendetta*, 18-19.

57. Donaly E. Brice. "The Good, The Bad, and The Ugly: A Comparison of Three State Police Captains," 10. Unpublished paper presented to the Texas State Historical Association annual meeting in Austin, March 1997. More recently much information on Helm's background has been published in *Brush Men and Vigilantes: Civil War Dissent in Texas* by David Pickering and Judy Falls.

58. This may be one E. McCormick identified as a carpenter in the 1870 census. He was a single white male born in South Carolina. Galveston County census, enumerated by J. G. Burnham, June 25, 1870, 184.

59. Lt. William Thompson to Capt. G. G. Huntt, 4th Cavalry Commanding, October 18, 1869, written from Helena in Barry Crouch Collection. Fulcrod's first name is unknown. He was probably the brother of Philip Fulcrod, who is found boarding in the household of Mary Jones and her family, in 1870. Goliad County census, enumerated July 13, 1870 by Edward S. Roberts, 363. Philip Fulcrod served as a 2nd Lieutenant in the artillery company of the 5th Texas Mounted Volunteers, and participated in General H. H. Sibley's campaign in New Mexico Territory in 1862. Jerry Thompson, ed., *Civil War in the Southwest: Recollections of the*

Sibley Brigade (College Station: Texas A&M University Press, 2001).

Chapter Four

1. Special Officer C. S. Bell to Capt. C. E. Morse, Assistant Adjutant General 5th Military District, from Austin, May 17, 1869. Original in National Archives, copy in Barry Crouch Collection.
2. *Galveston Daily News*, August 13, printing a letter from "Subscriber" written from DeWitt County, August 7, 1869.
3. *Galveston Daily News*, August 20, 1869, reprinting "further particulars" about the Choate killings in an undated issue of the *Gonzales Inquirer*.
4. *Daily Austin Republican*, August 27, 1869.
5. Telegram from C. S. Bell to Assistant Adjutant General H. Clay Wood, August 26, 1869. Original in National Archives, 5th Military District, copy in Barry Crouch Collection; the *Galveston Daily News*, September 1, and *Flake's Daily Bulletin*, September 1, 1869.
6. *Galveston Daily News*, September 1, 1869.
7. Although Westfall was seriously wounded, he survived. Jack Helm reported later that Westfall was among ten men arrested in late 1870. Westfall and William Dodd were arrested; Westfall was "Sent under Guard to Wilson Co—mortally wounded evading arrest" was his comment. Dodd was released as there were no charges against him. The list, reported on September 24, 1870, but giving no dates as to the actual arrest, consisted of, besides Westfall and Dodd, Elijah Ratcliff, John Newcomer, Albert Lacey, Lewis May, George Tison, George McCarty, John Benham, and one Chambers, first name not given. The arrests had occurred in Yorktown and in the counties of Live Oak, Bee, and Refugio. "Report of Arrests," 38-39 in State Police Ledger 404-1001 in Texas State Archives.
8. Special Officer C. S. Bell to Capt. C. E. Morse, from Campbell's Ranch, August 23, 1869. Original in National Archives. Barry Crouch Collection.
9. Special Officer C. S. Bell to Maj. Gen. J. J. Reynolds, written from Campbell's Ranch, Wilson County, August 23, 1869. Original in National Archives, copy in Barry Crouch Collection.
10. Thomas H. Stribling to Gen. J. J. Reynolds, written from San Antonio, September 19, 1869. Original in National Archives, copy in Barry Crouch Collection. In 1870, Stribling was a forty-

four-year-old lawyer with $20,000 in real estate and $3000 in personal estate. The Alabama-born man lived with his Illinois-born wife Helen and their three children in San Antonio. Creed Taylor was later quoted as saying that at Helena he was kept a prisoner one month, after which he was placed under a peace bond in the sum of $10,000 and only then turned loose. He buried Hays on the Ecleto near his old home in Wilson County. "Capt. Bell got the blood money for the killing of my son, but it burned his hands so bad that he quit Texas immediately to escape the righteous vengeance of the Taylors." Quoted in Sutton, *Feud*, 22.

11. *Dallas Herald*, October 9, 1869, "Outlaw Nabbed," reprinting an article from an undated *Denton Monitor*. Sheriff B. F. Greenlee had been appointed by Gen. J. J. Reynolds' Special Order # 105; he served until December 3, 1869. See Tise, 155.

12. Special Officer C. S. Bell to Capt. C. E. Morse, from Austin, October 4, 1869. Original in the National Archives, copy in Barry Crouch Collection.

13. Randolph W. Spencer and his brothers—William Addison, Theodore Frieling, and Alonzo O.—were the children of Elijah and Carroll W. Spencer. After the death of their parents the children went to live with their uncle, G. W. Brown in Karnes County, Texas. William married Caroline Hephzibeth Taylor in 1866. William A. Spencer was elected county clerk of Karnes County, and later was elected to the same position in 1878 in Kimble County. He served as county clerk until his election as sheriff of Kimble County on November 4, 1884; he was elected to two more terms and served until November 4, 1890. Randolph Spencer was killed by lightning while on a cattle drive from Texas to Kansas in 1870; his body was supposedly buried in a Hays County, Texas, cemetery but Hays County Cemetery inventories fail to list the name of any Spencer. See Tise, 307; M. G. Spencer, "Spencers from North Carolina to Texas," *Taylor Family News* 16, no. 1 (May 2006): 2–4; W. R. Massengale, "A Trip to Kansas in 1870," in *The Trail Drivers of Texas*, compiled and edited by J. Marvin Hunter (Austin: University of Texas Press, 1985), 1022; Dovie Dell Tschirhart Hall, "William Addison Spencer and Caroline Hepzibeth Taylor" in *DeWitt County*, 741–42.

14. Special Officer C. S. Bell to Capt. C. E. Morse, October 30, 1869. Original in National Archives, copy in Barry Crouch Collection.

15. The *San Antonio Daily Herald*, October 31, 1869, identified the dead as Christopher Kerlick Sr. and William Kerlick, H. G. Woods, and Deputy Faust. Additional details on the battle and genealogical information on the Kerlick family is from "Kerlick Family" by Beverly Kerlick Bruns in *The History of DeWitt County, Texas*, 526. Also see Paul N. Spellman, s.v. "Henry Gonzalvo Woods," *New Handbook*. The Kerlicks were buried in the small Jonischke Cemetery, south of Yorktown.

16. In 1870 James W. Cox was farming in DeWitt County. He was then forty-seven and had been born in Kentucky, claiming $1000 worth of real estate and $300 worth of personal estate. His household contained no wife, but five children ranged in age from seventeen to nine. The children were all born in Texas save the youngest, Rufus, who was born in California. DeWitt County census, enumerated June 1, 1870, by Willis Fawcett, 213. J. W. Cox was married a second time, to Mrs. Laura A. Hanks, on August 22, 1872, in Clinton. See DeWitt County Marriage Record Book D, License #1139, 44. After J. W. Cox's death she was again a widow. In 1880 she was farming and raising sheep, with her seventeen-year-old son from her first marriage and her seven-year-old son from her second marriage. Young Cox was another son who grew up never knowing his father due to the violence of the feud. DeWitt County census, enumerated by Wm. P. Huston, June 9–10, 1880, 434.

17. The Henry "Raglan," as Bell spelled the name, is certainly the Henry Ragland who in 1860 was a day laborer working for farmer A. C. Carothers in Refugio County, post office Crescent Village. He was then eighteen years old and had been born in Texas. See Refugio County census, enumerated June 9, 1860 by A. S. Thurmond, 129. In Victoria County a decade later, he was a farmer with a mere $350 worth of real estate and $100 worth of personal estate. See Victoria County census, enumerated August 5, 1870, by S. Sanford, 273. He was commissioned a private in the State Police on August 13, 1870.

18. Special Officer C. S. Bell to Capt. C. E. Morse, written from San Antonio, November 12, 1869. Original in National Archives, copy in Barry Crouch Collection.

19. Martin Luther Taylor was born February 16, 1845, and died November 23, 1869, in McMullen County. He married Sophronia Morris, daughter of W. B. "Dave" Morris on May 29, 1867, in

Atascosa County. Martin Luther was one of two sons of Rufus Taylor who were killed in the feud between 1869 and 1874. Ironically, another son of Rufus Taylor, Alfred P. Taylor, was with William E. Sutton when Charley Taylor was killed in Bastrop County.

20. Special Officer C. S. Bell to Capt. C. E. Morse, written from Laredo, November 28, 1869. Original in National Archives, copy in Barry Crouch Collection.

21. Day, *Feud*, 12–13.

22. Henry B. Yelvington, "Oakville Had Its Wild and Wooly Days—and, Its Mysteries Too," *San Antonio Daily Express*, August 27, 1933. This full-page article prints the two versions provided by Judge Andrew Dilworth. Dilworth discounts the version that they were both hanged, believing the pair were shot to death and their bodies left unburied. Dilworth is quoted as saying, "No one seems to know what report Bell's men turned in, but it was generally said that they claimed Taylor started to run and they had to kill him to stop him. They gave no reason for killing Morris or for leaving the bodies unburied." Yelvington's article does not clarify when the graves were first marked. He indicated the graves "were in good condition" when he first saw them, but by 1933 the stone slab at the head of each grave was "partially broken and the graves in a bad state." The original headstones read as follows: "In Memory of W. B. Morris, Born August 30, 1822. Died Nov. 23, 1869." and "In Memory of Martin L. Taylor, born Feb. 16, 1845, Died Nov. 23, 1869." The graves were originally covered with rocks, no doubt to protect them from wild animals. Through the years the stones were broken, but remained legible. In 1981 the area became part of the U.S. Bureau of Reclamation area. The remains of Morris and Taylor were removed and re-interred on February 13, 1982, to Hilltop Cemetery at Tilden with an "impressive ceremony" attended by several descendants of Taylor and Morris. The original burial land is now under the waters of the Choke Canyon Reservoir. Nonpopulation Schedule, 1870, McMullen County. Commissioners Court Minutes, Vol. 11, McMullen County, listing the "Monumented Graves" to be removed; "Reburial services for Taylor and Morris" by Mrs. A. E. Adolf, an article originally appearing in the *Beeville Bee-Picayune*, February 18, 1982, of Beeville, Bee County, Texas; *McMullen County History*, no publisher, no date (1980?), 412–13, entry "Morris-Taylor Killing."

23. The Nonpopulation Schedule for McMullen County, listing persons who died during the year ending June 1, 1870, does more than simply list their deaths. Besides showing that Taylor was twenty-seven and a white male born in Texas and married, and Morris was aged forty-nine, and also a white male, born in Mississippi, in the final column is written, "Assassinated/ gun shot wound" and across the writing in another hand, "Murdered."

24. Jack Helm, Sheriff of DeWitt County, writing from Concrete, Texas, June 14, 1870, to Gov. E. J. Davis. Original in Texas State Archives.

25. Ibid., June 26, 1870.

26. Hall represented District 18, which consisted of Freestone, Leon, Robertson, Bastrop and Fayette counties. The bill was introduced in the Called Session of 1870 of the 12th Legislature. *Members of the Texas Legislature 1846–1962*, Revised edition of 1939 (Austin, 1962), 58.

27. Carl H. Moneyhon, s.v. "James Davidson." *New Handbook.*

28. Besides the names of the captains, the names of the seven lieutenants and twelve sergeants were published in various newspapers. *Flake's Daily Bulletin* of July 21, 1870, for example, provided the names of those appointed captains, lieutenants, and sergeants. The force never reached its full capacity with the privates.

29. "Report of Arrests" (by the State Police), 32–33. Ledger 401-1001, Texas State Archives. A similar report appeared in the *Daily State Journal* of August 16, 1870. Commented the editor: "There are but a few men in the State Police, and they have not been at work more than three weeks, in which time upwards of *fifty malefactors*, who have hitherto evaded the civil authorities, and in many instances defied them, have been arrested and turned over to the authorities. This speaks well for the State Police."

30. *Daily State Journal* (Austin), June 26, 1870.

31. *Daily Herald* (San Antonio), July 27, 1870, reprinting an undated item from the *Gonzales Index.*

32. Oran Warder Nolen, "The Most Murderous Feud in Texas History," *True Frontier* magazine, September 1970, 55.

33. Chris Emmett, *Shanghai Pierce, A Fair Likeness* (Norman: University of Oklahoma Press, 1953), 57–58. Howard R. Lamar discusses the Lunn lynching as well, following Emmett closely, in *Charlie Siringo's West: An Interpretive Biography* (Albuquerque: University of New Mexico Press, 2005), 51–52.

34. *Flake's Daily Bulletin*, of Galveston, July 6 and 12, 1870, print-
    ing correspondence from "Trespalacios." This correspondent
    adopted his *nom de plume* from the community of Tres Palacios,
    a port community on the river of the same name. Rachel Jackson,
    s.v. "Tres Palacios, Texas," *New Handbook*. The Lunn family
    is listed in the 1860 census, head of household Josiah Lunn, a
    native of Pennsylvania, and wife Sarah A., from Mississippi,
    and six children. Matagorda County, Texas census, enumer-
    ated June 20, 1860 by (name illegible), 493. A decade later the
    only Lunn family is that of William Lunn, living with eleven
    others of the name of Lunn, Williams, Taylor, and Nail. Mata-
    gorda County, Texas census, enumerated by John Kimpe [?],
    August 4, 1870, 480. Their post office is shown to be Wilson's
    Creek and Tres Palacios. Also Matagorda County Historical Com-
    mission, *Historic Matagorda County* 1 (Houston: D. Armstrong
    Co., 1986), 183.
35. DeWitt County Marriage Book C, License # 951, 356. The
    license shows J. C. Taylor and Miss Mollie E. Kelly "both of
    said County, and he by the consent of his father & She of law-
    ful age." The license was issued and the marriage took place
    April 5, 1870, performed by Justice of the Peace L. W. Miller,
    in presence of a Mrs. Pratt and family. Attached was a permis-
    sion note dated April 4, 1870: "To the clerk of the county court
    of Dewitt county Sir you will let J C Taylor hav[e] licens[e] to
    mar[r]y this is my consent[.] P. B. Taylor." Brothers Eugene A. and
    Wiley Kelly, arrested at the same time with Henry and William,
    lived long lives. Eugene died in Odessa, Texas, in 1924 and
    Wiley died in Runge, Texas, in 1929. Both William and Henry
    left children who were mere babes at the time of their deaths.
    William B.'s daughter was Wilhemenia, born in 1870; Henry's
    son was Henry P., born in 1869.
36. *San Antonio Daily Herald*, September 4, 1870, reprinting an
    item from the *State Journal*.
37. The statements of Mrs. Amanda Kelly, wife of Henry Kelly,
    sworn before O. K. Tuton, on October 15, 1870, that of Mrs.
    Delilah Kelly, sworn on the same day before Tuton, appeared
    in the *Austin Daily Republican*, November 1, 1870, headlined
    "The Kelly Tragedy." Other affidavits followed. They appear
    with variations in Rose's *Vendetta*, 38–50.
38. District Court Records, True Bill, District Court, Lavaca
    County.

39. Sutton, *Feud*, 34–35.

40. "Report of Arrests." State Police Ledger 401-1001, 34-35. Texas State Archives, 34-35. Curiously there are charges against the Kellys dating back to 1859 and 1867 for disturbing public worship. An indictment charged Wiley Kelly with "Maliciously Disturbing Religious Worship" on June 10, 1859, a decade prior. The charge read that he did "disturb a congregation assembled for religious worship and conducting themselves in a lawful manner. ..." The charges against Henry Kelly, Thomas Franks, and Skipton were that at the Baptist Church on Mustang Creek near Sweet Home they "unlawfully and willfully did disturb a congregation then and there assembled for religious worship and conducting themselves in a lawful manner." This is dated as occurring on July 10, 1867. The indictment was not filed until November 8, 1869. Apparently the men who charged the Kellys with disturbing religious worship and/or disturbing a circus waited until the State Police force was created before attempting to bring them to trial.

41. "Report of Arrests," 4243.

42. Day, *Feud*, 13–14.

43. Ibid., 14.

44. Truitt, *Taylor Party*, 70.

45. *Daily Austin Republican*, November 1, 1870.

46. *San Antonio Daily Herald*, November 22, 1870.

47. *Galveston Daily News*, September 7, 1870.

48. *Honey-Grove Enterprise*, September 24, 1870, reporting news from Lavaca County.

49. *San Antonio Daily Herald*, September 11, 1870.

50. *Weekly Austin Republican*, September 14, 1870, reprinting an item from an undated *Gonzales Index*.

51. *San Antonio Daily Herald*, September 16, 1870.

52. *Daily State Journal*, September 17, 1870. Hunnicutt's appointment was revoked on September 1, 1870.

53. Helm's dismissal (November 30, 1870) and Haskins' appointment (December 1, 1870) are from the State Police Roster, Adj. Gen. Records, 134–35. Haskins served until August 31, 1872, 364–65.

54. *Weekly Austin Republican*, November 23, 1870.

55. James Davidson, *Report of the Adjutant-General of the State of Texas, June 24, 1870, to December 31, 1870*, (Austin: Tracy, Siemering & Co., 1870), 9–15.

56. *San Antonio Daily Herald*, April 21, 1871.

57. *Daily State Journal*, April 25, 1871.

58. *San Antonio Daily Herald*, May 3, 1871.

59. Ibid., May 19, 1871.

60. *San Antonio Daily Express*, December 13, 1871. The reward is noted in a letter to Capt. A. McCluny who inquired of such in correspondence to Gov. E. J. Davis, July 17, 1871. McCluny claimed to have arrested Doboy Taylor and inquired of the amount of the reward. Davis to McCluny, Co. D, 7th Regiment, State Guard, from Davis, Records of the Governor, RG 301, Letter Press Book (July 10, 1871–November 17, 1871), 55. That Taylor would probably have been found not guilty is surmised from Teel's claim "to have defended more than 700 clients charged with capital offenses and to have saved them all from execution." Thomas W. Cutrer, s.v., "Trevanion Theodore Teel," *New Handbook*.

61. J. B. Polley, "The Taylor Boys Made Things Interesting." Article reprinted from the *San Antonio Daily Express* in *Frontier Times* 9, no. 3 (December, 1931): 122.

62. Gonzales County, Texas census, enumerated June 30, 1870, by M. H. Beaty, 481. Their post office was Belmont.

63. Register of the Grand Central Hotel of Ellsworth, Kansas. Holstein is shown to have registered on June 3, 1873. Other well-known names on the same date include John Good, Pete Murchison, Ben Thompson, Neil Cain, Cad Pierce, and Crawford Burnett. Microfilm copy in author's collection. Of interest is that on the second of June J. G. McVea had registered; on the eighth J. F. McCrabb, Fred and John Duderstadt registered. On the Fourth of July G. W. Slaughter and W. D. Meador registered. Then on August 15 William Sutton and wife both registered. W. W. Davis registered several times in August and September. These men all either participated in the Sutton-Taylor Feud or else were close friends with men who did. Apparently the men who found conflict in Texas were able to avoid trouble in the Kansas cattle town of Ellsworth.

64. Minutes District Court of DeWitt County, Book B, Cause #548, 392.

Chapter Five

1. John Wesley Hardin, *The Life of John Wesley Hardin, From the Original Manuscript, As Written by Himself*, 13–14. Originally

published posthumously in 1896 by Smith & Moore of Seguin, Texas, and reprinted by J. Marvin Hunter in 1926 and serialized in *Frontier Times*, then reprinted by the University of Oklahoma Press in 1961 with an introduction by Robert G. McCubbin. Hereafter cited as Hardin, *Life*.

2. Frank L. Britton, *Report of the Adjutant General of the State of Texas, for the Year 1872* (Austin: James P. Newcomb and Company, 1873), 12. Hereafter cited as Britton.

3. Hardin's version of the killing of Smith, Jones, and Davis, "men calling themselves police" is in Hardin, *Life*, 32. The Christian name of General Bell is from the roster of State Police to be included in the unpublished manuscript by Barry Crouch and Donaly E. Brice: *The Governor's Hounds: A History of the Texas State Police*.

4. Britton's *Report*, dated December 31, 1872, provides a list of State Policemen killed or wounded. Eight had been killed, five wounded. Of the number killed, two were victims of Hardin, possibly three; two of the five wounded were victims of Hardin. Britton, 12.

5. Gonzales County Marriage Record, #1576.

6. The literature on Hardin is voluminous. The best biographies are Richard C. Marohn's *The Last Gunfighter: John Wesley Hardin* (College Station, Tex.: Creative Publishing Company, 1995) and Leon Metz's *John Wesley Hardin: Dark Angel of Texas* (El Paso: Mangan Books, 1996).

7. Hardin, *Life*, 61.

8. Record of Police Court of DeWitt County, 335–37. Copies provided to author by Karon Mac Smith.

9. Haldeman was the son of David H. and Candis Thompson Haldeman. They had five children, known: Mary E., born 1839; John T., who lived from 1846–1918; Tom, born August 1, 1848; Jesse E., born 1851; and Joseph, born 1858. DeWitt County census, enumerated September —, 1870 by Willis Fawcett, 268; and June 9–10, 1880, 434 by William P. Huston. The Salt Creek Cemetery, also known as the Old Davy Cemetery, where the Haldemans are buried, is a few miles north of Yorktown.

10. *Gonzales Inquirer*, May 18, 1878.

11. *Drag Net*, a short-lived newspaper of Gonzales, November 2, 1894.

12. F. L. Britton, *Report of the Adjutant General of the State of Texas for the Year 1873* (Austin: Cardwell & Walker, 1874), 122–23.

13. Details of the Haldeman killing are from the author's *Bowen and Hardin* (College Station, Tex.: Creative Publishing Company, 1991), 33–43.

14. F. L. Britton, *Report of the Adjutant General of the State of Texas for the Year 1873* (Austin: Cardwell & Walker, Printers, 1874), 116. Hereafter cited as Britton, *1873*. This report identifies the victim as John Morgan, although Hardin biographers Richard C. Marohn and Leon Metz both identify him as James B. Morgan. He may have served as a deputy at times, but the census identifies him as a stonemason. Years later, Hardin, while in prison, pled guilty to this killing, which resulted in his being sentenced to two years imprisonment to be served concurrently with the sentence for killing Charles Webb. Hardin's court appearance was held on January 1, 1892, at which he was treated as a celebrity. The *Daily Herald* of San Antonio reported the killing as taking place on Saturday, April 6 and identified Morgan as a stonemason by occupation and had been killed by "a man named Johnson, [who] then got on his horse and escaped." The *Herald* commented that it was believed Johnson was an alias of "West. Harding" and "in this instance" acted justifiably as Morgan "is said to have been the aggressor."

15. Hardin, *Life*, 79.

16. Letter from Pidge, in Austin's *Daily Democratic Statesman*, December 9, written from Clinton December 5, 1874.

17. Jack Hays Day informs us of his background. His grandfather, Robert Day, had brought his young wife Susan from Georgia to Texas where they first settled at St. Augustine. Three children blessed their union: John (Jack's father), Will, and Betty. Around 1840 the family moved to DeWitt County and about 1842 grandfather Robert Day was killed "at the hands of marauding Indians." The widow Susan Day became the wife of Pitkin Taylor on December 13, 1846.

18. Day, *Feud*, 7. DeWitt County census enumerated by Willis Fawcett, July —, 1870, 20. Not surprisingly Day identifies the two children as "Uncle Jim" and "Aunt Amanda" but enumerator Fawcett identified the daughter as Mary E. In 1860 the family is enumerated showing P. B. and Susan with two children: A. J. (Amanda Jane, age eleven years) and "Jas." (Uncle Jim, age eight years). DeWitt County census, enumerated by John R. Foster, June —, 1860, 466.

19. Day, *Feud*, 14.

20. Ibid., 14–15; and Truitt, *Taylor Party*, 95.

21. Truitt, *Taylor Party*, 82, 95. The only baby this could have been was Henry Peter Kelly Jr., born March 29, 1869.

22. Hardin, *Life*, 79-80. For material from the Hardin autobiography I have used only the 1896 first edition, since subsequent editions, such as the 1961 University of Oklahoma reprint, do not follow the original exactly.

23. Day, *Feud*, 15. Taylor's Christian name is frequently spelled "Pipkin." Apparently either Pitkin or Pipkin was acceptable.

24. Ibid., 15–16.

25. Ibid, 16.

26. Rose, *Vendetta*, 29. Unfortunately many early issues of the *Victoria Advocate* are no longer extant.

27. Day, *Feud*, 16. "Bud" Dowlearn was Patrick Hayes Dowlearn, son of Joshua M. and Jane Lowe Dowlearn, and was born July 24, 1854, and died January 10, 1924. Rosalie Key Myers, *Dowlearn Lowe* (no publisher, no place, 1992), 6.

28. Day, *Feud*, 17.

29. *San Antonio Daily Herald*, June 20, 1873.

30. Britton, *1873*, 116.

31. Hardin, *Life*, 77–81.

32. Britton, *1873*, 122. Adjutant General Britton here makes the remarkable statement that Texas was not the only state to offer a $1000 reward for Hardin. Missouri also offered a $1000 reward. There are no accounts of Hardin ever living in that state. *San Antonio Daily Herald*, March 25, 1873, also reported the $1000 reward offered for Hardin.

33. Day, *Feud*, 18–19.

34. Hardin, *Life*, 81.

35. Sonnichsen, *I'll Die*, 49.

36. Day, *Feud*, 19.

37. Rose, *Vendetta*, 29–30.

38. Ibid., 80.

39. John W. S. Christman and Mary E. Prather were married August 22, 1867, witnessed by James W. Cox and William Mitchell. DeWitt County Marriage Record Book A, License # 680, 221. Cox later married Mrs. Laura A. Hanks on August 22, 1872. DeWitt County Marriage Record Book D, License #1139, 44. From his first marriage Cox fathered six children. The 1870 census

shows Frank, William, Melissa, Perry, and Rufus. DeWitt County census, enumerated June 1, 1870 by Willis Fawcett, 213. The 1880 census shows James W. Cox, age seven years, was born in 1873, the year of his father's death, thus becoming another child who never really knew his father. DeWitt County census, enumerated June 9–10, 1880 by William P. Huston, 434.

40. Hyatt, *Fuel*, 35–36.

41. *San Antonio Daily Herald,* July 23, 1873. This report appeared essentially the same in the *Houston Telegraph* of July 30, 1873, giving further negative publicity to the DeWitt County area.

42. Letter from L. B. Wright to Gov. E. J. Davis, July 24, 1873.

43. Hyatt, "Littleberry Wright Family" in *DeWitt County*, 830. Wright is buried in the Upper Yorktown Cemetery, having died in 1882. This small cemetery contains the graves of Wright, the two Brassells killed in the feud, as well as feud victim Charles Heissig, although the latter's grave is not marked.

44. Identity of the weapon Hardin used is from David George, "Jack Helm Meets John Wesley Hardin," *The Texas Gun Collector*, Spring, 2003, 48–49. The weapon was examined by this writer at the Buckhorn Saloon in San Antonio. W. & C. Scott & Son were the firm of William and Charles Scott who operated a firearms factory at various addresses in Birmingham, England, until 1894. The company then joined P. Webley & Son to become Webley and Scott Revolver & Arms Co. Ltd., in 1897. The identification at the time of examination showed that Hardin later loaned or gave the weapon to Gonzales County Sheriff J. C. Jones. If accurate, Hardin gave the weapon to him prior to his becoming sheriff as his term was from 1880–1882. Most likely the weapon was given to Sheriff William E. Jones, a man elected several times to that office.

45. Hardin, *Life,* 81–82.

46. Day, *Feud*, 18.

47. Rose, *Vendetta*, 37. Helm may have used the blacksmith shop to work on his inventions. On November 16, 1872, his application was filed for an implement he termed a "new and Improved Cultivator" designed to destroy cotton worms. Patent number 139,062 is dated May 20, 1873. If indeed he was working on his invention he may have carelessly allowed his arms to be set aside, leaving him at a distinct disadvantage. Hardin and Day both recalled the date of the Helm killing incorrectly. Hardin

wrote his memoir, or perhaps dictated it to his mistress who acted also as his secretary, after sixteen years in Huntsville State Penitentiary. Naturally he would put his actions in the best favorable light. Hardin gave the date of the Helm killing as the seventeenth of May, almost two months too early. Day was writing his memoir some sixty years after the events occurred, which he knew of either first- or second-hand. His dating the killing as early March again indicates the weakness of memory, especially after that many years. Rose suggests that the killing was "[s]oon after the police act went into effect" which was in July of 1870, a serious error.

48. *San Antonio Daily Herald*, July 24, 1873.

49. *San Antonio Daily Express*, July 25, 1873.

50. *Houston Telegraph*, July 30, 1873.

51. *San Antonio Daily Express*, July 31, 1873.

52. *Bastrop Advertiser*, August 2, 1873, reprinting an item from an undated *Gonzales Index*. This same article was reprinted in the *Fayette County New Era* of La Grange, in its issue of August 8, 1873. The identical article appeared in the *Southwestern Index* (undetermined date) of Gonzales and the *San Antonio Daily Express* of August 9, 1873.

53. Hardin, *Life*, 81. Hardin wrote that Helm and fifty men entered "our neighborhood" inquiring about the location of Mannen Clements, George Tennille, and Hardin. Helm was "particularly insulting to my wife because she would not inform him of some of the Taylor party." This alone may have been the real reason Hardin wanted to kill Helm.

54. Joshua Robert "Brown" Bowen was becoming notorious. The *San Antonio Daily Express* described him as a "ruffian" who had committed rape "on a colored woman" and then "shot and killed one of the best colored men in the County, Bob Taylor, by name." *Express*, July 25, 1873.

55. L. B. Wright to Gov. E .J. Davis, July 24, 1873. Justice Wright was born December 4, 1830, in Perry County, Alabama. He died June 15, 1882, at Yorktown. Reading Wright's correspondence, one tends to consider him meek and shallow. Not so his son and grandson. His son, William L. Wright became a Ranger captain; his grandson E. A. "Dogie" became as well a Ranger captain.

56. One wonders what would have been the condition of Wright if he had also done the inquest on Helm's body. Wilson County Justice

James W. Dickey had that responsibility. For an unknown reason he did not submit his bill for $6.00 until some months later. The amount was approved at the November 20, 1873, commissioners meeting. Commissioners Court Minutes, Vol. "A," 229, Office of the County Clerk, Floresville, Wilson County. Unfortunately Dickey's inquest report has not been preserved. It would be extremely informative, probably revealing details such as the number and location of buckshot and bullet holes. "There Was An Inquest," in Karon Mac Smith, *On the Watershed of Ecleto and the Clear Fork of Sandies II*, 22–23. 1988.

57. John G. Johnson, s.v., "State Police." *New Handbook*.
58. C. S. Bell to Capt. C. E. Morse, Secretary for Civil Affairs, from San Marcos, May 14, 1870.
59. *Galveston Daily News*, June 15, 1870. Clinton's letter to the *News* was dated June 7, and written from Clinton.
60. Ibid., June 23, 1870.
61. J. G. Tracy, Chairman State Republican Executive Committee and State Senator 14th District, to Honorable O.C. French, Chairman Republican Executive Committee, State of Mississippi, written from Austin, May 28, 1873.
62. Requisition Papers, Texas State Library and Archives.
63. C. S. Bell to Gov. R. B. Hubbard, May 24, 1878, written from Washington, D.C.
64. *New York Times*, February 24, reprinting an obituary-article on Bell's death from the Dayton, Ohio, *Journal* of February 22, 1879.

Chapter Six

1. Sutton, *Feud*, 44.
2. DeWitt County census, enumerated August —, 1870 by Willis Fawcett, 255.
3. Letter from Pidge, written from Clinton, December 5 and published in the *Austin Daily Democratic Statesman*, December 9, 1874. A sketch of Tumlinson's life by this author is found in Shirley A. Karnei and Francis Hartmann, eds., *Yorktown, Texas: 150 Year Anniversary, 1848–1998* (Yorktown, Tex.: The Printery, 1997), 212–19.
4. State Police Records. Adj. Gen. James Davidson to Tumlinson, April 29, 1871, 32. Tumlinson had written to Davidson indicating he could not "comply with orders" and was discharged. Letterpress Book 401-1032.
5. Hardin, *Life*, 84.

6. Wright, although his spelling is atrocious, gave clear identification of the leaders of the besieging party. The "Mack Nickles" he mentions is Lazarus Nichols' son Morgan Oliver, who was born in 1851 and survived the feud, dying in 1897. Lazarus and his son are both buried in Lost Creek Cemetery in DeWitt County. Lazarus Nichols' life spanned from March 17, 1825, to December 30, 1882. A daughter, Elizabeth Ann, married one-time McNelly Ranger Roe P. Orrell.

7. Hardin, *Life*, 84.

8. Justice of the Peace L. B. Wright to Gov. E. J. Davis, August 16, 1873, written from Yorktown. The *Cuero Star* reported the "riot" slightly differently. The report indicated that Blair had gathered up "every man in town to suppress a riot four miles west of Yorktown; ... some of them on foot and most of them without arms. ..." Blair found "two distinct parties," one led by Tumlinson and the other by Hardin. "The sheriff was informed that no public disturbance was intended by either party, that the whole affair was of a personal nature, that a compromise had been effected and that both wished to repair to the county seat to draw up papers to keep the peace, to which the sheriff agreed." The entire group of feudists, about one hundred men, reached Clinton about four o'clock in the afternoon where the treaty was signed after which the parties dispersed. The *San Antonio Daily Express*, August 20, 1873, reprinting the item from the *Cuero Star*.

9. Sutton, *Feud*, 47. It is not clear from Sutton's work if what he had to include in his study was a photostatic copy of the original, a photocopy, or merely a handwritten copy. Several of the names appear incorrectly, such as "Jazanis Nichols," in reality was Lazarus Nichols. The name "Y. Hawks" may have indeed been a man named Hanks. Of special interest is the name of J. W. Brassell. His brother, George T. Brassell, was killed later in the feud along with his father.

10. *San Antonio Daily Express*, August 17, 1873. On April 22, 1873, the legislature repealed the law creating the State Police.

11. Undated *Victoria Advocate*, quoted in Rose, *Vendetta*, 32. Day incorrectly gives January 1, 1874, as the date of W. W. Pridgen's murder. The *Cuero Star* reported the killing was "about 11 o'clock yesterday morning" which would date the murder December 30, 1873. Day, *Feud*, 20, 40.

12. *Cuero Weekly Star*, January 9, 1874.

13. Ibid. A version of the treaty appeared in the *Galveston Daily News* of May 19, 1875, on the occasion of the arrival of twenty-two men indicted as Ku Klux Klansmen, an initial step in the prosecution of those for the murder of B. J. Pridgen's former slave Abram Bryant.

14. The spelling of the Sitterle name appears in a variety of ways. *Sitterle* is certainly the most accepted spelling, although some records use *Sitterlie*.

15. *Cuero Weekly Star*, January 9, 1874.

16. Robert J. Clow account book. The original, a 4" x 6" leather-bound booklet, is today housed in the Alice Clow Papers, Center for American History, University of Texas, Austin. Proprietors D. and W. R. Brown were the Brown brothers operating the Gulf Hotel in Cuero. According to one advertisement it was "a new and complete building in every respect. Rooms comfortable and well ventilated. Table supplied with the very best the market affords." *Cuero Weekly Star*, December 31, 1873.

17. *Cuero Weekly Star*, January 23, 1874, reprinting an item from an undated *Indianola Bulletin*.

18. Hardin, *Life*, 85–86.

19. The name is spelled in a great variety of ways. Alexander Henry Barekman is how Walter Clay Dixson spells it in his *Richland Crossing: A Portrait of Texas Pioneers* (self published, 1994). Among many others who provided genealogical information to his study was Joseph Anderson Barekman; since he is of the same line I have used that spelling except in direct quotations.

20. Rose, *Vendetta*, 51–52.

21. John Newbanks Keeran (1824–1904) was one of the most successful stockmen of Victoria County. After leaving his native Virginia he traveled to California where he made a fortune in ranching and gold mining. Locating in Texas in 1867, he established his 30,000-acre ranch in southeast Victoria County. He was among the first cattlemen to fence his pastures in the area. Among other accomplishments, he founded and was director of the Victoria National Bank. Thomas W. Cutrer, s.v. "John Newbanks Keeran" in *New Handbook*.

22. The idea of Mrs. Sutton being aware of the Taylors and then attempting to shield her husband from the danger is from Rose. "But the lynx eyes of the Taylors never lost sight of him. Jim and Bill Taylor, implacable as fate, followed him," he wrote.

"Sutton's noble little wife suspicioned their intentions, and so assiduous was her solicitude for her husband that she remained at his side, and thus shielded him from the murderous lead already molded and consecrated to his destruction." The idea of Laura Sutton trying to shield her husband is further embellished in the *Indianola Scrap Book*, edited by George French, first published in 1936 and reprinted with an index by the Jenkins Publishing Company, San Felipe Press of Austin in 1974. There the Taylors are described as "shaggy-bearded men" who had followed the Suttons and Slaughter from Clinton. Sutton's "noble little wife clung to his side and tried to keep herself always between them and her husband. Just as she was mounting the gangplank to the steamer in front of her husband, Bill and Jim came up. Several shots cracked in rapid succession," 90–91. The testimony of witnesses make no mention of this heroic action of Mrs. Sutton. The book was originally published on the 50th anniversary of the Indianola storm of August 26, 1886.

23. Hardin, *Life*, 86; Day, *Feud*, 23; 3 Texas Court of Appeals (1878). "William Taylor v. The State," 393–94. The pistol in question was a Smith & Wesson, serial number 21418. John Meador testified that he knew the pistol belonged to Sutton as he saw him buy it in Ellsworth, Kansas.

24. Hardin, *Life*, 87.

25. Day, *Feud*, 22.

26. *Victoria Advocate*, June 4, 1874.

27. "William Taylor v The State", 393–94.

28. James Monroe Bockius was born in Ohio about 1831 but left home to go to Texas due to a difficulty about which the details have been lost. Prior to the Civil War's outbreak he was mustered into the Mounted Rangers on the Rio Grande commanded by Colonel John S. "Rip" Ford. He attained the rank of sergeant by March of 1861. During the war he served as a spy and apparently was captured but paroled. He studied medicine to some degree, as he later was considered a doctor, at least by those who knew him. When he was arrested with Hardin's other cowboys in May of 1874 he was not charged with any crime, but was held on "suspicion." On May 13, 1884, Bockius married the widow of George C. Tennille, killed in July of 1874. He later was postmaster in Sedan, Gonzales County, named to that position on January 19, 1885. Bockius died in 1909 at the

age of 78. He is buried in the Billings Cemetery in Gonzales County. See Chuck Parsons, "Doc Bockius Survived Civil War, Texas Feud," *Newsletter* of the National Outlaw and Lawman History Association (hereafter NOLA) 2, no. 4 (Spring 1977): 9–12.

29. Hardin, *Life*, 87.
30. Ibid., 89.
31. Jim Anderson was not a medical doctor but was named in full *Doctor James Thomas Lee Buchanan Anderson*. His brother was Alexander Hamilton Anderson. They were the sons of Dr. William Nicks and Susanna Louisa Dixson Anderson. See Walter Clay Dixson, *Richland Crossing: A Portrait of Texas Pioneers*.
32. Hardin, *Life*, 92–93.
33. *Cuero Weekly Star*, June 11, 1874, reprinting items from the *Comanche Chief* of May 30, 1874. The *Star* headlined its report "More Lawlessness and Crime."
34. Ibid.
35. "Memorial of citizens of Comanche county relative to out-laws and asking for protection" to Gov. Richard Coke from Comanche citizens, dated May 28, 1874. Adj. General's Papers, Texas State Archives.
36. Monthly Return of Captain John R. Waller, prepared at Comanche, June 30, 1874. Waller's command consisted of himself, one lieutenant, three sergeants, four corporals, and sixty-seven privates, for an aggregate of seventy-six men. With this number of Rangers he was able to send out numerous scouts simultaneously.
37. Dixson, *Richland Crossing*, 123–24.
38. *San Antonio Daily Express*, June 19, reprinting an item from the *Daily Democratic Statesman* of June 15, 1874; J. D. Stephens to Gov. Richard Coke, June 10, 1874; John Waller to J. D. Stephens, June 10, 1874.
39. Gov. Richard Coke to Sheriff of Calhoun County (F. L. Busch), June 15, 1874. Adj. Gen. William Steele Letter Press Book, No. 1, 1874, 246. V. C. Giles, a veteran of General John B. Hood's Texas Brigade, was later employed at the Texas General Land Office. It is probable that Governor Coke respected Giles's ability to safely deliver the prisoners.
40. Adj. Gen. William Steele to Sgt. J. V. Atkinson, June 15, 1874, in Letter Press Book, No. 1, 1874, 248.
41. Adj. Gen. William Steele to Sheriff of DeWitt County (William J. Weisiger), June 16, 1874, 249.
42. Day, *Feud*, 29.

43. *Cuero Weekly Star*, June 27, 1874.
44. Sgt. J. V. Atkinson to Adj. Gen. William Steele, written at Austin, June 24, 1874.

Chapter Seven

1. Rose, *Vendetta*, 52; DeWitt County census, enumerated August —, 1870 by Willis Fawcett, 17. The headstone shows R. H. Brown was born November 28, 1851, and died November 18, 1875. He was buried in the Epperson-Brown-Jonischkies Cemetery, near Yorktown, where other Brown family members are buried. See Henry Wolff, Jr., "Group of Friends Discovers Old Cuero Marshal's Grave," *Victoria Advocate*, February 28, 1993; also Chuck Parsons, "Reuben Brown Headstone Discovered," *Newsletter* of NOLA 15, no. 4 (June 1, 1990): 3. For inventory see Patsy Goebel, *Cemetery Records of DeWitt County, Texas*, Vol. 3 (Cuero, Tex.: Privately printed, 1992), 54–55.
2. Archibald and Mary Spencer McVea had traveled from South Carolina to Tennessee to Texas, settling in Gonzales County in the early 1850s. In 1870 Archie McVea was head of household, farming with sons William, thirty-three, and James, twenty-seven, all born in South Carolina. Younger son Archibald was twenty-two and born in Alabama. Gonzales County census, enumerated August 23, 1870, by M.H. Beaty, 450.
3. Day, *Feud*, 31.
4. *Cuero Weekly Star*, January 23, 1874. In the McVea family cemetery, near Waelder, Gonzales County, there is a damaged headstone. Only the words "McVea [illegible] d. [?] 1874" can be read; this is perhaps the grave of James G. McVea. *Cemeteries Located in Gonzales County*, extracted from the *Quarterly* of the South Texas Genealogical and Historical Society, compiled by The Gonzales Public Library, Vol. 2 (no place, no date).
5. DeWitt County Marriage Records, Book D, License #1197, 64. The marriage was performed March 18, 1873, at Clinton by Rev. J. T. Gillett. Anna Taylor's sister Persia H. Taylor would marry Basil's brother John R. F. Brown in 1876. Book D, License #1514, 171. Reuben H. Brown never married.
6. Oran Ward Nolen, "The Most Dangerous Feud in Texas," *True Frontier Magazine*, September 1969, 14–17, 55–57. See also James C. Hatch, "More About the Career of John Wesley Hardin," *Frontier Times*, June 1924, 6–7.
7. *Cuero Weekly Star*, April 8, 1874.

8. *Galveston Daily News*, April 15, 1874.

9. *Bastrop Advertiser,* April 11, 1874.

10. Hardin, *Life*, 87-88.

11. DeWitt County census, enumerated July 27, 1860, by John R. Foster, 487. F. M Buchanan was from North Carolina; mother Nancy from Alabama. William F., and siblings Mary, Margaret, and Frances were all Texas-born.

12. Day, *Feud*, 29–30. Augustus Washington Pridgen was the son of Henry and W. E. Pridgen, and was born September 8, 1838, and died February 2, 1876. Bolivar Jackson Pridgen was the son of Wiley Washington and Mary Baker Pridgen, and lived from February 14, 1829, to February 15, 1903.

13. *Daily Picayune*, New Orleans, June 5, 1874.

14. *Cuero Weekly Star*, June 4, 1874. Pridgen's wife, Martha Anne Williams Pridgen, died February 2, 1872, leaving Pridgen with seven children. From an unpublished typescript, a history of the Pridgen family, courtesy Jack S. Pridgen and letter dated May 3, 1984. Jack S. Pridgen is the great-grandson of B. J. Pridgen.

15. Both B. J. and A. W. Pridgen were charged with the murder of Buchanan. Case No. 1047 in DeWitt County District Court shows the Pridgens were charged "with the murder of one William Buchanan ... on the 17th day of May AD 1874." The pair were able to provide bond of $1000 to appear in court on the first Monday of August 1875 to answer the indictment. James W. Maddox made the complaint against the Pridgens. *Taylor Family News* 5, no. 1 (February 1995): 6–7.

16. *San Antonio Daily Express*, April 12, 1874.

17. *Austin Daily Statesman*, July 14, 1874.

18. Ibid., July 16, 1874.

19. *Brenham Daily Banner*, July 16, 1874.

20. *Cuero Weekly Star*, July 4, 1874.

21. *Galveston Daily News*, July 1, 1874. Upon his arrival in Clinton, McNelly also found fault with Sheriff Weisiger. He reported to Adj. Gen. William Steele that on his arrival in Clinton the sheriff turned over come capiases "for parties that have been here all the time. ... I can't help thinking that the Sheriff is in sympathy with these people. The capture of Hardin & Taylor would go a long way to quiet things in this county." McNelly to Steele, September 2, 1874. William Jordan Weisiger was born October 16, 1832 in Danville, Boyle County, Kentucky, and died October 23,

1885, and is buried in the Weisiger Family plot, Hillside Cemetery, Cuero. As a soldier he participated in the last battle of the war at Palmito Ranch in May 1865. Weisiger was elected several times as sheriff, serving from 1873 to 1881. Thus the comments that he was a weak sheriff seem harsh. Sidney R. Weisiger, "William Jordan Weisiger," Typescript copy in Weisiger Family file, Box 22, Folder 411, Victoria College, Special Collections; and Tise, 157.

22. *Galveston Daily News*, July 1, 1874.

23. DeWitt County census, enumerated by Willis Fawcett, September —, 1870, 269. The 1870 census shows Tennille as born in Texas, whereas the 1850 census shows his birth state as Missouri. DeWitt County census, enumerated by A. W. Hicks, August 31, 1850.

24. Pidge provided a colorful word-picture of the community of Cuero: "The town is situated almost in the center of the county, near the banks of the beautiful Guadalupe river, as pretty a stream as there is in Texas." He then provided factual information as well as revealing his sense of humor: "DeWitt county, as everybody knows, is bounded on the north by Gonzales, on the east by some county the name of which I do not remember, on the south by one which I do not recollect, and on the west by another, the name of which I have since forgotten." Of the town of Clinton, then the county seat, Pidge wrote that the population was about 400 "when they are all at home from 'out of the hurly-burly.'"

25. Pidge to Austin *Daily Democratic Statesman*, written from Clinton November 8, and published November 12, 1874.

26. Hardin, *Life*, 107.

27. Tennille was buried in the Billings Cemetery in Gonzales County, his grave originally marked only by a stone. Today there is a simple home-made marker inscribed "George C. Tenille [*sic*], Jr. 1825–1874." For a sketch of Tennille's life see Parsons, "Forgotten Feudist," *Frontier Times* 50, no. 1 (December–January 1976): 28–29, 44–45.

28. Adj. Gen. William Steele to Gov. Richard Coke, July 10, 1874, Letter Press Book, 401-621, 297.

29. Ibid., 297.

30. Daniel Brinkley Peavy, Alabama native, born March 10, 1822, farmed and raised stock in DeWitt County. At the time of the 1870 census he was listed as forty-six years old. Among others

living in his household was his eighteen-year-old son, W. W., a farm hand. DeWitt County census, enumerated by Willis Fawcett, June —, 1870. D. B. Peavy died in Cuero on January 12, 1897. He had served in Captain Stapleton's Company A, 24th Brigade, during the Civil War. Margaret Peavy Heisig, "Daniel Brinkley Peavy," *DeWitt County History*, 651–53.

31. Civil Minutes Book F, DeWitt County, Texas, final trial and judgment August 9, 1875, 564. According to historian Nellie Murphree, when Bolivar J. Pridgen was married, on his twenty-first birthday, he was given two-hundred acres of land and some slaves, one of whom was Abram Bryant. After emancipation Abram chose to remain with his former master. See Nellie Murphree, *History of DeWitt County*, edited by Robert W. Shook (Victoria: The Rose International Imprints, 1962), 101. In 1870 Bryant was listed as a sixty-one-year-old black man, "Farmer on Shares" with two other farm hands. He is shown to be a native of North Carolina, as was Senator Pridgen. DeWitt County census, enumerated by Willis Fawcett, July —, 1870, 285. The men did go to trial in May 1875. The *Galveston Daily News* of May 21 gives extensive coverage to the indictments and the demurrer by the defendants. In that issue the names of Joseph Tumlinson, James E. Smith, Ed Parkinson, Christopher T. Hunter, David Haldeman and W. H. Lackie are omitted with no explanation. *Galveston Daily News*, May 21, 1875.

32. Capt. L. H. McNelly to Adj. Gen. William Steele, August 31, 1874. McNelly cited his location as "Hd. Qrs. Co. A." Presumably he was camped between Clinton and Cuero.

33. Ibid.

34. The identity of these three men who sought protection in McNelly's camp comes from the letter of Lt. T. C. "Pidge" Robinson, written at Clinton on August 28 and printed in the *Austin Daily Democratic Statesman*, September 2, 1874.

35. Charles M. Middleton, one of the forty men in the newly formed company, was born in Chapel Hill, Washington County, Texas, on April 15, 1852, a son of Thomas Jefferson and Mary Ann Meek Middleton. One family story indicates he killed a man while still a youth and was on the run when he joined up with Captain McNelly. Middleton enlisted on July 25, 1874, along with Privates Chalk, James T. Irvin, and J. F. Turner. Middleton remained with McNelly until early 1875, but the three privates

were discharged later that autumn of 1874. Middleton married Cora Chisholm on October 26, 1875. She was the granddaughter of Richard H. and Hardinia Taylor Chisholm, thus he was another Ranger who "married into the Taylor family" as did A. R. Hendricks. In 1880 the Middletons were ranching in Kimble County where Creed Taylor and several of the Clements men also ranched. Much later, on July 17, 1900, in Bastrop County, he was convicted of cattle theft. He entered Huntsville prison as convict # 19497 and was discharged on September 6, 1907. Middleton died in Phoenix, Arizona, on August 17, 1927, and is buried there in Forest Lawn Cemetery.

36. This is how McNelly spelled the exchange in his report. It is a corruption of the Spanish exclamation, ¡cuidado!

37. Capt. L. H. McNelly to Adj. Gen. William Steele, August 31, 1874.

38. Letter from Pidge, written at Clinton, August 28, and printed in the *Statesman*, September 2, 1874.

39. Ibid.

40. Presumably the Tuggle, only identified by his surname, is Lodwick. Two Tuggles had signed the January 3, 1874, treaty of peace: A. Tuggle and L. Tuggle. The Tuggle family consisted of patriarch Thomas J. Tuggle, a blacksmith from Georgia, his wife Amelia, and children John A. (Alfred), Lodwick, Catherine, Nathaniel, Thomas, Ettie, and Adeline. DeWitt County census, enumerated August —, 1870, by Willis Fawcett, 224. Their post office was Clinton.

41. Letter from Pidge, written at Clinton, August 28, and printed in the *Statesman*, September 2, 1874.

42. Letter from Pidge, written at Clinton, August 4, and printed in the *Statesman*, August 8, 1874. The complete letters and other writings of T. C. Robinson are in Parsons, *"Pidge" A Texas Ranger from Virginia: The Life and Letters of Lieutenant T. C. Robinson, Washington County Volunteer Militia Company "A"* (Wolfe City, Tex.: Henington Publishing Co., 1985).

43. From Coleridge's *The Rime of the Ancient Mariner*, written in 1798, which begins: "It is an ancient Mariner,/ And he stoppeth one of three./ 'By thy long grey beard and glittering eye,/ Now wherefore stopp'st thou me?'" The Pidge paraphrase appears in the letter written from Clinton on September 18 and printed in the *Statesman* of September 24, 1874.

44. *Galveston Daily News*, September 24, 1874.

45. Ibid., September 25, 1874.

46. Ibid., September 26, 1874.

47. McNelly to Steele, written from Clinton, September 30, 1874.

48. Letter from Pidge, written in Clinton on October 13 and printed in the *Statesman*, October 14, 1874.

49. Ibid.

50. McNelly to Steele, October 18, 1874.

51. Mrs. G. C. Mayfield. "Interesting Narrative of Capt. W. L. Rudd, Ex-Ranger," *Frontier Times* 10, no. 3 (December, 1932): 124. The same article although in abbreviated form, entitled "Capt. W. L. Rudd of Yorktown, Ex-Ranger," appeared in *Frontier Times* 9, no. 12 (September 1932): 561–66.

52. Letter from Pidge, written in Clinton on October 13 and printed in the *Statesman*, October 14, 1874.

53. Ibid. The expression "Let us have peace," which Pidge quotes here, is from the 1868 acceptance speech made by U.S. Grant at his nomination for president.

54. Letter from Pidge, written in Clinton November 8 and printed in the *Statesman*, November 12, 1874.

55. *Herald and Planter* (Hallettsville, Lavaca County) December 10, 1874, reprinting an item from Yorktown dated November 24, appearing in an undated *Cuero Weekly Star*. Tumlinson was born February 16, 1811. The broken headstone in the small family cemetery indicates Tumlinson was sixty-three years, nine months, and seven days old.

56. The *San Antonio Daily Express*, March 26, 1875.

57. *Herald and Planter* (Hallettsville, Lavaca County) December 31, 1874.

Chapter Eight

1. L. H. McNelly to B. Pridgen, Galveston, written from Clinton, March 3, 1875. Issues of the *Pittsburg Dispatch* newspaper are no longer extant for this time period, so it has been impossible to read what Pridgen wrote. Pittsburg, the county seat of Camp County, is in northeast Texas, some 350 miles from DeWitt County. Why that newspaper printed Pridgen's letter is unknown.

2. McNelly to Steele, written from Clinton, March 4, 1875.

3. Itemization of charges against various feudists appears in Truitt, *Taylor Party*, 140–42.

4. *Galveston Daily News*, May 14, 1875.

5. Ibid., May 19, 1875.

6. James W. Hatch states that the borrowed horses were returned. See his "Destructive Storm at Indianola, 1875," *Frontier Times* 3, no. 1 (October, 1925): 37–39. Hatch was not a juror for the Taylor trial, but his brother D. W. Hatch was, and presumably told this story to James W. Hatch. The freedman Guy Michot has not been found on census records, but the 1870 Calhoun County census shows a white Michot farm family, consisting of head of household Julius Michot with five children. Their post office was Indianola. Calhoun County census, enumerated June 3, 1870 by S. Sanford, 365. Guy Michot was perhaps a former slave of this family.

7. Sonnichsen, *I'll Die*, 67.

8. Lelia Seeligson, *A History of Indianola* (Cuero, Tex.: *Cuero Record*, no date), 12.

9. John Fitzhenry, "Fifty Years A Policeman," in *The Trail Drivers of Texas*, ed. J. Marvin Hunter (Austin: University of Texas Press, 1986), 827.

10. Marjorie Burnett Hyatt produced three editions of her genealogical study of the conflict, the first two entitled *The Taylors, The Tumlinsons and the Feud* (1978, 1988). The third revised edition is entitled *Fuel for a Feud* (1990). In her foreword to the third edition she writes of her original interest in the family histories and making her materials available to other researchers, but "was somewhat distressed that the general public felt it was a feud between the Sutton and Taylor families, when I knew it was not" (ii). Robert C. Sutton Jr. wrote: "When the Helm-Tumlinson-Taylor trouble finally came to be called by the shorter name of the 'Sutton-Taylor Feud,' it was because there was one man, but only one, by the name of Sutton involved. [But] the Taylors wanted him worst of all," Sutton, *Feud*, 28. Also, cattleman James T. Johnson recorded his memoirs of the trail driving days for J. Marvin Hunter, which were included in *The Trail Drivers of Texas*. Johnson recalled having worked some fifteen years for John Taylor, and in the early 1870s "experienced quite a lot of difficulty trying to play neutral in the Taylor, Sutton and Tumlinson feuds, as my sole desire was to work for wages and not get mixed up with either side." Johnson, then a resident of Charco, Goliad County, added that at the age of seventy, "as old as I am, I feel like I

could go through all those hardships again if necessary." James
T. Johnson, "Hardships of a Cowboy's Life in the Early Days
of Texas," 760–62.

11. *Galveston Weekly News*, November 22, citing a report from
Indianola, dated November 18, 1875. Brown's death is also described in Parsons, "Rube Brown and the Atmosphere of Violence" in the English Westerners Society *Brand Book* 24, no. 1
(Winter 1986): 13–20.

12. *New York Times*, "Two Men Murdered in Texas," November 19,
1875, citing "Galveston Dispatches" through New Orleans.

13. R. H. Brown's grave was marked but the headstone through
the years sank to below ground level—until recent years. On
April 13, 1990, several lay historians and genealogists explored
the Epperson Cemetery in DeWitt County, in hopes of finding
Brown's grave. In a previous visit a footstone had been found
marked "R. H. B." and a portion of an obelisk and a broken
stone with only the letters "e Brown" remaining. With the aid of
probes a stone was discovered just below the surface. After careful digging the base for the obelisk was discovered, and care-
fully lifted to ground level for examination. The birth and death
dates for three family members were legible on this base: Miriam
Brown, Reuben's mother; T. Josephine Brown, a sister; and R.
H. Brown, "born/ Nov. 28, 1851/ Died Nov. 18, 1875." The
group who "discovered" the base of Reuben Brown's grave
marker consisted of Robert S. Giles, Patsy Goebel, Marjorie
Hyatt, Robert Alman, and this author. See "Reuben Brown
Headstone Discovered" in the *Newsletter* of NOLA 15, no. 4
(June 1990): 3.

14. Day, *Feud*, 31.

15. *Austin Daily Democratic Statesman*, January 6, 1876. See also
Chuck Parsons, "Bill Sutton Avenged: The Death of Jim Taylor,"
Quarterly of NOLA 3 (March 1979): 3–5.

16. Lavaca County census, enumerated September 22, 1850 by James
Kerr, 308.

17. The *Daily State Journal*, February 21, 1873. This was probably the Henry *Steinberg* family. In 1870 he was a successful
farmer in Washington County. He survived the stabbing as he
was still a resident of Washington County when the 1880 census was enumerated. Washington County census, enumerated
June 19, 1880, by G.P. Burke, 183-84.

18. A. L. Roy to Adj. Gen. F.L. Britton, written from Winchester, Fayette County, April 3, 1873. Original in Texas State Archives.
19. Confederate Service Record of A. R. Hendricks, National Archives.
20. Fayette County Marriage Record Book, 284. "A. R. Hendricks and Mrs. E. J. Kelly," rites of matrimony "duly celebrated" by Thomas W. Glass. And Hyatt, *Fuel*, F-52, F-53.
21. Bennett's grave marker in the Taylor-Bennett Cemetery indicates only that his death came after the amputation of his leg, the doctor having "sawed his leg off without anesthetics." Photo of grave marker courtesy Robert W. Shook.
22. Hyatt, *Fuel*, F-51.
23. Day, *Feud*, 33. T. T. Teel claimed to have defended 700 individuals charged with capital offenses during his career, and did not lose one case. Thomas W. Cutrer, s.v. "Thomas Trevanion Teel," *New Handbook*.
24. Day, *Feud*, 33–34.
25. Delony was the son of Lewis Henry and Sarah Ann Delony, and was three years old in 1860. At the time of the census the Delony family was living in the household of James Norman Smith, Clerk of County Court. DeWitt County census, enumerated June—, 1860 by John R. Foster, 457. Delony, *40 Years a Peace Officer: A True Story of Lawlessness and Adventures in the Early Days in Southwest Texas* (No place, no date, but possibly privately printed at Abilene, Texas, 1937), 13. This book was reprinted in the Western Publications periodical *Old West* 7, no. 2 (Winter 1970): 69–96, with slight variations. Hereafter cited as Delony.
26. Martin V. King, Georgia-born blacksmith, in 1870 resided with his wife Margaret and five children. The eldest child, Thomas Jefferson King, was thirteen and born in Texas, suggesting the Kings had long been residents of Texas. The name of Ed Davis, the "adopted son," does not appear in the King household. DeWitt County census, enumerated June 1, 1870, by Willis Fawcett, 296. King acted occasionally as a deputy. In November he and a deputy sheriff of Guadalupe County arrested a freedman named Russ Booth, allegedly part of a gang of horse thieves who operated in the DeWitt and Guadalupe County areas. Booth's friends resisted but King managed to settle the matter without bloodshed. *San Antonio*

Daily Express, November 16, 1875. This is a summary of a report originating in an undated *Cuero Star*.

27. Reference to this hanging immediately before the street fight is not found in any other writings dealing with the feud, nor has Charles Page been found on the census.

28. Delony, 13.

29. Ibid., 14.

30. *Brenham Banner* (Washington County), January 21, 1876, reprinting an item from an undated *Cuero Weekly Star*.

31. *Galveston Daily News*, January 1, 1876; and the *San Antonio Daily Express*, January 7, 1876.

32. Elizabeth Hendricks survived the feud's violence. She died in 1887, although an exact date is unknown. She is buried beside her first husband in the Taylor-Bennett Cemetery near Cuero.

33. Louise and Fullen Artrip, *Memoirs of Daniel Fore (Jim) Chisholm and The Chisholm Trail* (Booneville, Ark.: Artrip Publications, 1949), 49–50. Daniel Fore Chisholm was born in 1865 and died October 1, 1954.

34. This is the first (and only) time the name of Chamblin appears in feud literature. Perhaps he was the J. A. Chamblin enumerated in the 1860 census, identified as a planter from South Carolina, living with his wife and six children. The next household visited was that of N. J. Ryan. In that household was the McCrabb family, one of whom was their fifteen-year-old son J. F., who is better known as "Buck" McCrabb, also with the Hudson posse in Clinton that day. DeWitt County census, enumerated June __, 1860, by John R. Foster, 459.

35. Eddie Day Truitt, "Grand Jury Indicts Sutton Gang for Murder of Jim Taylor, A. L. [*sic*] Hendricks and Mason Arnold," *Taylor Family News* 5, no. 3 (August 1995): 1–2.

36. Daniel Jefferson White was the youngest son of Daniel J. White Sr. and Elizabeth McCullough White. A daughter, Mary Elizabeth White, married feud participant James DeMoss. *DeWitt County History*, 815. Another brother was Joseph Priestly White, better known as "Doc" White.

37. Henry Junius White was another son of Daniel Jefferson White Sr. He married Mattie Brown, no known relation to R. H. Brown. See note 36 above.

38. Christopher Taylor "Kit" Hunter, the son of Robert and Cyrene Sutton Hunter, was born January 6, 1856, and died November 7,

1923. He married Marietta Blair, a daughter of the DeWitt County Sheriff James Francis Blair, on January 25, 1882. *Feud*, F-19 and F-152.

39. *Galveston Daily News*, July 7, 1877.

Chapter Nine

1. *San Antonio Daily Express*, February 26, 1876; the *Galveston Daily News*, March 27, 1876, reporting "Special Correspondence" to the *News* dated March 21 from Gonzales.

2. Hyatt, *Feud*, 27–34. One family Bible, now in the Sutton Family Collection, shows: "August W. Pridgen died on 2nd of Feby A.D. 1876[.] He was in humanly murdered near Burns Station in DeWitt County[.]" In another family Bible the same is expressed only with the added note that his death marked the downfall of the Sutton party. This cousin of B. J. Pridgen was born September 8, 1838, the son of Henry and Willey Eatman Pridgen.

3. It is believed this is the son of C. W. and Margaret Allen, who, in 1870, were farming in DeWitt County. Their children included fifteen-year-old Joseph and three younger siblings, Sarah Jane, Claiborn, and Alfred. Willis Fawcett enumerated this family as household and family # 199; household and family # 200 was A.J. Allen, also farming, with his wife Mary and their three children. Both Allens, presumably brothers, were from Alabama as were their wives. All their children were born in Texas. DeWitt County census, enumerated August —, 1870, by Willis Fawcett. Their post office was Clinton.

4. James E. Lampley was, in 1876, about twenty-seven-years-old. When the 1870 census was taken his mother, Appline, is shown to be head of household. The widow Lampley and all five children were born in Alabama. She is listed as a farmer and James, Edward, and Harry listed as "Farm hand." Daughter Christian and seven-year-old Franklin are shown to be "At home." DeWitt County census, enumerated June 2, 1870, by Willis Fawcett, 213.

5. *Galveston Daily News*, March 7, 1876, printing news from DeWitt County, and the *Galveston Weekly News*, March 13, printing a report from Cuero dated February 29, 1876.

6. *Galveston Daily News*, March 8, 1876, citing "Special Correspondence" from Cuero dated March 4, 1876.

7. *Galveston Daily News*, March 8, 1876, reporting "Special Correspondence" to the *News* from Cuero on March 4.

8. North Carolina native Alonzo T. Bass resided near Belmont in northwestern Gonzales County. In 1870 he is listed as a forty-four-year-old farmer with two daughters. Gonzales County census, enumerated September 1, 1870 by M. H. Beaty, 458. He was elected sheriff of the county four times: first on August 6, 1860 but served only until April 1862 with no reason known for discontinuance. He was elected again on February 15, 1876, and then again on November 5, 1878 and again on November 2, 1880. Tise, 209. Bass died on June 27, 1891, and is buried in the Masonic Cemetery in Gonzales. *Gonzales Inquirer*, July 2, 1891.

9. *Galveston Daily News*, March 16, reporting news from Gonzales of March 15, 1876.

10. Ibid., March 22, 1876, reporting news from DeWitt County.

11. *San Antonio Daily Express*, March 25, 1876. Of the four Clements brothers, although all had signed at least one treaty of peace, the only one charged with anything more serious than gambling or wearing a pistol was Mannen who was indicted for murder in at least one case. For a brief biography of the man see Robert W. Stephens, *Mannen Clements: Texas Gunfighter* (privately printed, 1996).

12. *Galveston Daily News*, March 21, 1876, reporting "Special Correspondence" from Gonzales dated March 21. The same item appeared in the *Galveston Weekly News* of March 22, 1876.

13. Ibid.

14. McNelly's testimony on border troubles is found in "Texas Frontier Troubles," *House of Representatives Report* No. 343, 44th Congress, 1st Session, 1876.

15. Capt. L. H. McNelly to Adj. Gen. William Steele, March 8, 1876, written from King's Ranch. The original of this letter has not been found; the typed copy was discovered in the papers of Dr. Walter Prescott Webb, now archived in the Center for American History, University of Texas. Apparently Dr. Webb made a typed copy of numerous documents housed in the Texas State Archives during research for his study of the Texas Rangers. A few of the originals were misplaced and since lost.

16. The name is spelled in various ways in contemporary literature as well as secondary sources. I have used the Brassell spelling as that is how the name is spelled on their headstones in the Upper Yorktown Cemetery.

17. DeWitt County census, enumerated June --, 1870 by Willis Fawcett, 252–53.

18. *Galveston Daily News*, October 4, 1876.

19. The statements are from the actual record of *Cases Argued and Adjudged in the Court of Appeals of the State of Texas during the Latter Part of the Galveston Term, 1880, and the Early Part of the Austin Term, 1880*, Vol. 8, 257–63. The "Surround the house, boys," quotation appears on page 258.

20. Ibid., 259.

21. Ibid., 259.

22. Ibid., 259.

23. Ibid., 260–61. The graves of Dr. Brassell and his son George, as well as Mary Ann Brassell, are marked, and are to be found in the Upper Yorktown Cemetery on 13th Street and Reidel Avenue in Yorktown, DeWitt County.

24. Ibid., 261–62.

25. Ibid., 262–63.

26. William Steele, *A List of Fugitives from Justice*, A list compiled from official records on file in the office of the Adjutant General of Texas, 1878, facsimile (Austin: State House Press, 1997), 16.

27. Day, *Feud*, 34.

28. C. L. Douglas, *Famous Texas Feuds* (Dallas: Turner Company, 1936; repr., Austin: State House Press, 1988), 86.

29. "Kuklux Law at Cuero," *Galveston Daily News*, September 22, 1876.

30. N. A. Jennings. *A Texas Ranger* (New York: Charles Scribner's Sons, 1899; facsimile, Ruidoso, N. Mex.: Frontier Book Company, 1960), 279. Hereafter cited as Jennings.

31. *Victoria Advocate*, October 5, 1876. Curiously, this report indicated Dr. Brassell had only recently left Georgia, and "sought the inviting land of DeWitt county for a home for himself and family." This is clearly in error as the family was in Texas in 1870 for the federal census.

32. *Cases Argued and Adjudged ...* , 278.

33. DeWitt County Court Records, Marriage Book D, License # 1548, 182.

34. DeWitt County Court Records, Marriage Book D, License # 1527, 175. Bob Thomas is no doubt the same man who was with the Sutton posse in Bastrop when Charles Taylor was killed.

35. *San Antonio Weekly Express*, September 28, 1876, citing a "Special to the Galveston News" from Cuero.

36. Day, *Feud*, 40.

37. *Victoria Advocate*, October 5, 1876.

38. L. B. Wright to Adj. Gen. William Steele, October 8, 1876. Of interest is that M. V. King signed the January 3, 1874, treaty of peace as a member of the Taylor faction. W. W. Davis also signed as a Taylor man, but was he the "Doly" Davis who killed King?

39. Hall was placed in command of McNelly's Special State Troops on January 1, 1877. McNelly was dismissed not because of any malfeasance or inefficiency, but his medical bills were simply too high to justify retaining him. Due to McNelly's popularity with the public and his Rangers, Steele received such criticism that he felt obligated to justify his decision. Hall was considered "the right man in the right place, and who was in the full vigor of early manhood and health" according to Adjutant General Steele's report, which was printed in the *Galveston Daily News* of February 6, 1877.

40. Lt. J. L. Hall to Adjutant General Steele, December 10, 1876.

41. Although some members of the Brassells may have "left the country" in 1880 the widow Brassell was still in the county. She was head of household, living with sons Theodore C., Sylvanus S., Jefferson D., John M., and daughters Martha J., "Leonard L." (possibly "Leona"). In the same household are her niece Margaret A. and nephew Phillip B. Moses. DeWitt County census, enumerated June 1, 1880 by W. H. Littleton, 457. At least three of the children married in neighboring Gonzales County: Sylvanus S. married Mary S. Stroman on May 6, 1885; Theodore married Georgia K. DeBerry on May 26, 1896; Leonard L. (or Leona) married C. F. Shindler on November 12, 1883. Mary Ann Brassell never remarried. She died on April 20, 1883, in Gonzales County.

42. Lt. J. L. Hall to Adj. Gen. William Steele, from Clinton, December 10, 1876.

43. Jennings, 280.

44. George Durham, as told to Clyde Wantland, *Taming the Nueces Strip: The Story of McNelly's Rangers* (Austin: University Press of Texas, 1962), 165.

45. Jennings, 283.

46. Durham, 166.

47. Monthly Return of Lt. J. L. Hall, prepared at Clinton, December 31, 1876. Original in the Texas State Archives, Austin.

48. Frederic Remington, *How the Law Got Into the Chaparral: Conversations with Old Texas Rangers*, ed. John H. Jenkins (Austin: Jenkins Publishing Company, 1987), 25. Remington visited Texas

in 1896 in order "to gather material for his paintings and writings." In San Antonio, among other interesting people, he met and
interviewed John S. "Rip" Ford, William A. A. "Bigfoot" Wallace,
and Lee Hall. His article, with illustrations, appeared in the December 1896 issue of *Harper's Magazine*. It later appeared as a chapter in his book *Crooked Trails*, published in 1898.

49. John Andrews is listed as a thirty-year-old farmer with a wife,
Susan A. E. in the 1880 census. Living with them were a niece and
nephew and two laborers, all Texas born. DeWitt County census, enumerated July 2, 1880 by Robert A. Pleasants, the son
of Judge Henry Clay Pleasants, 398.

50. *Victoria Advocate*, December 23, 1876.

Chapter Ten

1. *Daily Democratic Statesman*, May 5, 1877.
2. Ibid.
3. DeWitt County census, enumerated June —, 1870 by Willis
Fawcett, 230. Hudson, listed as forty-nine, is shown to be a native
of Texas, his wife Mary S. from North Carolina, and their one
daughter Rebecca A. born in Texas about 1857. On April 20,
1875, Rebecca married W. C. "Curry" Wallace who served in
the same posse that killed Taylor, Hendricks, and Arnold. Information found in DeWitt County Court Records, Cuero, Marriage Record Book D, License #1395, 130. Mary S. Hudson was
born on May 27, 1827, and died on January 26, 1879. Her headstone in Cuero's Hillside Cemetery identifies her with her dates
and adds "Wife of R. B. Hudson." On June 1, 1882, Hudson was
married to Mrs. Rachel F. Cox in Gonzales County. Gonzales
County Marriage Record Book C-1, License # 3067, 265–66.
Their marriage was performed by Alanson Brown, O. M. G. The
marriage ended in divorce. Jack Hays Day wrote that Hudson, "at
heart a coward," later "inveigled a widow in Gonzales to marry
him. She was a propertied woman who soon learned his weakness and dispensed with him. He went down to Cuero and loafed
around some of his relatives, finally dying a pauper." Day, 34.
This is partly confirmed in an interview with the late Mrs. Eva
Wilson, a granddaughter of Mrs. Rachel Robinson Cox Hudson.
The date of Hudson's death, and burial place, is unknown.
4. Delony, 14.

5. *Galveston Daily News*, July 7, citing a report from Cuero dated June 30, 1877.

6. *Daily Democratic Statesman*, printing a lengthy interview with Hardin, August 29, 1877.

7. Ibid., headlined "Casting Out of Devils—How Texas Does It."

8. Hardin, *Life*, 125. Gladden and Ringo were both incarcerated for their part in the Mason County troubles, the so-called "Hoo Doo War" of 1875.

9. Anonymous, *Life and Adventures of Sam Bass the Notorious Union Pacific and Texas Train Robber* (Dallas: Dallas Commercial Steam Print, 1878), 68.

10. Joshua Bowen to Mrs. Jane Swain (Mrs. Jane Hardin), May 6, 1877, written from Zadlers Mill [*sic*: Zedler's Mills], Gonzales County. Original letter in the John Wesley Hardin Letter Collection, Texas State University, San Marcos.

11. *Gonzales Inquirer*, May 15, 1878.

12. William W. Davis was a Gonzales County stock raiser. He also had served as postmaster of the Albuquerque post office. More importantly he served in the State Police with the rank of sergeant, from April 6, 1872, until his resignation on October 31, 1872.

13. For Bowen's trial and the subsequent alteration of testimony see Chuck Parsons and Marjorie Parsons, *Bowen and Hardin* (College Station, Tex.: Creative Publishing Co., 1991).

14. *Galveston Daily News*, December 16, 1877, citing a report from an undated Cuero *Bulletin*.

15. Telegram dated June 5, 1877, from Duval Beall in Cuero to Adjutant General Steele.

16. *Galveston Daily News*, December 23, citing a report from Cuero dated December 18, 1877.

17. Ibid., December 30, 1877, citing a report from Cuero dated December 24, 1877.

18. Jackson and Jackson, reporters, *Cases Argued and Adjudged in the Court of Appeals of the State of Texas* (St. Louis: F. H. Thomas and Company, 1880), 278–79. Contrary to Judge Pleasants' statement that a reign of terror still existed in the county, a Cuero newspaper reporter, in discussing the December trial, stated that one of the "most remarkable features" of the grand jury's report, was "that there has not been a single murder committed in the county within the past twelve months." And the reason for that unusual record was "owing no doubt to the presence of a portion of Capt.

Hall's command, which is stationed in the county. The presence of this command has had a salutary effect in preserving order throughout this and the western counties." *Galveston Daily News*, December 30, citing a report from Cuero dated December 24, 1877.

19. *Cases Argued and Adjudged*, 279.
20. Ibid., 305–10; Sonnichsen, *I'll Die*, 85–86.
21. Day, *Feud*, 39.
22. David E. Luddeke. "Carl Heinrich and Henriette Sperling Heissig," in *DeWitt County History*, 477.
23. Application for Executive Clemency # 5473, Secretary of State Papers, Record Group 307, Box 2-9/305. Augustine's pardon is dated October 3, 1899.
24. *New York Times*, February 24, reprinting a lengthy article about Bell from the Dayton, Ohio, *Journal* of February 22, 1879.
25. Wyatt Anderson, "A Pioneer in West Texas," in J. Marvin Hunter's *Frontier Times* 3, no. 5, 14–15.
26. L. C. Williamson to Adj. Gen. William Steele, telegram from Coleman County, April 15, 1877. Adj. Gen. Correspondence.
27. J. R. Fleming to Major J. B. Jones, April 21, 1877. Adj. Gen. Correspondence. See also *Frontier Times* for reprint of an article from the *Comanche Chief* newspaper, undated, of the arrest as recalled by Private J. W. McCullom, then serving under Lt. B. S. Foster. McCullom first served under Lt. J. W. Millican from May 25 through December 23, 1874, in Company A; then in Company E from September 1, 1875, until his honorable discharge on October 31, 1877.
28. DeWitt County census, enumerated June 17, 1880, by R. M. Forbes, 368.
29. For a discussion of Hanks' life see Chuck Parsons, "O. C. Hanks and the Texas Connection," *The Outlaw Trail Journal*, Summer 1994, 19–29. Hanks was killed in San Antonio by a police officer named Josehp A. "Pink" Taylor, who was no relation to the DeWitt County Taylors. The body of Hanks was identified positively by Thomas Stell of Cuero.
30. John D. Stephens to Gov. R. B. Hubbard, November 17, 1877. A note from Hubbard on the document indicates it had been paid "in fall of 1876." Original documents in the Texas State Archives.
31. Hyatt, *Feud*, F-164, prints the affidavit in full. It is recorded in Deed Book 18, 543, and signed on June 29, 1916.

Chapter Eleven

1. Capt. L. H. McNelly to Adj. Gen. William Steele, August 31, 1874.
2. *Cuero Daily Record*, January 21, 1895, from the "Clinton Matters" column.

Epilogue

1. The wooden boards marking numerous graves in the Taylor-Bennett Cemetery were replaced either by granite markers or by new boards in 1973 at the time state historical markers were placed at the graves of Josiah and Hephzibeth Taylor. Milton O. "Uncle Bill" Bennett was the unofficial caretaker of the cemetery for many years. See *Taylor Family News* 7, no. 3 (August 1977): 6.
2. *Gonzales Daily Inquirer*, July 26, 1988.
3. Ibid.
3. Quotations from transcript of the program in author's collection.

Selected Bibliography

Books and Published Pamphlets

Artrip, Louise, and Fullen Artrip. *Memoirs of Daniel Fore (Jim) Chisholm and the Chisholm Trail*. Tulsa, Okla.: Patrician Press, 1949.

Awbrey, Betty Dooley, and Claude Dooley. *Why Stop? A Guide to Texas Historical Roadside Markers*. 4th ed. Houston, Tex.: Gulf Publishing Company, 1999.

Blanton, Joseph Edwin. *John Larn*. Albany, Tex.: Ventura Press, 1994.

Britton, Frank L. *Report of the Adjutant General of the State of Texas, for the Year 1872*. Austin, Tex.: James P. Newcomb and Company, 1873.

———. *Report of the Adjutant General of the State of Texas for the Year 1873*. Austin, Tex.: Cardwell & Walker, Printers, 1874.

Burnett, Marjorie Lee, comp. *Taylor Family History: Descendants of Josiah Taylor and Hephzibeth Luker*. Smiley, Tex.: Sandies Creek Press, 2003.

Cases Argued and Adjudged in the Court of Appeals of the State of Texas during the Latter Part of the Galveston Term, 1880, and the Early Part of the Austin Term, 1880. Vol. 8. Np: no publisher, 1880.

Cases Argued and Adjudged in the Court of Appeals of the State of Texas. Dallas, Tex.: F. H. Thomas and Company, 1880.

Cemeteries Located in Gonzales County. Extracted from the *Quarterly* of the South Texas Genealogical & Historical Society, Vol. 2. No place. No date. Copy in Gonzales Public Library, Genealogy Department.

Cox, Ross J. Sr. *The Texas Rangers and The San Saba Mob.* San Saba, Tex.: C & S Farm Press, 2005.

Crouch, Barry A. *The Freedmen's Bureau and Black Texans.* Austin: University of Texas Press, 1992.

Crouch, Barry A., and Donaly E. Brice. *Cullen Montgomery Baker: Reconstruction Desperado.* Baton Rouge: Louisiana State University Press, 1997.

Davidson, James. *Report of the Adjutant General of the State of Texas, June 24, 1870, to December 31, 1870.* Austin: Siemering & Co., 1870.

Day, Jack Hays. *The Sutton-Taylor Feud.* San Antonio, Tex.: Sid Murray & Son Publishers, 1937.

DeArment, Robert K. *Bravo of the Brazos: John Larn of Fort Griffin, Texas.* Norman: University of Oklahoma Press, 2002.

Delony, Lewis S. *40 Years a Peace Officer: A True Story of Lawlessness and Adventure in the Early Days in Southwest Texas.* Abilene, Tex?: no publisher, 1937; repr. in *Old West* magazine, Winter 1970.

DeWitt County Historical Commission. *The History of DeWitt County.* Dallas, Tex.: Curtis Media Corporation, 1991.

Didear, Hedwig Krell. *Karnes County and Old Helena.* Austin: San Felipe Press, 1969.

Dixson, Walter Clay. *Richland Crossing: A Portrait of Texas Pioneers.* Everman, Tex.: Peppermill Publishing Co., 1994.

Douglas, C. L. *Famous Texas Feuds.* Dallas, Tex.: Turner Company, 1936; repr., Austin, Tex.: State House Press, 1988.

Emmett, Chris. *Shanghai Pierce: A Fair Likeness.* Norman: University of Oklahoma Press, 1953.

French, George, ed. *Indianola Scrap Book.* Austin, Tex.: San Felipe Press, 1974.

Frontier Times. Edited by J. Marvin Hunter. Facsimile edition.

Goebel, Patsy. *Cemetery Records of DeWitt County, Texas.* 3 vols. Cuero, Tex.: Privately printed, 1992.

Hardin, John Wesley. *The Life of John Wesley Hardin, from the Original Manuscript, as Written by Himself.* Seguin, Tex.: Smith & Moore, 1896.

Heitman, Francis B. *Historical Register and Dictionary of the United States Army, from its Organization, September 29, 1879, to March 2, 1903.* Washington, D.C.: Government Printing Office, 1903; repr., Urbana: University of Illinois Press, 1965.

Hyatt, Marjorie Burnett. *Fuel for a Feud. A Third Revised Edition of The Taylors, the Tumlinsons and the Feud.* Smiley, Tex.: Privately printed, 1990.

———. *The Taylors, the Tumlinsons, and the Feud.* rev. ed. Smiley, Tex.: Privately printed, 1988.

Jackson, Jack. *The Lost Cause: John Wesley Hardin, The Taylor-Sutton Feud, and Reconstruction Texas.* Northampton, Mass.: Kitchen Sink Press, 1998.

James, Glenn, and Henri Rupe Capps. *The Life of Thomas W. Gamel.* Annot. Dave Johnson. Ozark, Mo.: The Dogwood Printing, 2003.

Jennings, N. A. *A Texas Ranger.* New York: Charles Scribner's Sons, 1899; repr., Ruidoso, N. Mex.: Frontier Book Company, 1960.

Jones, Virgil Carrington. *The Hatfields and the McCoys.* Chapel Hill: University of North Carolina Press, 1948.

Karnei, Shirley A., and Francis Hartmann, eds. *Yorktown, Texas: 150 Year Anniversary.* Yorktown, Tex.: The Printery, 1997.

Lamar, Howard R. *Charlie Siringo's West: An Interpretive Biography.* Albuquerque: University of New Mexico Press, 2005.

Lasswell, Mary. *Rags and Hope: The Recollections of Val C. Giles, Four Years with Hood's Brigade, Fourth Texas Infantry 1861–1865.* New York: Coward-McCann, 1961.

Life and Adventures of Sam Bass the Notorious Union Pacific Train Robber. Dallas, Tex.: Dallas Commercial Steam Press, 1878.

Marohn, Richard C. *The Last Gunfighter: John Wesley Hardin.* College Station, Tex.: Creative Publishing Company, 1995.

Matagorda County Historical Commission. *Historic Matagorda County.* Houston, Tex.: D. Armstrong Co., 1986.

Members of the 12th Legislature 1846–1962. Rev. ed. Austin, Tex.: no publisher, 1962.

Metz, Leon C. *John Wesley Hardin: Dark Angel of Texas.* El Paso, Tex.: Mangan Books, 1996.

———. *Pat Garrett: The Story of a Western Lawman.* Norman: University of Oklahoma Press, 1974.

Moneyhon, Carl H. *Texas after the Civil War: The Struggle of Reconstruction.* College Station: Texas A&M University Press, 2004.

Murphree, Nellie. *History of DeWitt County.* Victoria, Tex.: The Rose International Imprint, 1962.

Myers, Rosalie Key. *Dowlearn-Lowe.* Np: Privately published, 1992.

Newsletter of the Kimble County, Texas Historical Survey Committee. May–June, 1967.

O'Neal, Bill. *The Bloody Legacy of Pink Higgins: A Half Century of Violence in Texas.* Austin, Tex.: Eakin Press, 1999.

———. *War in East Texas: Regulators vs. Moderators.* Lufkin, Tex.: Best of East Texas Publishers, 2006.

Parsons, Chuck. *Captain L. H. McNelly: Texas Ranger—The Life and Times of a Fighting Man.* Austin, Tex.: State House Press, 2001.

———. *"Pidge" A Texas Ranger from Virginia. The Life and Letters of Lieutenant T.C. Robinson, Washington County Volunteer Militia Company "A."* Wolfe City, Tex: Henington Publishing Co., 1985.

Parsons, Chuck, and Marjorie Parsons. *Bowen and Hardin.* College Station, Tex.: Creative Publishing Company, 1991.

Pruett, Jakie L., and Everett B. Cole. *The History and Heritage of Goliad County.* Austin, Tex.: Eakin Publications, 1983.

Ramey, William Neal, ed. *The Texian.* Austin, Tex.: no publisher, 1886.

Ray, G. B. *Murder at the Corners.* San Antonio, Tex.: Naylor Company, 1957.

Raymond, Dora Neill. *Captain Lee Hall of Texas.* Norman: University of Oklahoma Press, 1940; repr., University of Oklahoma Press, 1982.

Remington, Frederic. *How the Law Got into the Chaparral: Conversations with Old Texas Rangers.* Ed. John H. Jenkins. Austin, Tex.: Jenkins Publishing Company, 1987.

Rose, Victor M. *The Texas Vendetta; or, the Sutton-Taylor Feud.* New York: J. J. Little & Co., 1880; repr., Houston, Tex.: Frontier Press of Texas, 1956.

Seelingson, Lelia. *A History of Indianola.* Cuero, Tex.: The Cuero Record, no date.

Smallwood, James M. *The Feud That Wasn't: The Taylor Ring, Bill Sutton, John Wesley Hardin, and Violence in Texas.* College Station: Texas A&M University Press, 2008.

Smallwood, James, Barry A. Crouch and Larry Peacock. *Murder and Mayhem: The War of Reconstruction in Texas.* College Station: Texas A&M University Press, 2003.

Smith, Karon Mac. *On the Watershed of Ecleto and the Clear Fork of Sandies.* Seguin, Tex.: Tommy Brown Printing, 1983; rev. ed. 1984.

———. *On the Watershed of Ecleto and the Clear Fork of Sandies Volume II.* Seguin, Texas: Tommy Brown Printing, 1987.

Sonnichsen, C. L. *I'll Die Before I'll Run: The Story of the Great Feuds of Texas.* New York: Harper & Brothers, 1951.

———. *Ten Texas Feuds.* Albuquerque: University of New Mexico Press, 1957.

———. *Tularosa: Last of the Frontier West.* New York: Devin-Adair Company, 1960.

Sowell, A. J. *Early Settlers and Indian Fighters of Southwest Texas.* Austin, Tex.: Ben C. Jones & Co.; repr., Austin, Tex.: State House Press, 1986.

Steele, William. *A List of Fugitives from Justice.* Facsimile reprint, Austin, Tex.: State House Press, 1957.

Stephens, Robert W. *Mannen Clements: Texas Gunfighter.* Np: Privately printed, 1996.

Sutton, Robert C. Jr. *The Sutton-Taylor Feud.* Quanah, Tex.: Nortex Press, 1974.

Taylor Family News, edited by Bena Taylor Kirkscey.

Tise, Sammy. *Texas County Sheriffs.* Hallettsville, Tex.: Privately printed, 1989.

Truitt, Eddie. *The Taylor Party.* Wortham, Tex.: Privately printed, 1992.

Tyler, Ron C., editor-in-chief. *The New Handbook of Texas.* 6 vols. Austin, Tex.: Texas State Historical Association, 1996.

Waller, Altina L. *Feud: Hatfields, McCoys, and Social Change in Appalachia, 1860–1900.* Chapel Hill: University of North Carolina Press, 1988.

Articles and Chapters

Baensiger, Ann Patton. "The Texas State Police During Reconstruction: A Reexamination." *Southwestern Historical Quarterly* 72, no. 4 (April 1969).

Fitzhenry, John. "Fifty Years a Policeman" in *The Trail Drivers of Texas.* Comp. and ed. J. Marvin Hunter. Austin: University of Texas Press, 1986.

"Fought with Ben Milam." in *Texas Field and Sportsman.* 1904(?).

George, David. "Jack Helm Meets John Wesley Hardin." *The Texas Gun Collector.* Spring, 2003.

Hatch, James C. "More About the Career of John Wesley Hardin" in *Frontier Times.* June 1924.

Johnson, James T. "Hardships of a Cowboy's Life in the Early Days of Texas" in *The Trail Drivers of Texas*. Comp. and ed. J. Marvin Hunter. Austin: University of Texas Press, 1986.

Nolen, Oran Warder. "The Most Murderous Feud in Texas History." *True Frontier*. September 1970.

Parsons, Chuck. "Bill Sutton Avenged: The Death of Jim Taylor." *Quarterly* of the National Association for Outlaw and Lawman History, Inc. (NOLA) March 1979.

———. "Doc Bockius Survived Civil War, Texas Feud." *Newsletter* of the National Association for Outlaw and Lawman History, Inc. (NOLA) 2, no. 4 (Spring 1977).

———. "Forgotten Feudist." *Frontier Times*, December–January 1976.

———. "Mason Arnold—'He Came from Schulenberg'." *Quarterly* of the National Association for Outlaw and Lawman History, Inc. (NOLA) 21, no. 4 (October–December 1997).

———. "O. C. Hanks and the Texas Connection." *The Outlaw Trail Journal*. Summer 1994.

———. "Reuben Brown Headstone Discovered." *Newsletter* of the National Association for Outlaw and Lawman History, Inc. (NOLA) 15, no. 4 (June 1990).

Shook, Robert W. "Bolivar J. Pridgen." *Texas Bar Journal*, April 1965.

Smallwood, James. "Sutton-Taylor: A Feud?" *South Texas Studies* 3 (2005).

Yelvington, Henry B. "Morris-Taylor Killing." *McMullen County History*. Np: no publisher, no date (1980?).

Newspapers

Texas

Advertiser (Bastrop)
Bee Picayune (Beeville)

Banner (Brenham)
County Bulletin (Burnet)
Daily Democratic Statesman (Austin)
Daily Express (San Antonio)
Daily Herald (San Antonio)
Daily Inquirer (Gonzales)
Daily News (Galveston)
Daily Republican (Austin)
Daily State Journal (Austin)
Daily Telegraph (Houston)
Drag Net (Gonzales)
Enterprise (Honey Grove)
Fayette County New Era (LaGrange)
Flake's Daily Bulletin (Galveston)
Herald (Dallas)
Herald and Planter (Hallettsville)
Junction Eagle (Junction)
Times Herald (Dallas)
Tri-Weekly Republican (Austin)
Union (Houston)
Victoria Advocate (Victoria)
Weekly News (Galveston)
Weekly Republican (Austin)
Weekly Star (Cuero)

Other States

Daily Picayune (Louisiana)
New York Times

Government Documents

Davis, E. J. "Report of Special Committee on Lawlessness and Violence in that State." U. S. Senate Journal, *Miscellaneous Document,* No. 109, 40th Congress, 2nd Session, 1868.

Pease, E. M. "Communication from Governor Pease of Texas, Relative to the Troubles in that State." *House Miscellaneous*

Document, No. 127, 40th Congress, 2nd Session, U. S. House of Representatives, 1868.

Federal Census Records
Nonpopulation Census Schedules ("Mortality Schedules")
DeWitt County, 1870
Goliad County, 1870
McMullen County, 1870

Population Census
Calhoun County, 1880
DeWitt County, 1860, 1870, 1880
Goliad County, 1870, 1880
Gonzales County, 1870, 1880
Refugio County, 1860
San Patricio County, 1860, 1870
Victoria County, 1870, 1880

Unpublished Materials

Ainsworth, Mary Elizabeth Humphries. "The First One Hundred Years." Typed memoirs dictated to her son George Otis Ainsworth, 1951. Copy in author's possession.

Bastrop County. District Court Records, Minute Book F. Bastrop, Texas.

Clow, Robert J. Account Book. In Center for American History, Austin.

County Special Policemen, Ledger 401-1058.

"Dedication of Official Historical Grave Markers for Josiah Taylor and Hephzibeth Taylor." Printed program. Cuero, Texas, April 29, 1973.

DeWitt County. Civil Minutes Book, Book F. Cuero, Texas.

———. District Court Minutes, Book B. Cuero, Texas.

———. Marriage Records, Vols. A, C, D and E.

Dietz, John F. "Descendants of John and Mary Miller McCrabb." Copy in author's collection.

"Ellsworth Hotel Register." Microfilm reel # 5554. Kansas State Historical Society, Topeka, Kansas.

Gonzales County. Marriage Records, Vols. A, C-1.

Hunter, John W. "Literary Effort" Manuscript relating events of life of Creed Taylor in Texas State Library and Archives, Austin.

Lavaca County. District Court Records. Hallettsville, Texas.

Pridgen Family Bibles. Sutton Family Collection. Texas Ranger Hall of Fame and Museum, Waco, Texas.

"Register of Elected and Appointed State and County Officials August 1866-1870." Microfilm Reel # 3501. Texas State Library and Archives, Austin.

Report of Arrests. Texas State Library and Archives, Austin.

Roster of State Police. Prepared by Barry A. Crouch and Donaly E. Brice.

State Police Ledger. Texas State Library and Archives, Austin.

Steele, William. Letter Press Book. "Adjutant General William Steele. No. 1. 1874."

Stell, Thomas. "The Taylor-Sutton Feud." Typed manuscript in the C. L. Sonnichsen Collection, Special Collections, University of Texas-El Paso.

Sutton Family Bible. Sutton Family Collection, Texas Ranger Hall of Fame and Museum, Waco, Texas.

Sutton, Mrs. Laura E. Widow's Application for Pension. National Archives.

Sutton, Mark C. Correspondence and genealogy charts on Sutton family to author, October 30, 1981.

Tumlinson, S. H. "Tumlinson: A Genealogy." Typed manuscript, 1994?

Wilson County. Commissioners Court Minutes, Vol. A. County Clerk Records, Floresville, Texas.

———. Marriage Records, Vol. A.

Wyatt, Frederica, Junction, Texas. E-mail to author, December 1, 2006.

Video

Vendettas: Sutton vs. Taylor. VHS Documentary of A & E Television, 2001, The History Channel.

Index

Page numbers in **bold** refer to illustrations.